# The Loves of Catherine the Great

*Also by Vsevolod A. Nikolaev*

*Series in Russian:*

Sophia Paleologue: The Byzantine Princess Who Became
The First Queen of Russia
Ivan the Terrible: His Life, His Diplomacy,
His Secret Police
Boris Godunov and the 'False Demetrius'
Martha Skavronskaya: The Lithuanian Country Woman
Who Became Empress of Russia
Catherine the Great's Childhood and Youth
The Tragic Destiny of Tsar Ivan VI
Emperor Paul: Unhappy Life and Terrible End
Alexander I: The Tsar-Beggar


*Also by Albert Parry*

*Books in English:*

Terrorism: From Robespierre to Arafat
Russian Cavalcade: A Military Record
Russia's Rockets and Missiles
The New Class Divided: Science and
Technology Versus Communism
The Russian Scientist
Whistler's Father
Tattoo
Garrets and Pretenders

# The Loves of Catherine the Great

by

## Vsevolod A. Nikolaev

and

## Albert Parry

Coward, McCann & Geoghegan
New York

Library of Congress Cataloging in Publication Data

Nikolaev, Vsevolod.
The loves of Catherine the Great.

Bibliography: p.
Includes index.
1. Catherine II, Empress of Russia, 1729–1796.
2. Peter III, Emperor of Russia, 1728–1762. 3. Saltykov,
Sergeĭ Vasilévich, 1726–    . 4. Stanisław, II August,
King of Poland, 1732–1798. 5. Orlov, Grigoriĭ
Grigor′evich, graf, 1734–1783. 6. Russian empresses—
Biography. 7. Soviet Union—Kings and rulers—Biography.
8. Favorites, Royal—Soviet Union—Biography. I. Parry,
Albert, Date.   II. Title.
DK171.5.N54   1982      947′.063′0924  [B]  82-7406
ISBN 0-698-11201-6                              AACR2

Printed in the United States of America

# Contents

# The Loves of Catherine the Great

# Authors' Note

This is not a work of fiction. It is based on authenticated eighteenth-century Russian, French, and German memoirs, correspondence, diplomatic reports, and other historical documents. No situations or dialogue have been invented, and the quotations that appear in our narrative are taken directly from research sources. An occasional indirect quotation has been changed to a direct one for stylistic reasons.

The authors would like to express their warm gratitude to Irene Bulazel, of Greenwich, Connecticut, who suggested the possibility of a book on this subject and brought the authors together.

Vsevolod A. Nikolaev
Albert Parry

# Prologue

They slept in the same bed the first eight years of their marriage, but not once did they touch each other conjugally. For eight years he remained a virgin, she did not.

This curious couple consisted of Grand Duke Peter and Grand Duchess Catherine of Russia. Years later, for six brief months, he was Emperor Peter III. She, having overthrown and crushed him, reigned as Empress Catherine II—Catherine the Great—for thirty-four years.

Throughout her stormy career, Catherine was an awe-inspiring figure—the builder and absolute ruler of a domain that at its height numbered 36,000,000 souls and claimed lands stretching from Central Europe across the heart of Asia to Alaska. How did a minor German princess emerge from her obscure origins to become both a passionate and hedonistic woman and the sovereign of an immense and heterogeneous realm?

This is the story of Catherine's first three lovers—Sergei

Saltykov, Stanislas Poniatowski, and Gregory Orlov—and the roles they played in her erotic life and rise to power. Each man was responsible for awakening passions lying dormant in Catherine. And these passions, the source of her indomitable will, combined with her innate gift for intrigue to propel Catherine along the road to despotism and empire.

ಹ

By 1742, when the future Peter III, then a boy of fourteen, was first brought from his native Kiel in northern Germany to Russia, the Romanov dynasty had precious little Russian blood left in its veins.

Empress Elizabeth, who in November 1741 had seized the throne from a baby cousin and his mother, the Regent, was herself only half-Russian. Her father, Peter the Great, was a genuine Romanov, but her mother, Martha Skavronskaya, who reigned for only two years as Catherine I, was a plebeian—a wartime camp-follower of Lithuanian origin.

Elizabeth's nephew was born Karl Peter Ulrich, son of the Duke of Holstein-Gottorp and of Elizabeth's sister Anna, the elder daughter of Peter the Great. Half-German through his father, one-quarter Russian and one-quarter Lithuanian through his mother, he was summoned from Kiel to St. Petersburg by Empress Elizabeth to be her heir apparent, a Grand Duke and the Crown Prince of Russia. The Empress, despite one secret husband of peasant origin and an abundance of lovers, had no acknowledged children.

Converted from his staunch Lutheranism to the Russian Orthodox Church, which he promptly began to hate as deeply as he detested this barbaric Russia, the boy Peter—now, in Russian, Pyotr Fyodorovich—awaited his bride.

For this prize at least two competing cliques at the Russian court had their candidates, both of them German princesses. Of the two, Elizabeth chose Sophie Augusta Fredericka of Anhalt-Zerbst, in north-central Germany, a region close to both Prussia and Saxony by blood and state service ties, as well as by geography.

Through her mother, Sophie belonged to the Holstein-Gottorp princely clan, one of the multifarious collections of petty north German sovereigns. Peter was also a part of one of this clan's branches. Anhalt-Zerbst, of Sophie's paternal line, was a noble family on a slightly lower level than Holstein-Gottorp, but influential nonetheless.

Sophie's father, Prince Christian August, from the Zerbst-Dornburg side of the house of Anhalt, was some thirty years older than her mother. Like so many of his neighbors, minor German princes, he served King Frederick William I of Prussia. He began by commanding a regiment of the King's, continued as the Commandant of the annexed province of Stettin, and reached the post of Provincial Governor.

The King's son, Frederick the Great as he was to be known, made Prince Christian August a field marshal when Frederick ascended to the throne of Prussia. The young philosopher-warrior-king may have thought that by elevating Christian August he was repaying the elderly man for the festivities he had enjoyed in Stettin castle. In any case, the promotion was the summit of Christian August's career.

Christian August unknowingly made his only really important contribution to history on May 2, 1729, when his daughter Sophie Augusta Fredericka was born—the future Catherine the Great. Nine months earlier, the future Frederick the Great, then the seventeen-year-old Crown Prince, had been a welcome houseguest of Christian August's and his young wife, and there are dark hints in the literature of the time, and later, that the baby girl was not the offspring of the old Governor, but of the witty Crown Prince, who had been ordered away from the fleshpots of Berlin by his stern father. Certainly, when Frederick became King, he did his best to advance Sophie's candidacy as Russia's Crown Princess—and succeeded.

Whatever her parentage, the baby Sophie was the relatively insignificant product of two minuscule princely houses in provincial Germany. This area of Europe, however, had one important attribute—its titled young men and women were sent forth to other, mightier lands to marry, and, frequently, to wield immense power.

Karl Peter Ulrich of Holstein-Gottorp and Sophie Augusta Fredericka of Anhalt-Zerbst both belonged to this procession. Their origins were similar, but fate marked Sophie for fame and Peter for an early and sordid death.

# Marriage as Disaster

Empress Elizabeth made her choice of the bride-to-be with what she thought was due caution and forethought. For months prior to the marriage her ambassadors, agents, and spies gathered information about Sophie and her kinfolk. The candidate's portraits in varying sizes were ordered and delivered, and found favor in Elizabeth's eyes. Finally, invitations were issued for Sophie and her mother to come to Russia.

Elizabeth's informants bungled the investigation of Sophie's mother, for the dossier on Princess Johanna Elizabeth that reached St. Petersburg was incomplete and inaccurate. For years to come, Johanna Elizabeth gained a dubious notoriety throughout the courts of Europe. The Russian historian Vasily Klyuchevsky later characterized her as neurotic, restless, unsettled as if haunted, with a pathological need to quarrel with all around her and to slander anyone she fancied was in her way. She was, writes Klyuchevsky, "an adventure incarnate, an embodiment of intrigue ever on the move, who felt at

home everywhere but not in her own house"—in short, a
busybody. During her lifetime Johanna Elizabeth traveled all
over the Continent, visited most of the European capitals, and
"served as Frederick II's agent in such diplomatic machinations that even genuine diplomats shied away from them, and
for this she earned the great King's considerable respect." Yet
she was to die years later an exile in France, shortly before her
daughter became Empress of all the Russias. She died, according to Klyuchevsky, in straitened circumstances because Frederick was so niggardly about paying his agents.

At least one other Russian historian calls Klyuchevsky's
scorn for Johanna Elizabeth excessive. Research seems to indicate that the Princess, in all her opaque moves in Russia and in
the West, hardly ever took pay, regular or not, from Frederick. Nor did she write any secret dispatches from Russia to
him directly. She conveyed colorful dirt about the Empress-
Tsarina in a more roundabout way, by telling the Prussian envoy in St. Petersburg, who then included her revelations in his
confidential reports to Berlin. Not that this method dimin-
ished her role as Frederick's informer. Generally, except for a
few details, Klyuchevsky, with his ready access to a wide range
of Imperial archives in both St. Petersburg and Moscow, knew
whereof he wrote and lectured.

As for the penury at the close of her life, there is testimony
from other reliable sources that when in time Frederick's
Prussia and Elizabeth's Russia went to war against each other,
and Johanna Elizabeth with one of her sons had to flee to
Paris, her Zerbst castle was confiscated by Frederick. An exile
deep in debt, Johanna Elizabeth had to sell whatever diamonds and furniture she still had. Her daughter, Russia's
Crown Princess, succeeded in persuading Elizabeth to buy the
furniture on the quiet, through trusted intermediaries, to
avoid a scandal.

Sophie grew up at first with no special attention paid to her.
Her elders in the Stettin household, mainly servants and tutors, treated her well enough. On the rare occasions when
Johanna Elizabeth was home, she kept to the simplest rules as
to what her daughter should or should not do. If the Princess

felt that Sophie was at fault, she did not chide her but merely slapped her face.

Fortunately for Sophie, she had a knowledgeable and understanding governess, Mademoiselle Elizabeth Cardel, or Babette, a Frenchwoman of Huguenot origin. Attached to the Stettin household as practically a member of the family, for years she was *in loco parentis* to Sophie and gave her affection while teaching her the French language and classics and even the rudiments of philosophy. Discovering and sharpening Sophie's quick mind and lively curiosity as well as her considerable industry, Babette instructed the child so well that at the beginning of her teens Sophie not only spoke, read, and wrote French fluently but even thought in that language. She also imbued Sophie with gentle manners and delicate feelings. The future Catherine the Great would remember Babette with sunny gratitude to the end of her turbulent life.

At thirteen, Sophie began to fill out in a promisingly agreeable way, and her attractive little figure was soon noticed by males in the castle and in Stettin. When she was fourteen, one of her young Holstein uncles, her mother's junior brother, George, then in Saxon service, fell in love with her. Goodlooking, exuding charm, he made the niece promise that someday she would marry him.

But in far-off St. Petersburg the Empress-Tsarina decided otherwise.

୨

To consolidate the throne she had so recently usurped from the baby Emperor Ivan VI, this daughter of Peter the Great's desperately needed a crown prince of illustrious blood, closely related to her. Karl Peter Ulrich of Holstein seemed to Elizabeth a perfect choice, being the only child of her elder sister Anna, and an orphan. She thought she could manage him at will. And she would soon bring him a suitable bride, a sturdy, fertile German princess to continue the Imperial line of succession.

In choosing Sophie as her nephew's bride, the Empress may have been prompted, in part at least, by the sweet memory of a certain man in Sophie's family.

As a young princess, Elizabeth had once and briefly been betrothed to an uncle of Sophie's, the eldest brother of Johanna Elizabeth, the dashing, handsome Prince Karl August of Holstein-Gottorp. Declared Elizabeth's fiancé, he had arrived in Russia, and on beholding him, the Princess said that she was indeed smitten, that, yes, she loved Prince Karl August dearly and would marry him. Then smallpox suddenly struck the visitor and he died. Elizabeth was wont to say that her grief over his horrible and unexpected death compelled her to remain unmarried. But as if to assuage the pain, she became promiscuous, trying one lover after another, well into her two decades as Empress.

In choosing Sophie, the Empress would also faithfully follow the precept of her father, the Great Westernizer, for Emperor-Tsar Peter preferred Germans to any other nationals as brides and grooms for his young kin. At one time Peter had tried France. While in Paris after his brilliant victories over Sweden, the Tsar tentatively proposed that he and the Duke of Orléans, the Regent, arrange to marry the young King Louis XV to Peter's own equally young daughter Elizabeth. Peter needed such an alliance with a powerful European dynasty to underscore his new Russian power, to speed up his country's Westernization.

But, politely and firmly, the French declined Peter's bid. To them, this Tsar and his realm were mere upstarts, of foggy antecedents and an uncertain future. Elizabeth's mother, Martha Skavronskaya, that erstwhile laundress and mistress of veritable rabble of Russian soldiery—until Tsar Peter picked Martha up to make her his regal consort—was especially distasteful to the French. After his death, Martha—then Catherine I—renewed negotiations with the French, but her overtures were declined even more emphatically. In their disdain, the Bourbons would not offer from their resplendent stock even a substitute husband for young Elizabeth, not even a minor prince or a duke. Their family tree was more than a thousand years old. It dated back to the Crusades—even further—and was deep in the soil of Western Europe. The King of France, to be sure, embraced lower-class beauties, some taken from the dregs of his subjects, but solely as bed-companions, never as royalty. So the rulers of eighteenth-century Russia turned to the more complaisant Germans in their search for titled and eligible young men and women.

෫෧

Sophie was four months short of fifteen when, on January 10, 1744, she left Zerbst for Berlin, and on the twentieth of February (which, by the Russian calendar was the ninth of February) arrived in St. Petersburg.

During this journey, her mother and traveling companion worried about the girl's future and complained about the discomforts, which included primitive accommodations and the bitter cold of the Russian winter. But Sophie, on the surface timid, was hopeful and sharply observant of her new impressions.

Near Riga they had encountered a strange convoy of black carriages, with window curtains tightly shut, guarded by forbidding-looking horsemen. Sophie asked who they were.

The answer was at first silence, followed by a gruff explanation that the gloomy carriages contained the Braunschweig family of the deposed baby Tsar, the former Emperor Ivan VI, being transported from one place of captivity to another even more wretched, farther east. Not an auspicious beginning for Sophie's Russian sojourn.

She cheered up when, later, a large escort of gaily attired cavalry joined them. Sophie gazed at the riders with delight. The Russians saw a shy young girl with irregular features, not a beauty but sufficiently good-looking, her deep-blue eyes strikingly set off by black eyelashes. She had full lips and a chin that jutted out ever so slightly. They of course were unaware that back home a number of men were sighing for her, including her dashing Uncle George.

At Riga a delegation from the Empress met the mother and daughter, among them General Vasily Saltykov, a member of one of Russia's most venerable families. Eight years later, the General's younger son, the handsome and volatile Sergei, Chamberlain to the Crown Prince, would become Sophie's first lover.

*        *        *

In St. Petersburg, the Empress, having carefully examined her guest, decided that she had made a good choice. Elizabeth displayed considerable benevolence toward Sophie, but was cooler toward the mother, whom she soon determined to be meddlesome and demanding. Both women were showered with costly gifts, and initially Sophie thought that her aunt-to-be was kindness itself, a paragon of virtue, love, and solicitude.

Young Peter treated his future bride to a variety of moods, now friendly, now surly. Sophie thought him immature and far from handsome, and a bout with smallpox soon rendered him so ugly that Elizabeth did not want the sensitive girl to visit him during or immediately after the illness. When Sophie finally did see him after his convalescence, she reassured the Empress that she would indeed go through with the marriage. The Empress had feared that upon beholding the awful mask of Peter's face, she would plead to be sent back to Germany. But Sophie held firm—after all, she was not marrying her boorish Holstein cousin, she was marrying the crown of Russia.

On June 28, 1744, in a glittering, slow-paced ceremony, the young German visitor was admitted to the Russian Orthodox Church and received her new name—Catherine, or, in Russia, Yekaterina Alekseyevna. The Empress would thus honor the name and memory of her mother, Martha Skavronskaya, who became Catherine, daughter of Alexis, when she converted to Orthodoxy.

Young Catherine had prepared for her new faith diligently. For months since early 1744, under the tutelage of zealous priests, she had studied the recondite Church dogma and ritual in addition to the difficult Russian language, and showed considerable success. She was determined to be as devoutly Russian and Orthodox as her new status demanded. The Empress was delighted, and so were the priests. Her bridegroom-to-be sneered.

To her somewhat anxious father, the girl wrote reassuringly that there was really very little difference between Lutheranism and Russian Orthodoxy, which of course was not true.

Her mother, on the other hand, didn't seem to care. From

the time of their arrival in Russia six months earlier, Johanna
Elizabeth jealously counted and compared the jewelry, the
money, and the rich attire presented by the Empress to her
and her daughter. She complained that more honors and
other attentions were given to her daughter than to her, and
she tirelessly plunged into this or that dubious corridor of
court intrigue.

The Princess flirted outrageously with several handsome
chamberlains, especially one, Ivan Betsky. Some at the court
even said that she went to bed with him, and several of Catherine's ladies-in-waiting, those who felt quite at ease with her
by now, gently teased the girl that soon enough she might
have a little Russian half-brother or half-sister. Catherine was
shocked and embarrassed.

At the same time, her mother gleefully collected juicy court
gossip about Elizabeth's many affairs and relayed these tidbits
to King Frederick's Ambassador in St. Petersburg, Baron Axel
von Mardefeld. Early in Elizabeth's reign the Ambassador was
liked and trusted by the Empress. He was among those who
had helped in his King's advocacy of the little Princess of
Anhalt-Zerbst as the Russian Heir Apparent's bride.

But von Mardefeld was detested by the seemingly all-powerful Chancellor Alexis Bestuzhev-Ryumin, great-grandson of
an English immigrant in Russian service. The Chancellor had
vigorously intrigued in favor of another German princess as
the future bride, but in spite of his influence with the Empress, had lost. He was still hopeful, even at a late date.

A lucky break came his way, or so he thought for a time.
Robbers stopped von Mardefeld's special courier on his westward route and relieved him of his pouch. The highwaymen
were Bestuzhev-Ryumin's masked servants. In the pouch
brought to the Chancellor were von Mardefeld's dispatches to
Frederick, quoting copiously from Johanna Elizabeth's scandalous tales about Elizabeth's bedroom antics.

Triumphantly, Bestuzhev-Ryumin carried to the Empress
these gleanings from von Mardefeld's diplomatic pouch, with
a few judicious comments of his own. The Empress exploded.
She summoned mother and daughter before her and showed
them the evidence, then one outraged tirade followed an-

other. She shouted curses and threats: "The ingratitude, the lies! Even if this were true, what business is it of yours? I will destroy you!"

She would not listen to Johanna Elizabeth's abject, tearful apologies.

For a time it seemed as if the marriage would be called off and both women sent packing back to Berlin and Zerbst in disgrace. But the Empress disappointed Bestuzhev-Ryumin's fond hopes. She made it clear that her anger was aimed at Johanna Elizabeth, not at her daughter. In fact, Catherine, after the initial terror and confusion, regained her courage and Elizabeth's confidence, and adroitly soothed the Empress, who eventually calmed down enough to postpone Johanna Elizabeth's expulsion from Russia until after the marriage.

The betrothal ceremony was held on June 29, 1744, the day after Catherine's conversion to Russian Orthodoxy. But nearly fourteen months more had to elapse, for one reason or another, before the wedding. Catherine had been in Russia for a year and a half when, on August 21, 1745, she was married to Peter. He was seventeen and a half; she, just past sixteen.

&.

All through 1744 and up to the date of the wedding there were problems. At times the Empress seemed to be postponing the preparations, and she even hesitated to set the date. Then she appeared to be in a rush. She tried to be gracious with Johanna Elizabeth, despite the woman's misbehavior at court, evidently because she was afraid, groundlessly, that the eccentric German would take offense at something or other, pack her bags, and take Catherine back home.

Elizabeth was also worried by the coolness developing between the betrothed pair, which contrasted with their correct conduct toward each other during the early stages of their acquaintanceship. After Peter's recovery from smallpox, the two had got along quite well. They would often sit side by side on a windowsill, swinging their legs and chatting in German. Peter was pleased that Catherine did not then insist on speaking

Russian, which was difficult for him but apparently came easily to her, though she always spoke with an accent.

But for months now, Peter had been clearly hostile toward his future wife. He envied her looks, her *politesse,* which charmed all those around her. Instead of pride in her success, he felt acute resentment. The mirrors in the palaces he visited told him how repulsive his face and figure were. Everyone bowed before him, the Crown Prince, but there wasn't the fond attention that Catherine now received. He craved it for himself and did not get it.

The Empress realized that the wedding had to take place at once, before the two were totally estranged. And Elizabeth wished no other bride for her nephew. Perhaps more than anyone else, the Empress was beguiled by Catherine—by her looks, promising in their bloom a real beauty, by her tact, her obedience to the Imperial will of her aunt, her diligence in learning both her new Orthodoxy and her new tongue, so strange and perplexing with its endless declensions, conjugations, tenses, participles, and gerunds. During one winter, Catherine rose regularly from her bed in the middle of the night to bend over her desk for hours, memorizing words and phrases. She caught a bad cold that nearly deteriorated into pneumonia.

Early in the summer of 1745, Elizabeth moved to the Summer Palace, taking the nephew with her; Catherine had to remain with her mother in the Winter Palace. Peter at once took advantage of the parting: now he visited his bride rarely, explaining rudely that it was too far for him to walk or even ride from one palace to the other. At one of his infrequent visits he laughed unpleasantly as he told Catherine, "My lackey Romberg the Swede has been teaching me how to handle women. He says that the wife must keep her silence and always tremble before her husband, and the husband must beat her constantly."

The worsening of the relationship was reported to the Empress by her informers at court. "We must marry them immediately!" she cried out in horror. But Her Majesty's personal physician, the clever descendant of Huguenots, Count Johann Hermann Lestocq, a sometime lover of Elizabeth's while she was a princess, and who had helped her to the throne in the November 1741 coup, now warned her, "Please wait, Your Majesty. The Crown Prince is too young, he is not really developed yet."

"Nonsense, my friend, you are wrong. The young man's only trouble is that he drinks too much. Once we make him stop his drinking he will be an excellent husband and father, and all will be well."

She then named the fateful date: August 21.

Meanwhile, Catherine was growing more and more apprehensive. She who had wanted this marriage so much was hesitant now. In her memoirs she recalls, "The closer the date of my wedding approached, the greater the melancholy in my heart. I wept often, myself not knowing why."

For all her curiosity and eager anticipation, the young bride-to-be was frightened and naive. Catherine had known some of the facts of life since early childhood, but in the essential areas she was basically ignorant. Her mother had told her nothing until the eve of the first night with Peter.

She was passionate—that much she knew. As a preadolescent, she had fallen into the delicious habit of jumping up and down on her bed almost every night, embracing those voluminous German pillows and featherbeds with her entire unformed body, mounting the pillows spread-eagle until she reached a state of sweet and voluptuous relief. Only then could she sleep.

Less than a year before her departure for Russia she had turned the head of her handsome eighteen-year-old Uncle George, and she had had some naughty dreams at the time.

And in Russia, while waiting over a year for her wedding to be arranged and celebrated, Catherine often spent long evenings with her young chambermaids, most of whom were of hearty peasant stock, and would lie back in her bed and drink in their salacious tales of what their brothers and sisters had told them about initial marital bliss.

At last, on the evening of August 20, 1745, Johanna Elizabeth secreted herself with her daughter Catherine and began to tell her of the magic and misery of the night when a virgin becomes a woman. For once they were loving and intimate, and they cried on each other's shoulder.

At six the next morning Catherine entered her bathroom, where the chambermaids had made everything ready. Just then the Empress appeared for her obligatory surveillance of the bride's nudity, to make sure that Catherine had no physical defects that might prevent her from being the Crown Prince's proper wife and the worthy mother of their children. Satisfied, the Empress left.

Bathed and perfumed, Catherine stepped into her boudoir, where Elizabeth was awaiting her. The hairdresser labored on the future bride's head for a full hour while the Empress supervised the progress, punctuating the work with her peremptory instructions.

She kept up her rapid fire of orders as Catherine was being dressed. The result was enchanting, as Johanna Elizabeth later reported to her husband in Stettin: "Exquisite jewels and ornaments, which literally covered her from head to toe, made my girl glitter with beauty. Her cheeks were slightly rouged. . . . Her glossy black hair was a particularly fine contrast to her soft white skin. No powder was placed on her; her skin was naturally white. I have never in my life seen such magnificent attire, brilliant with silver and with wonderfully patterned embroidery."

The erratic yet fond mother concluded, "The Empress with her own hands placed the Imperial crown on our daughter's head."

Catherine's bridal gown was of silk imported from Naples. The Empress wore a similar dress, but in chestnut brown instead of silver. Italian silk was used for the Crown Prince's wedding suit. The buttons of his jacket were large diamonds, and his sword was studded with them as well.

The principal wedding train consisted of twenty-four gilded court carriages, the first of which was occupied by the Empress and the bridal pair. A file of other vehicles of varying degrees of splendor followed. To show her displeasure with the bride's mother, the Empress allotted to Johanna Elizabeth a secondary seat in a lesser-ranking carriage. Christian August was absent—he was not invited, much to Catherine's carefully concealed chagrin, for she had wanted her father to be a guest on this day of all days. But Johanna Elizabeth's young brother, Prince Ludwig of Holstein, was present, as was one of the Hesse princesses, bidden to come on Elizabeth's whim.

The procession rolled solemnly from the Summer Palace to the Kazansky Cathedral, escorted by a glittering troop of Guards officers and another contingent of court retainers in their Imperial liveries. Block after block was lined with Guards regiments, townspeople, and peasants from nearby villages.

The processions and ceremonies marking the three major events of her youth—the conversion, the betrothal, and the wedding—stayed with Catherine as vivid memories to the end of her life. Describing in her memoirs an early recollection of Russians thronging the route of an Imperial progress toward a cathedral, she tells of her astonishment at the enormous number of onlookers in rags, of cripples and beggars, all bowing humbly before the jewel-bedecked aristocrats, passing in their fantastically adorned carriages, escorted by richly clothed lackeys, all of this preceded by bishops and priests in gold and silver robes, carrying icons and crosses encrusted with diamonds and emeralds.

To such events the head of the Chernyshev clan, an illegitimate son of Peter the Great and incredibly rich, came with a swarm of retainers, outriders, and other manservants, every one of them clad in livery of gold brocade.

And to this Grand Ducal wedding on August 21 an exalted elder Naryshkin, from whose clan the mother of Peter the Great had stemmed, rode in a carriage studded with mirrors and costing all of 50,000 rubles. His caftan from collar to hem scintillated with precious Ural and Oriental stones.

The wedding ceremony was long and tedious. The clergy, led by Metropolitan Amvrosy and lesser hierarchs, filled the cathedral with their chanting, now sonorous, now shrill or booming. In her memoirs Catherine remembers how heavily her bridal gown and crown weighed on her.

As the service dragged on, the Crown Prince fidgeted. At one point a Chernyshev lady tiptoed up to him and whispered

into his ear, "Do stand still, Your Highness. You are not on
your life to turn your head. It is our Russian folk belief that
whichever of you does so will die first."

In response the Crown Prince cursed the Countess under
his breath, then repeated to Catherine by his side, raising his
voice suddenly, with a short, loud laugh, "The damned fool
says that whichever of us turns his head will die first!"

And he did just that, glaring balefully.

At last it was over. The procession regrouped to reverse its
steps and wheels to the Summer Palace for the ball.

But the Empress said she was fatigued. After a mere half-
hour of dancing she announced that the newlyweds were now
to be taken to the bedchamber in the apartments set aside for
them in the palace. The bridal pair, with their closest relatives
and highest courtiers, marched to the bedroom.

In her letter to Stettin, Johanna Elizabeth took care to note
that the walls of the bedroom were lined with bright-red velvet, and that the baldachin over the bed was huge and
gorgeous. The closest relatives entered the room with the pair,
but, in accordance with ancient custom, the bridegroom and
all the other males left immediately.

The ritual of unclothing the Imperial bride began. Catherine's mother wrote to Christian August, "Her Imperial Majesty herself removed the crown from our daughter's head,
then yielded to the Hessian Princess the honor of undressing
her and putting the nightgown upon her."

Presently all were gone. The door was closed. Catherine was
alone and awaited her husband.

She did not love Peter. He was unattractive, his formerly
moonlike face by then made gaunt and even more disagreeable by his illness. He was crude, unpleasant, and unpredict-
able. But one day he would be Emperor of all the Russias, and
she would rule with him as Empress. She was resigned and
prepared for her wifely duty.

Lying in her exquisite nightgown, Catherine waited in an
emotional state of fear mixed with elation. But the bridegroom did not arrive. In her memoirs, thirty years later, she
recalls how restless she became, now lying in bed, now jump-

ing up in despair and searching for her clothes, to dress and
go—where?

Peter walked in two hours later, staggering drunk after
many bottles shared with Andrew Chernyshev and other cronies. He struggled into a nightshirt and declared with a stupid
laugh, "The lackey would have been amused to see us together in bed!"

Without a further word, he chose a spot on the bed as far
away from Catherine as he could find, turned his back to her,
and fell asleep, snoring loudly, his body reeking of wine and
tobacco.

๏

For days and weeks afterward, receptions, dinners, and balls
followed one another in a mélange of native Russian and imported Western European splendor. No one knew of Catherine's anguish and bitterness.

Her mother wanted to stay on and on, but the Empress was
firm. Surely, she said, Christian August wanted his wife back
in Stettin. So Johanna Elizabeth at long last left, on September
28, 1745. Catherine was destined not to see either her or her
father again.

On the specific orders of the Empress, the carriage was
ready early that morning, and Johanna Elizabeth departed
while her daughter still slept. The day before, mother and
daughter did not even have a chance to say a proper, crying
goodbye in each other's arms. In fact, though she missed her
mother and felt even more alone, Catherine was also vastly
relieved that her life-complicating parent was finally gone.

The last audience had been given by the Empress to
Johanna Elizabeth in mid-September. It had been very official,
in the throne hall, the Empress sitting high above the Princess
in a tall armchair, a diamond diadem on her proud head, the
blue ribbon of the Order of Saint Andrew across her heavy
shoulder and ample bosom, a dry smile on her sensuous lips.
She extended her plump hand to be kissed.

Pressing the Imperial hand to her trembling lips, Johanna
Elizabeth fell to her knees. In her best French, she begged the

sovereign's forgiveness "For all the unpleasantness caused Her Majesty willfully or inadvertently . . ."

There was for a tiny moment something like a friendly glance from the Empress. Then, no doubt recalling what Chancellor Bestuzhev-Ryumin had brought to her, Elizabeth grew cold. She lectured testily: "It is too late to talk of this, Madame. You should have thought about it sooner. Had you shown from the very start this modesty and humility, everything would have been different."

She wished the Princess bon voyage and extended her hand to be kissed once more. Johanna Elizabeth made the deepest curtsy possible. The Empress, already risen from the armchair, turned to leave. There was no forgiveness.

A passionate gambler, Johanna Elizabeth on the eve of her departure was appalled to learn that her card debts had reached a tremendous sum, and that in addition her extravagant dress purchases in St. Petersburg had resulted in piles of unpaid bills. Altogether she owed 160,000 rubles. She had believed that all these obligations would be discharged by an Imperial ukase. But the Empress willed that only 60,000 rubles of the total be paid from the Romanov treasury. Catherine came to the rescue. She signed a promise to her mother's creditors that she would personally pay back the remaining 100,000 rubles, in periodic installments, out of her own Grand Ducal allowance.

On arrival in Berlin, Johanna Elizabeth experienced one wild flash of hope when a messenger from the Russian embassy delivered a letter with Elizabeth's personal seal. The Empress was at last pardoning her, was sending her one more rich gift! But her hope turned to ashes when she read a request, to be relayed by Johanna Elizabeth to Frederick: His Majesty was to recall his envoy, Axel von Mardefeld.

Of her wedding night, Catherine was to write three decades later, "That very first impression entered my sensitive heart deeply, and remained there for the rest of my life."

Similar nights followed, for years, as a terrible ordeal. Catherine recalls that, while she bathed daily, Peter rarely washed, and his odor was high and revolting.

Nonetheless, she was ready and willing. He was not. As to who, if anyone, had prepared the Crown Prince for the crucial phase of his nuptials, no memoir or other deposition tells us. It is unlikely that any competent physician had ever examined him.

At the age of seventeen, when he was wed, Peter knew the joys of intoxication, but was totally incapable with women. He may have been a passive homosexual. In any case, Dr. Lestocq had guessed correctly about the boy. And even as Peter slowly matured and gradually learned, by way of his rough-and-tumble friends at court, about a man's way with a woman, his tightly grown foreskin, a condition known as phimosis, prevented him from enjoying the practical experience until well into his mid-twenties.

At night, lying next to his young wife, the Crown Prince played with his toy soldiers for hours on end, setting them up and moving them about on the blanket. He owned many such soldiers, made of lead, wood, sugar, starch, and other materials, whole companies and battalions of them. Sometimes Peter forced Catherine to participate in the childish maneuvers and battles.

Another passion of the Crown Prince's was his puppet theater, and with this too he would amuse himself for long stretches of time, usually in a special vestibule of the palace, but occasionally in their bedroom. He fancied himself a violinist and scraped his fiddle mercilessly, assailing his wife's ears.

In their bedroom, behind the resplendent bed, he kept several of his pet dogs. Catherine loved animals, but even her patience wore thin. The hounds were restless, ran around the chamber, jumped over the bed, and barked or whined incessantly. On one occasion Peter became incensed by the improper behavior of a small, pedigreed dog. He would train the brute right, he vowed. So he hung the unfortunate animal up and began to lash it cruelly. As the dog yelped and howled, Catherine, in tears, implored Peter to stop, but he went on till it died.

In her memoirs she was to write, "What a misfortune to be

married to a man who is altogether too young." And: "No, there have never been in the world two persons so unlike mentally."

In spite of all this, she might have become used to Peter, might have even learned to love him, "had he been willing to be pleasant to me." She went on:

> But already in the very first days of our marriage the heavy thought came to me: should you fall in love with this man, you will be the unhappiest woman on earth, for there will be no harmony whatsoever between you and him. . . . He pays you no attention at all, he talks of hardly anything except his puppet theater, and to any other woman he is more attentive than to you. . . . And you are too proud to complain aloud. And so, do not display any friendliness to this gentleman, take care only of yourself, Madame.

When not drooling over his marionettes or his toy soldiers, Peter, though still a virgin, began to babble about his exploits with various ladies of the court, and even pretended to ask his wife's advice on how to manipulate them to his best advantage. Catherine was still too naive to understand that it was all braggadocio, that he was incapable of using his member, that he fantasized his conquests because of his inadequacies, to compensate for his many weaknesses and failures. And although he continued to be repulsive to her, she was nonetheless jealous as he boasted of his successes while she suffered his monstrous neglect. For years Catherine remained ignorant of her husband's phimosis.

Still not truly a beauty, Catherine was now well formed, with an early hint of the eroticism soon to blossom forth. It was difficult for her to remain a married virgin when the entire court around her was so dissolute, when fornication was the order of the day. Particularly notorious was her aunt and sovereign, the Empress Elizabeth, who openly carried on her affairs with three or four steady lovers at the same time, allotting each his hour or two, and taking to her bed any well-built Guardsman she spotted, often summoning a soldier from his sentry post to amuse her.

And there was Peter's passion for King Frederick. The two corresponded, mostly in Peter's later years, but never met. Peter idealized the King from afar. He wore a ring with Frederick's cameo portrait on it, and often pressed it to his lips reverently. Peter knew by heart every battle in which Frederick had fought, in all its details, especially those engagements in which the Prussian had defeated his opponents. Frederick, hearing of this, marveled at the Grand Duke's adulation and said laughingly, not without a touch of smugness, "Peter sees me as his Dulcinea."

Upon learning of a military innovation or reform in Prussia, Peter studied it carefully. Even though Russian uniforms, introduced half a century earlier by his grandfather, Peter the Great, were far more comfortable and practical than those decreed by Frederick, the Grand Duke—even as Heir Apparent, not yet Russia's Emperor—insisted on Prussian models, and never mind their irksome rigidity: they looked so imposing on the parade ground.

This became evident when Peter grew bold enough to import a few units of his own Holstein soldiers from Kiel. He dressed them in Frederick's awkward cut of uniform and had a diminutive fort built, also on the Prussian pattern. Now he could push his toy soldiers aside, play real war games, and stage parades with live warriors. Prince Nicholas Repnin, a sensible man appointed by the Empress to supervise the Grand Duke, goodnaturedly let him have his way, hoping that Peter would leave behind some of his childish foolishness if he had weightier pastimes.

But the Empress soon showed her concern, seeing her throne threatened. She did not want foreign soldiers, particularly Germans, so close to her seat of power, and in 1747 she ordered the Holsteiners sent home. Elizabeth also decreed the dismissal and departure of a number of Peter's Holstein officials. There were entirely too many of them, she felt, and they made free of the Grand Ducal court (also called the small court and the young court). The Empress was angry: "These

Germans openly mock our Russian customs and particularly our Orthodox faith."

But here she encountered a dilemma: Peter was, after all, the hereditary Duke of Holstein, and while in St. Petersburg, had to rule his cabinet ministers sitting at Kiel. For this he needed his advisers and liaison men at his elbow in the Russian capital. Elizabeth had to relent.

As the new Duchess of Holstein, Catherine found herself involved in the matters of that distant German land. Peter, especially in their first years together, when the pair got along better, sometimes sought her advice on problems, most often those having to do with Holstein. He was pleased by her judgments and even called her Madame la Ressource.

But in these and other things Catherine was opposed by some of his retinue, most vehemently by his Chief Chamberlain (*Kammerherr*), General von Brocktorff. The Grand Duchess and the Holsteiner hated each other; because of his ugly, birdlike appearance she dubbed him, in the folksy Russian she was constantly expanding, *Baba Ptitsa*—the Pelican.

In addition to his older advisers from Holstein, there were enough younger officers from Kiel left in Peter's entourage, and it was with them, as well as with some native Russians, that Peter behaved like the chieftain of a gang of overripe delinquents. Wild, tough, unkempt, they roughhoused all over the palaces and nearby royal parks; chased one another when they weren't marching around or playing at military maneuvers; drank, played cards, shot their pistols aimlessly, or beat dogs.

The tamest of Peter's amusements was his puppet theater, to which he invited his cronies and even his servants and lackeys. One late evening he unveiled a most unexpected treat for his boon companions.

A tightly fitted and securely locked door led from the vestibule into one of the intimate rooms of the Empress. Moved by curiosity, the Grand Duke had three holes drilled through the door, so tiny as not to be easily detected, yet affording a clear view of what was taking place within.

The Empress was supping with her secret husband, Alexis Razumovsky (in court whispers irreverently spoken of as "the Night Emperor"), and her two younger lovers, Ivan Shuvalov and Nikita Beketov, among other guests. All were in attire customarily worn in bed.

In feverish excitement Peter called his guests to come enjoy the show. They looked and marveled, doubled over with suppressed laughter. He tried to induce a passing court lady to have a peek, then summoned Catherine. But she, after one brief glance, turned away in disgust from her husband and his gang and lectured them for their licentiousness and temerity. She implored Peter to plug up the holes, but he refused.

Catherine did not report any of this to the Empress, but from her own informers the Imperial aunt learned of the holes and the voyeurism. Livid with rage, Elizabeth ordered both Peter and Catherine summoned to her presence.

The couple, roused from their bed, were quick-stepped—almost dragged—to the Empress in their nightclothes. In shrill indignation she tore into her nephew—but spared Catherine. For her informers had told the Empress of Catherine's sense of propriety and her refusal to join in the lark.

As Peter, in stunned silence, twirled his nightcap in his trembling hands, Elizabeth shouted at him to remember what his namesake, his grandfather and her father, Peter the Great, did to his own son and heir, Alexis, for his insubordination and treachery—had him tortured to death. "Those who do not show respect for crowned persons will be thrown into prison!"

Her nephew was truly frightened now. Above all things, he feared a dungeon like that in which for years his ill-fated cousin, former Emperor Ivan VI, overthrown by Elizabeth, was languishing. The Grand Duke's nightmares were filled with visions of himself, chained to a wall as a result of his aunt's wrath or a palace coup. He tried to mumble an explanation or apology, but the Empress cut him short with curses and obscenities.

Catherine, shaken by the scene, began to cry. Elizabeth turned to her abruptly, with sudden calm, to reassure the young woman that her virtuous behavior at the door was known and appreciated, and that the curses and threats were for Peter only.

Peter shivered; the danger was grave. In St. Petersburg, the palaces and dungeons were near each other and, as the historian Klyuchevsky observed, frequently exchanged tenants.

In early 1744, when Catherine, barely fifteen, first met her future aunt, Elizabeth was thirty-four and still very handsome. Tall, heavily but majestically built, with an attractive face and a good figure, she often dressed in tight-fitting uniforms for riding, masquerades, and parades, the better to display her charms. A diplomat wrote, "You cannot imagine how well a military uniform sets off her looks. I am confident that those not knowing her identity could easily take her for an officer were it not for her beautiful feminine face."

Her ample chestnut-brown hair contrasted well with her large brown eyes and white teeth. In her agreeable moods she liked to show off her teeth and her sensuous mouth in a charming smile—particularly to good-looking young males whom she wanted for her bed. The Spanish envoy, though generally hostile toward her, wrote extravagantly of her "supernatural beauty."

Unfortunately, in her late thirties Elizabeth was becoming not just stylishly stout but excessively fat. She began to drink to excess, kept irregular hours, and neglected to exercise except in bed. She took after her father in more than stature; like Peter the Great she had a quick temper but usually cooled off right away. Like her magnificent father, she was promiscuous. Nor had her mother lagged far behind Russia's first Emperor: Martha, the peasant girl and camp follower, later destined to be Empress Catherine I, was also beautiful and sexually proficient.

Exceedingly vain, first as Grand Duchess and later as Empress of all the Russias, Elizabeth spent hours selecting robes and hairdos for court functions and still more time dressing, once the choice was made. Sometimes diplomats and courtiers marking time in the reception halls were requested to go home and return another day—Her Majesty was not ready and did not know at what hour she would be prepared to make her appearance.

On one regrettable occasion Elizabeth decided to have her lush brown hair dyed black. But the dye was defective. Instead of the desired change, it flowed over her scalp and down her face and neck. Her hair had to be shorn and she would have to wear a cap until it grew out. Not wishing to suffer alone her sorry condition, the Empress decreed that every woman in court, from the ladies-in-waiting to the chambermaids, had to have their heads shaved. In spite of the weeping and wailing, the ukase was carried out, but Catherine was spared this indignity.

Elizabeth began her erotic career in her mid-teens, a few years before the reign of her cousin Empress Anna Ivanovna (daughter of Ivan V, who was a half-brother of Peter the Great). Mortally afraid of Ernst Johann Biron (Buehren), Anna's Baltic lover and the despotic and cruel deputy ruler of Russia, young Elizabeth avoided the main palaces and Machiavellian politics of the empire. Hearing from time to time rumors that Biron and other Germans around him were making ready to strike at Elizabeth by making her a nun, their would-be victim distanced herself from the court by moving to her estate of Alexandrovskaya Sloboda near Moscow. There, in the mid-1720s, she tried out her earliest lovers, one after another, "shamelessly doing things which caused even the least modest persons to blush," wrote the well-known Tsarist-era historian Vasily Bilbasov, "and then fervently praying before a Holy Virgin icon." For she was indeed pious.

Bilbasov names A. B. Buturlin, a good-looking Guardsman, the very first "slave of her heart." From him she switched to an even more handsome Sergeant Ivan Shubin of the Semyonovsky Guards Regiment. The Sergeant's most halcyon year was 1726, when Elizabeth was seventeen and her mother, Catherine I, was still alive and on the throne. This bliss apparently lasted past her mother's death in 1727, and through the short reign of her nephew Peter II (1727–1730), but came to grief when her cousin Anna Ivanovna ascended the throne upon the death of Peter II in 1730.

Lover Shubin boasted about his luck too much and too openly, and Empress Anna was displeased. Never having transcended his peasant origins, the Sergeant behaved, according to Georg von Helbig, a German memoirist, so ostentatiously that Anna "roughly and impolitely" ordered him to be arrested and shipped off to Siberia. Several sources state that by the same decree, the Sergeant's tongue was cut out, a rather decisive way of stopping his bragging, but this is disputed by Helbig, who relates the scandal as follows:

In 1741, at five o'clock in the morning following the November night of her coup d'état, the newly ascended Empress Elizabeth sent a special courier to Siberia, promising him a suitable reward if he found Shubin. The courier's problem was that before being chained and sent off, Shubin had his name changed by one more order of Empress Anna's, so that now, in 1741, no one could find him. Nor were any documents left behind in any chanceries as to what new name Shubin had been given.

The courier searched all the Siberian prisons and places of exile diligently but to no avail. Many fruitless months passed, and the man was ready to return to St. Petersburg and report his failure. As he was turning away from the last dungeon of the last jail, he exclaimed in despair, "What will our Empress Elizabeth Petrovna say if I don't deliver Shubin to her?"

"What?" a prisoner from the back of the cell called out. "If Elizabeth is the Empress now, I am Shubin!"

So he was, indeed, with his tongue intact.

Shubin reached St. Petersburg in the summer of 1743. The reunion was touching. The Sergeant was immediately promoted to the rank of major and decorated with the Order of St. Alexander Nevsky, for past services rendered and sufferings endured.

Elizabeth was overjoyed to see her former lover, but she did not summon him to her bed, for the unfortunate soldier retained few traces of his former good looks and virility. Elizabeth soon realized that Shubin could be of no use to her as a courtier or official either, for it was plain to everyone that he was hopelessly stupid.

Besides, since 1726, she had had a succession of lovers that included Andrew Vozhzhinsky, a stableman; a page named Lyalin; and, most prominently, a chorister from the Ukraine, Alexis Razumovsky, who now (mildly) objected to Shubin's reappearance.

And so, the Empress granted Shubin extensive estates, to

which he soon retired with his new rank of lieutenant general. There he lived out the rest of his years in peaceful obscurity.

Elizabeth took the chorister to her bed while she was still a Grand Duchess, a full decade before her seizure of the throne. This was his story:

An officer of the Imperial army, a certain Colonel Vishnevsky, was returning to Russia from a wine-buying mission to Hungary. His route lay through the Ukraine. Early in January 1731, he briefly halted his journey in the village of Chemery in the province of Chernigov. The stop coincided with a holiday, and the pious Colonel walked into the local church. During the service he noticed a youthful chorister whose voice and looks were out of the ordinary.

After the service, the officer talked to the priests. They told him that the young man, then twenty-two, was from a poor Cossack family named Razum. His mother, known locally as Razumikha—Razum Woman—owned and ran a tavern in the nearby village of Lemeshi, a ramshackle enterprise, as such rural establishments were. In his boyhood, the Chemery village clergy had singled out Alexis Razum for his voice and had taken him over from his family to sing in the church and live at the priests' expense.

The Colonel bluntly announced that the young man was going with him to St. Petersburg. The flattered clergymen were willing to let Alexis go, but Mother Razum still had the final say in the matter, and it was not without difficulty that the Colonel won her consent.

In the capital, Colonel Vishnevsky handed over Alexis to the proper authorities, who, having tested the newcomer's voice and clothed him appropriately, placed him in the choir of the Imperial court chapel. Grand Duchess Elizabeth happened to be in her St. Petersburg quarters, not at her retreat near Moscow. One day she saw and heard Alexis as he was singing a liturgy. She was at once spellbound by his voice and by his splendid physique. Her decision was immediate: she ordered him to appear before her in a private audience.

The young couple were the same age, having been born in 1709. The Ukrainian was tall, statuesque, with a smooth, slightly swarthy skin. His black eyes were of an exotic cast and seemed to resemble those of figures seen on timeless Egyptian bas-reliefs. The Grand Duchess melted in his presence.

She requested and obtained his transfer to her entourage. He was now officially called "Her Highness' personal singer." But his untutored voice soon slid into mediocrity, and he was transferred to the post of Imperial bandurist—player on the bandura, a multistringed Ukrainian folk instrument. Razum's talent again proved to be feeble, and one more change was made. Appointed to be manager first of one of Elizabeth's estates, then of all of them, he was in time the undisputed master of her bed as well as her fields, mansions, and serfs. Alexis' family name, Razum, though meaning "mind" or "cleverness," somehow did not sound dignified enough to Elizabeth, so by her decree, it was lengthened to Razumovsky, which was considered far more genteel.

On that November night in 1741 when Elizabeth deposed Ivan VI, her lover Alexis did not accompany her in her busy rounds of the Guards barracks that led to her capture of the main Romanov palace. He was told to stay behind and guard her own small palace at the Tsaritsyn Meadow. All went well, and it was to the Meadow palace that Elizabeth first brought her royal captives—the overthrown Regent Anna Leopoldovna with her baby, Ivan, now the former Emperor, and his newborn sister.

On her first day as the Empress of all the Russias, the triumphant Elizabeth brought her lover, Alexis, out into the open. She elevated him to the rank of chamberlain, then made him a lieutenant general—although he had never seen a battle—and gave him the title of count. Later she promoted him to field marshal and secretly married him. At that point malicious tongues at court dubbed him the Night Emperor. Elizabeth presented Alexis with thousands of serfs. His estates, including those in his native Ukraine, equaled Bavaria in size.

After her seizure of power, Elizabeth commanded that her lover's mother and younger brother Cyril be brought to the capital, together with whatever close relatives could be rounded up. An officer was put in charge of a caravan of sleds and carriages, filled with sable coats and rich clothing. At

Lemeshi, the officer inquired as to where he could find Lady Razumovskaya. The villagers scratched their heads in puzzlement. There were no ladies in the vicinity, they said. Finally they surmised that the gentleman meant the old Cossack Natalia Razumikha, the tavernkeeper—Razum Woman.

When Elizabeth's messenger found Natalia, the old woman listened to his story in amazement, then, according to the legend, cried: "Noble sire, you seem to be kindhearted. Please don't look at me so. What wrong did I do to you?"

But the officer carried out his mission, and soon the entire Razum tribe—Natalia, Cyril, Natalia's daughters and their children—were bundled into furs and crammed into the vehicles. Terrified by this combination of wealth and brutality, off they went on the long northward journey to St. Petersburg.

In the capital Natalia was tidied up, dressed, and over-dressed to be presented to the Empress. Her hair was teased and powdered, her face was amply rouged, she was tugged and pulled into a costly brocade, and thus was she fetched to the Imperial palace with the instructions that she was to kneel the moment the Empress appeared before her. En route to the audience, there was in one of the palace halls a tall mirror in which Natalia beheld her own new image for the first time. Thinking she was at last in the presence of her sovereign, the poor befuddled peasant woman reverently dropped to her knees.

Alexis' mother and her numerous kin were installed in splendor. Young Cyril was particularly favored. He was sent abroad to be educated in the best schools, but on returning after two years was rumored to be as abysmally ignorant as before. Nevertheless, in 1746, at the age of eighteen, he was appointed by Elizabeth to be president of the Imperial Academy of Sciences. He was also made a count, a field marshal, and the Hetman of the Ukraine. The Empress married him off to Catherine Naryshkina, a girl from one of Russia's oldest and noblest families. (The mother of Peter the Great was a Naryshkina.) Later, Cyril Razumovsky became one of the lovers of Catherine the Great.

Although Elizabeth married Alexis Razumovsky in secret, this became widely known both at home and abroad. The Imperial adviser who reportedly first suggested this marriage, and after much scheming brought it about, was Bestuzhev-Ryumin. The Chancellor was a feared figure at court because of his gift for intrigue. Yet he seemed unable to win allies and was uncertain of his influence. To strengthen it he master-minded his sovereign's marriage, hoping to become Alexis' favorite. He enlisted the aid of a cabal of high clergy who sought to enhance their own standing at court as well as sanctify and legitimize the goings-on in the Imperial bedchamber.

As word of the marriage spread, Alexis savored the delights of ever-increasing power. On his saint's day, groups of ambassadors from every nation made their obligatory pilgrimage to his chambers, where Elizabeth's protégé received them in his bathrobe. He even attended her state functions in less than suitable attire.

At times Alexis knew his limitations. When late in her reign Elizabeth named him Field Marshal, he said, "My Empress, you may call me Field Marshal, of course, but you cannot make even a simple colonel out of me."

His riches were immense, but when he knew it was politic to part with some of them, he did so with an unstinting hand. When Elizabeth died, and her nephew Peter, now Emperor Peter III, moved into the Winter Palace, Razumovsky presented him with a diamond-studded walking stick and one million rubles in gold.

Alexis Razumovsky loved cards. He frequently held the bank, a stack of gold coins in front of him. Fellow players were permitted to borrow coins, but their host made no effort to collect the debts. Some abused his generosity. One evening Prince Ivan Odoyevsky, high at court and one of the empire's richest men, thus "borrowed" 1,500 rubles, dropped the gold into his capacious hat, and carried the hat to the vestibule. From there his servant took it home.

The Night Emperor set the new trend of using diamonds as coat buttons and belt studs. He gave magnificent balls on his estates and in his Anichkov Palace in the capital. Hunting with falcons or hounds was a frequent source of joy to him as well as to Elizabeth.

Alexis was an openhanded, benevolent host, but when

drunk (and this happened often) he could be cruel, ordering the caning of even his best friends with *batogi,* special sticks used for corporal punishment. Whether for chastizing those who crossed him or to help him during attacks of gout, Elizabeth presented him with a semi-cane, semi-crutch, whose handle was of onyx and held a miniature image of herself. The carving of her face was astonishingly true to the original, and the body of the Empress was depicted as a siren, with a bare bosom and a diamond-studded crown.

When Elizabeth went on an inspection visit to Razumovsky's native Ukraine, the local authorities provided 4,000 horses for her Imperial caravan, yet her lover upbraided his subordinates. As many as 23,000 horses would be needed, he thundered. So herds of additional steeds were confiscated from well-to-do Ukrainians.

As she entered Kiev, students of the theological seminary awaited her at the city gates, dressed as ancient Greek gods and heroes, and some even as mythical beasts. An old man with a magnificently long beard, in rich medieval vestments, crowned, a scepter in his right hand, played the role of the tenth-century Grand Duke Vladimir—Saint Vladimir, who converted the Russians to Christianity. Greeting Elizabeth as his heiress and declaring that he was placing the entire Russian nation at her feet, he bade her enter his ancient capital.

Cyril was also rather good-natured and accessible, but had eccentricities of his own. His annual salary as Hetman of the Ukraine was 100,000 gold rubles, and his wife, Naryshkina, made him yet richer with the 44,000 serfs she brought as part of her dowry. Nonetheless, he stretched out his hand for more wealth, complaining of his "extreme shortages" and begging the Empress for more estates. He also borrowed money from courtiers and other noblemen, and seldom if ever paid his debts. His headquarters, where he lived in splendor theretofore unknown among the simple Cossacks, were at Glukhov, in the Ukraine, but he regarded the town as too boring and provincial and returned to St. Petersburg and its glitter for long stays. The scientists of the Academy, whom he ordered about from the age of eighteen, were appalled by his near-

illiteracy, but he ran that distinguished institution, at least
nominally, for almost two decades.


Having Alexis Razumovsky as her principal lover and secret
husband did not prevent Elizabeth from savoring other affairs
of varying durations. Occasionally she had three or even four
lovers at a time, alternating their nights or even their hours of
the same night, and maintaining a *ménage à trois,* a *ménage à
quatre,* and even on one occasion a *ménage à cinq.*

Sometimes Elizabeth slept with diplomats or other foreigners at her court when she liked them sufficiently or felt
the need to repay a political debt. Earliest among these were
Jacques Joachim Trotty, Marquis de la Chétardie, the French
Ambassador to St. Petersburg, and Count Johann Hermann
Lestocq, Elizabeth's personal physician. It was Chétardie who
in 1741, secretly, through Lestocq, supplied Elizabeth with his
government's money to facilitate her seizure of power. Then
and later he freely boasted of sharing Elizabeth's bed.
Whether or not Lestocq bragged about his similar luck with
her, business came before pleasure in Elizabeth's court. In
1748, catching him in behind-the-back scheming with Frederick against what she considered to be Russia's interest, the
Empress had Lestocq arrested, grilled by her secret police,
and sentenced to death. But she commuted the sentence, exil-
ing him first to an Upper Volga region and, after three years,
farther north to the area of Arkhangelsk. He was returned to
civilization only after her death.

In time Razumovsky grew accustomed to this male procession stomping or tiptoeing through his wife's bedchamber.
He became philosophical about it and learned not to protest.
He came to accept, among the others, Ivan Shuvalov, the lover
who seemed the most permanent of Elizabeth's paramours.

Shuvalov had the advantage of being a younger and more
virile man. The son of Elizabeth's friend Countess Shuvalova,
he could easily have been mistaken for the Empress' son
rather than her bed-companion. Athletic-looking, his face expressive, his nose a trifle too long, but his lips hinting of passion, an appealing dimple on his chin, he was indeed
attractive.

As none of her steady lovers prevented Elizabeth from enjoying the embraces of incidental bedmates, the diplomats' reports of her behavior shocked, amused, or awed Europe's other sovereigns. A few crowned heads grimly jested about the goings-on. While entertaining a French guest at Sans Souci, Frederick pointed to a vigorous young Hussar who had just entered the room: "That fellow has the handsomest penis in my dominions. I am going to send him as Ambassador to Russia!"

He said this without the least flicker of a smile.

Through the French and Austrian diplomats the story was at once relayed to Chancellor Bestuzhev-Ryumin and, naturally, to Elizabeth herself. The Chancellor was livid, the Empress furious.

Young Catherine, naive and disbelieving in the very first months of her Russification, soon learned that her aunt's excesses were far from being hearsay. Initially baffled, then angered, still later saddened, Catherine found herself—by degrees—aroused. In time, of course, she would become as dissolute as her aunt. In her memoirs she was to write approvingly of Elizabeth's choice of Ivan Shuvalov as her paramour. By that time Catherine was attuned to court mores: "I was happy about his success because I had observed him since the days when he was a page. He had seemed diligent; he was always seen with a book in his hand."

Nonetheless Catherine's insatiable royal aunt extended her stable of lovers. To Razumovsky and Shuvalov she added a chorister from the Imperial cappella named Kashinvsky and an equally young and virile lover, the cadet Nikita Beketov. Beketov, whom Elizabeth discovered when the boy was eighteen, became a serious contender for her prolonged favors.

Prince Boris Yusupov, director of the military academy, had founded an amateur theater in which his students put on plays in Russian and French. Elizabeth took a fancy to the theater and had it transferred from the academy to her palace. Female as well as male roles were performed by the cadets, and Elizabeth was fond of dressing the actors with her own Imperial hands. To be fitted into feminine costumes, the youths had to be stripped naked first, and this is how the Empress had her initial view and feel of Beketov in all his mas-

culine glory. From the dressing rooms of the theater to his
sovereign's bed was but a short step for the exotic-looking
young soldier, who was soon made Alexis Razumovsky's aide-
de-camp, then colonel.

At the height of her infatuation with her latest bedmate,
Elizabeth personally selected the most costly and richly ornamented coats and breeches for him and adorned these with
her own diamonds and gold jewelry. Soon the formerly
obscure cadet strutted into court in attire that included more
sophisticated French imports such as shirts with elaborate
lacey *jabots*. His sovereign's diamond rings and gold watches
completed this tableau of ostentatious splendor.

Beketov's fall from grace was sudden and total when Elizabeth heard from her informers that he was in the habit of
inviting Imperial choristers and other court favorites to his
palace apartment, treating the youths to lavish food and
drink, and taking walks with them through the Peterhof park.
In her memoirs Catherine was to defend Beketov, writing that
he was a poet and needed those lads as his audience while
reciting his verses and songs. Elizabeth thought otherwise.
Catherine reminisces: "She unexpectedly left Peterhof, ordering Beketov to stay behind. He fell ill with a nervous fever,
nearly dying. However, he recovered, but from then on remained in the shadows and left the scene. He was transferred
to the army, where he made no career."

Catherine was certain that it was Ivan Shuvalov and his two
uncles, the Counts Alexander and Peter, both powerful at the
court, who blackened Beketov's reputation by spreading the
rumor that young Nikita was a homosexual, that his youthful
guests were his lovers, and that he was thus unworthy of Elizabeth's bed.

Other sources state that Ivan Shuvalov's sister had a part in
Beketov's dismissal. Fearing that Nikita might soon displace
her brother, she gave Beketov a salve which, she assured him,
would make his face even more alluring. But the creme
caused his skin to erupt in repulsive sores, and this frightened
Elizabeth into suspecting that her lover had syphilis. Or so the
Shuvalovs whispered into her ear. Hence his banishment.

*        *        *

The Shuvalov family rode high at court for many years. Of the uncles, Count Alexander Shuvalov rose to the position of chief of the secret police. For a long time he headed the anti-Catherine faction in Elizabeth's entourage. His brother, Count Peter, died comparatively early in this game, but during his years in the Imperial corridors of power he tried hard to diminish Alexis Razumovsky's standing with the Empress.

The two Shuvalovs, singly and together, were far more clever than Alexis. Yet, with all their brains, and though close to Elizabeth, they could never elbow aside Razumovsky, who seemed to be a Cossack simpleton but in actuality knew how to defend his interests.

But the Shuvalov uncles could do one thing that no one else managed with the same effectiveness: they constantly frightened Elizabeth with talk of plots and conspiracies brewing against her. She who had climbed to the throne with the help of Guardsmen's muskets and swords feared that her enemies might use other praetorians to unseat her.

With such dark rumors and reports, and sometimes concrete evidence, swirling about her, Elizabeth decided early not to allow the former Emperor Ivan and his family to leave Russia for their native Braunschweig (which had been, briefly, her original intention). Moreover, she decided, it would be necessary that they be shifted deeper into Russia, away from her vulnerable Western frontiers. Theirs was the caravan young Sophie of Anhalt-Zerbst and her mother encountered in February 1744, upon entering the Baltic provinces of Russia. Elizabeth also decreed that none of Ivan's siblings were to marry. She did not wish any of his collateral descendants to scheme for the throne.

In her anxiety, especially during her early reign, Elizabeth tried to sleep in a different bedroom each night, and took the additional precaution of carefully choosing guards—all of lower ranks, with no ambitions—to sleep nearby on cots or on the floor. One such guard, upon being awakened in the middle of the night when his sovereign felt the call of nature, was in the habit of touching her leg from his prone position on the floor, thus ensuring that it was indeed she, Her Imperial Majesty, who was stepping over him. As he did this, he would

exclaim, "Ah, my white swan!" Because of this he was in time
officially given the name Lebedev—"of the Swan."

On that night in November 1741 when she seized the
throne, Elizabeth had knelt before an icon and had solemnly
sworn that in her reign no death sentences would be carried
out, and insofar as we can tell from memoirs and other documents, throughout the two decades of her rule no one was
executed in her empire. However, her early oath not to take
life was replaced by the almost equally cruel procedure in
which her enemy was taken to the scaffold, his head was
placed on the chopping block, and the executioner raised his
ax. At the last moment an official would halt the execution,
read an Imperial commutation of the sentence, and bundle up
the psychologically broken victim in furs prior to exile in
Siberia.

Elizabeth permitted torture to extract confessions and occasionally decreed that tongues, ears, and noses be removed
from those who particularly displeased her, prior to their exile
beyond the Urals.

The Lopukhin case was an apt illustration. Natalia
Lopukhina had been a court favorite and a ranking attendant
at the coronation of Empress Anna in 1730. A leading beauty
of her time, she was the mistress of *Hofmarschal* Rheingold
Loewenvold. In November 1741, upon seizing power, Elizabeth ordered the arrest of Natalia and her husband, Stepan
Lopukhin, but released them. In July 1743, both Lopukhins
were rearrested on charges of conspiracy, and with them their
son, Lieutenant Colonel Ivan Lopukhin, as well as Countess
Anna Bestuzheva-Ryumina, a kinswoman of the Chancellor's.
On August 29 Elizabeth decreed all of them to be exiled—
after their tongues were cut out and their bodies flogged with
knouts, publicly.

This was done, on one of the capital's prominent squares.
As they were being driven in carts from the bloody scaffold,
Natalia saw a group of Elizabeth's senators (an appointive office in Tsarist Russia) stare at the procession in curiosity out of
their office windows. It was they who had cosigned the dreadful sentence. Raising her hands heavenward, Natalia spat her
blood at the administrators and turned away with a gesture of

disgust. (Three of the sentenced were destined to die in exile, but Natalia survived, and on Elizabeth's death was returned to her relatives in Russia. She died soon afterward, in March 1763.)

To the Guards officers who had helped her to the throne, Elizabeth presented vast estates, thousands of serfs, gold, jewels, and other gifts and privileges. The Empress, in a policy to be emulated by Catherine in 1762, distributed Crown lands to her favorites, allowing them to multiply and fatten at the expense of the peasantry. She permitted her nobility to use extortion, blackmail, and outright thievery to exploit the Eastern tribes under her sovereignty. She closed her eyes to the depredations of officers and officials who, like the medieval robber barons of Western Europe, armed their more aggressive serfs with the latest and best of weaponry and led them in forays against weaker, less influential fellow aristocrats.

A law unto themselves, the Russian nobility imprisoned and tortured their serfs in dungeons on their estates. Others were banished to Siberia or conscripted into the army. Public notices of the day offered serfs for sale—a coachman along with a carriage, a pretty wench as a package deal with a racehorse, a wife torn from her husband. The *droit du seigneur* was an accepted practice. Many aristocrats exercised it indiscriminately; others, more fastidious, required that the objects of their favors be certified as virgins.

The Russian empire was vast and rich in resources, yet the economy was constantly ailing. One reason for this was the appalling ignorance of its ruler. Elizabeth's ideas of geography were primitive: she thought one could travel from Russia to London overland. Her grasp of economics was no better. In 1742 she revived an old ukase ordering the few Jews who lived there, illegally, to be deported. This was a continuation of Peter the Great's policy that it was premature to allow Jews into Russia—doing so would only harm the Jews themselves. They could be admitted only if they were baptized. It is noteworthy that one of Peter's closest and cleverest aides was Peter Shafirov, the son of a Polish Jew baptized in Moscow. In 1710 Peter made Shafirov Russia's first baron. The family's original name was Shafir, for sapphire; apparently because their ancestors were jewelers.

Elizabeth's Senate recommended that it would be profitable for the empire if Jewish merchants were occasionally allowed to enter and trade in Russia and the Ukraine. On this document the Empress scribbled her celebrated resolution: "From the enemies of Christ, I wish no interesting profit."

Since so much money was lavished on the court, and to a lesser extent on the army and navy, very little was left over for anything else, and the chronic shortages of the state treasury were a scandal known to all.

Expenditures for the court were lopsided. For example, in addition to jewels and sumptuous attire, there were rows of extremely expensive mirrors, most of which dated back to Peter the Great's time. Peter knew that the common people had a superstitious fear of mirrors, and may have had this in mind when he spent so much for them. The court could never get enough furniture and furnishings. When the royal family and other nobility traveled about the immense country, their beds and chests, tables and chairs, cutlery and crockery, went with them.

Penury and shabbiness showed up in surprising places. Catherine writes in her memoirs that even the palaces were badly constructed. Doors and windows fitted badly and were drafty. Rainwater and melted snow dripped from the cracked ceilings. Rats and other vermin abounded. When a Moscow palace of Elizabeth's caught fire, Catherine was astonished to see hundreds of rats and mice fleeing down the front staircase.

While on the road with the Empress, Catherine found accommodations slipshod and worse. There were pools of water on the floor of the Grand Ducal bedroom and huge holes in the walls. Often Catherine had to be satisfied with overnight stays in peasant huts. In the morning the serf women would pull their freshly baked bread out of the ovens while the Grand Duchess was dressing at their very elbows. Better quarters were reserved for the Empress and her lovers, of course.

When the Grand Ducal court visited Moscow, no one bothered to make decent preparations for Catherine's servants.

During one visit, as many as seventeen of them were jammed into one small room—a sheer horror in the summer heat. To make it worse, the only passage to and from the room was through Catherine's chambers. Her servant girls frequently had to sleep on mattresses piled on the floor of her dressing room.

Hoping to curry favor with the Empress, some aristocratic families tried to ape her extravagances. They dressed from head to foot in jewels they could ill afford and purchased priceless equipages decorated with gold. Gold and velvet tapestries, silk curtains, and Gobelin textiles made their houses vulgarly ostentatious. Thoroughbred horses were bought and kept not for transportation or even sport, but because they demonstrated the opulence of their owners. Serfs were taken from their labors in the fields to become idle and unneeded town servants.

Valets, outriders, and other flunkeys wore splendid but stiff and uncomfortable uniforms embroidered with the coronets and other emblems of their masters, often without underclothing between their gorgeous attire and their unwashed bodies. Less favored serfs shuffled across elaborate mosaic or parquet floors barefoot, in tatters, and verminous.

The aristocrats dressed according to the latest fashion of Paris and Vienna, and spoke French, which gradually their children's imported tutors had brought to the parents as well. Yet the mansions of many of these noblemen looked more like unkempt barns than royal residences. Civilized comforts were rare. Toilets, called *sortiry,* from the French *sortir,* to go out, were in the backyards.

The endless series of balls, soirées, and theatrical performances given in St. Petersburg and elsewhere called for apparel that accorded with each event. Elizabeth owned an astonishing number of dresses. When a huge fire struck Moscow, 4,000 of them were destroyed. At her death her wardrobe contained 15,000 dresses, 5,000 pairs of shoes, and two trunkfuls of silk stockings. (By contrast, in 1744, Sophie and her mother brought three dresses each with them to Russia.)

In her memoirs, Catherine, in high indignation, laments the

crude level of entertainment and conversation at Elizabeth's court:

> The day after our arrival there was a card game for high stakes. . . . This was necessary at a court where there were no exchanges of opinion, where everyone hated everyone else, where malicious chatter passed for wisdom, and where any sort of serious conversation was considered a crime against the state. The silliest gossip was accepted as artful subtlety. Since all of them were ignoramuses, they avoided the arts and sciences as topics of conversation. You could wager that one-half of this assembly could barely read, and I am not sure that even one-third could write.

Few at court read books. Peter at times bought them, "but oh, what books those were! One-half of them were Lutheran prayer books and the other half courtroom accounts of the trials of highwaymen."

All of them were in German, but where her husband found them she did not know. Catherine complained that it was difficult to find serious French books in St. Petersburg, but she did manage to get some from foreign envoys and from non-diplomatic foreigners who lived in the capital, mostly physicians, apothecaries, and tradesmen. From Paris she ordered eleven volumes of *The Universal History of Germany,* and she also collected the French classics—Montesquieu, Voltaire, and others. "Usually," she continues, "I sat in my room by my lonesome self and read."

# Sergei Saltykov:
# The Deceiver

**B**ut the Imperial court, and especially the Empress, refused to leave Catherine alone with her books. Busy as she was with her intrigues, pleasures, and duties, Elizabeth found time to worry about Catherine and Peter's sex life. What on earth was wrong? Why wasn't the couple producing the heir Elizabeth needed? Ivan VI was now growing up in Elizabeth's dungeons. The Empress refused to have the boy killed—she was too devout for that. Nonetheless, for years, and to her life's end, she feared plots to free him, overthrow her, and restore him. A firmer line of succession, preferably male, was urgently needed.

Had she asked, she might have learned from her secret agents that in her vast domains there were folk rumors and predictions by crazy monks that she, Elizabeth, would wait just a few more years, till Ivan reached young manhood, then would release and marry him after dumping Alexis Razumovsky and her assorted lovers, thus legitimizing her own rule and obtaining a rightful husband-heir in one bold stroke. But Elizabeth had no such intention. What she wanted was for Peter and Catherine to get busy!

No one as yet had told her of Peter's phimosis, so she blamed Catherine for the fiasco. In an audience, the Empress castigated the young Grand Duchess: enough time had elapsed for Catherine to become pregnant, yet there was no sign of a blessed event. In her memoirs Catherine recalls, "She accused me of being the only cause of the barren state of this marriage. I attempted to say that the wife cannot alone be held responsible for this. The Empress interrupted me by asserting that her own experience told her that everything depended on the woman."

In rising agitation Elizabeth screeched her condemnation: "It is not my fault that you do not love the Grand Duke, but I married you off to him not at all against your will. I know you love another!"

The Empress was apparently referring to Andrew Chernyshev, the merry *valet de chambre* at the Grand Ducal court. Catherine's liking for the young man was freely whispered about among the ladies-in-waiting. Less known was the attraction Catherine felt for Andrew's cousin, Zakhar Chernyshev, also a handsome, robust Guardsman.

To continue with Catherine's memoirs: "Raising her voice yet higher, she began to charge me with thousands of sundry horrors, of which by now I hardly remember half."

From her near-hysterical lectures on morality, the Empress moved on to accusations of high treason.

"She now insulted me, asking whether I had not been receiving instructions from my mother to spy for the King of Prussia. She added that she knew everything, that she was well aware of all my wiles and camouflages."

As she listened to her angry aunt in despair, Catherine was certain that Bestuzhev-Ryumin's machinations were at the bottom of all these charges. She already saw herself shackled in a fortress dungeon whence there was no return.

The Empress was now practically foaming at the mouth.

She was in reality excoriating the stupid, mischief-making Princess Johanna Elizabeth, safe in far-off Prussia, not the frightened young woman standing before her. Finally losing control of herself, crimson with rage, Elizabeth was crowding Catherine toward the door, fists clenched high over her head, her eyes flashing dangerously. Catherine writes, "I knew well that in her temper tantrums she was wont to beat up women close to her at the court, and even some of her male admirers. I waited for her blows, and there was nowhere for me to escape to, as by then I was pushed to the very door."

And then the door opened and Peter walked in. The Grand Duke had been standing on the other side, listening tensely, and at last decided to come to his wife's rescue.

Elizabeth stopped short. She was apprehensive of her nephew's eccentricities, which could lead both of them—and the entire dynasty—to disaster. Longing to quit Russia, he might decide to use this cruel and unwarranted tirade by his volatile aunt as an excuse. Peter would beseech his adored Frederick to insist on his, Peter's, departure for Germany once and for all. A scandal on an international scale might result.

The Empress' wrath subsided; Catherine was permitted to return to her rooms unharmed. She later wrote that her knees were so weak she could hardly walk or even stand up. She went to bed and her physician bled her. She wept through the night.

By then, many at court knew of Peter's phimosis, but no one dared tell the Empress, who was at her wits' end. She finally concluded that she needed someone close—very close—to the sterile couple who would find out just what was going on—or more likely not going on—in their bed, and who would somehow induce them to start behaving like a normal man and woman. She considered Prince Nicholas Repnin, the sober, honest gentleman whom she once appointed to supervise Peter. But this sort of integrity would not do for such a delicate mission. A couple was needed, and she presently found the likely pair—the Choglokovs.

Maria Choglokova, née Hendrikova, was a cousin of the Empress' and at times her trusted confidante. Like Elizabeth, Maria was, through her mother, of half-peasant origin. Her

mother, Christina Skavronskaya, was Catherine I's sister. And
Elizabeth fondly remembered Cousin Maria after seizing the
throne in 1741: to celebrate her subsequent coronation, the
Empress, among other favors to her relatives, elevated Maria
to the title of countess and included her among her closest
court attendants.

Her husband, Nicholas Choglokov, born in 1718, as a youth
had enjoyed the protection of Ernst Biron's elder son, whom
he served in a vague and minor capacity. His father was an
impoverished Russian nobleman; his mother a German "of a
plain calling," as contemporary documents described her,
which meant that she was of plebeian origin. As a young cadet, Nicholas had caught the eye of Elizabeth, mainly because
of his remarkably graceful dancing. She married him off to
Cousin Maria Hendrikova, who had fallen in love with him.
He was made Grand Duke Peter's *Kammerherr* and
*Oberhofmeister*—Senior Chamberlain—a post he held from
1747 until his death in 1754.

By the end of the 1740s, Nicholas Choglokov was neither
wasp-waisted nor otherwise attractive. Ignorant, tactless, with
a self-confidence that verged on arrogance, he was known at
court as a passionate hunter, cardplayer, and, above all, despite his married state, a persistent womanizer. His lurid affair
with a lady-in-waiting named Kosheleva brought the wrath of
Elizabeth upon him, but Maria, on her knees, begged her Imperial cousin to forgive him, and the Empress, mollified, pronounced her mercy.

But that near-disgrace happened almost at the end of
Choglokov's career and life. In 1747, he began his—and his
wife's—campaign to reform the Grand Ducal couple. At first
all went smoothly. When he replaced Prince Repnin as Peter's
mentor, the Empress issued two explicit guidelines to
Choglokov:

1. [You are] to be with the Grand Duke, not a step away, to
aid him by deed and counsel, to safeguard him from any and
all unpleasant adventures and unseemly undertakings, but on
the contrary demonstrate to him your concern in all possible
ways and exert your utmost efforts toward the encouragement
of his genuine happiness, honor, and welfare.

2. To concern yourself with his good health and see to his proper behavior in church, in society, and at home, in times of both occupation and repose, and to protect his person.

These instructions would have been ludicrous even had they been applied only to a notoriously irresponsible young adult male. But by the end of the 1740s they were extended to include a close watch over the proper, sensible Catherine.

The Empress' choice of the Choglokovs was based on a certain logic. Despite his dissolute life, Nicholas did not shirk his marital duties—he eventually sired eight children. Maria seemed always to be either pregnant or nursing. Elizabeth concluded that both husband and wife were experts on things sexual and could be counted on for an analysis of and solution for a case of sterility. She commanded them to work their way into the intimacy of the unhappy couple and report regularly to her.

Early in 1750 Maria came to the Empress with a triumphant air: she had found a key to the mystery: "The whole trouble is that His Highness is too smelly, and so Her Highness refuses his embrace. That is why there is no baby. His Highness reeks with sweat, he is redolent of tobacco and beer. He is positively noisome; he stinks. He has not had a bath in years. All he does is splash his face with water. I will make him take a bath and there will be a pregnancy and a baby!"

"That simple?" marveled the Empress.

"That simple," confirmed Maria. "That simple, Your Majesty, my dear cousin!"

So that was it: the foul smell emanating from the Crown Prince must have repelled his lovely wife so much that Catherine could not bear his mere touch, certainly not his body upon hers.

"Go ahead!" the Empress said, her eyes shining with relief.

Maria set about her plan.

It was February of 1750. Lent had begun. The first week was a preliminary period called *myasopust,* when the Orthodox were forbidden to eat meat. So they ate *bliny,* or pancakes, in profusion. These were filled with cottage cheese, cream, herring, and especially caviar.

Through the week carnivals and folk festivities roared full

blast. There were wild rides in sleighs, on carousels, and on contraptions that slid on the ice. Vendors offering nuts, spiced bread, fishcakes, and all sorts of hot-off-the-griddle pancakes were everywhere weaving their way between the swings and jerry-built stalls of the bustling fairs. In the palaces and the mansions the royal family and the aristocrats danced in endless balls and masquerades when they weren't gorging themselves on domestic and imported delicacies.

Then the week ended, and on Sunday evening all fell quiet. Theaters, dances, rides, and feasting stopped abruptly. The Great Lent was ushered in, to last the gloomy weeks until Easter.

Some counted *myasopust,* with its abstinence from meat but frenzied carnival and other festivities, as the first week of Lent. Others began the count of weeks with the Great Lent, the first week of which was called *syropust,* or abstention from cheese. Only vegetables were eaten then. Peasants drove into the cities with their carts and wagons loaded with barrels of brined cabbage, salted cucumbers, pickles, baskets heaped high with dried mushrooms, and boxes of chickpeas. These were to be the sole nourishment of true believers.

Solemn services, accompanied by the melancholy tolling of bells, filled the places of worship. Good Christians bathed themselves thoroughly so as to attend confession pure in body, and, presumably, in spirit.

Maria selected this opportune moment to bring Peter instructions from his aunt that at the end of the carnival, on the eve of the Great Lent, he was to take a bath. The Choglokovs' own quarters, near the Grand Ducal apartments, boasted one of the best traditional Russian bathhouses in the capital, where hot bricks raised clouds of steam, and birches were available for stimulating self-flagellation. This was to be the scene of the cleansing of the Crown Prince and the first step in the creation of an heir for the empire.

In her memoirs, Catherine recalls that in February 1750, having obeyed the injunction to avoid eating meat, she was planning to go to Madame Choglokova's bathhouse on Wednesday evening so as to be ready for her confession the following day. But the evening before, Maria strode into her room, where Peter was also present, and without further ado announced, "Her Majesty's will is that you too, Your Highness, are to go with your wife tomorrow to my place to take a bath, which will by that time be ready and waiting for both of you. High time for you, Your Highness, to grow accustomed to the rules of hygiene and cleanliness—to the ways of people of culture!"

The Crown Prince first blanched with shock and surprise, then turned purple with rage. "Leave me in peace!" he cried. "You and your gross Russian peculiarities! I have never been in one of your Russian bathhouses, but I have heard about them. Never will I descend to your barbaric customs—to steam my body with scalding water, flog myself with your birch-branch brooms, and then shower under those ice-cold streams! No—tell Her Majesty that I won't go! I don't intend to die!"

"So!" Maria screamed at him, thrusting herself close to Peter's trembling body, waving her arms, practically spitting in his face, "this means that you intend to show Her Imperial Majesty that her will and her decrees aren't worth a straw to you!"

"I hate all your barbarous customs and tricks!" Peter shouted back. "No civilized Westerner would ever agree to steam in one of your ill-reputed bathhouses. You must all understand that my life is the dearest thing in the world to me. Let Her Majesty at last realize that she cannot—no, she cannot—force me to do things that go against my very nature. You may report to Her Majesty that in this I will not give in either to her or to you! And that's final."

"Our Empress will find a way to make you submit to her Imperial will!" countered Maria. "And your refusal will be severely punished—you will see!"

"Yes, we will see, we will see, indeed!" Peter sputtered. "We will see just how she will compel me to go to your damned Russian bath! I am not a baby to be treated like this . . ."

Raising her voice to a yet higher pitch, Maria threatened: "Fine, Her Majesty will pack you off to a cell in the Peter and Paul Fortress! And in that dungeon you will have only yourself to blame . . ."

At this, Peter broke down and began to cry. But then, summoning his courage, he perked up enough to loose a string of curses at Maria, to which she at once responded with her own billingsgate.

Now in hysterics, Peter screamed: "You are a fool, a fool! You only know how to get pregnant and produce all those endless brats of yours. You only know gossip and backbiting. You turn people all around you against each other and then you carry tales about it all to the higher-ups! When I finally break out of this Russian hell and return to my beloved Holstein, to my civilized Europeans, I will leave behind this savage land with its bathhouses and ignorant priests, with all its superstitions and stupidities!"

"You are an idiot of little sense, if any!" Maria flung back. "Drunkard, you were retarded from your very birth—you are unable to have children!"

Finally, catching her breath and calming down somewhat, Maria retreated a step or two and announced: "I will relay this conversation to Her Majesty—every word of it!"

And with a haughty toss of her head, she left.

All through this ugly exchange, Maria had said not a word to Catherine, nor did Catherine try to interfere. She later wrote in her memoirs that she was shattered, numbed by it all.

Maria returned after a while. Apparently she had made her report to Elizabeth, telling the Empress of Peter's hysterics and of his reckless defiance of her orders. The Empress was at a loss. Now, again facing Peter, Maria said evenly, "The Empress is most distressed that you still have no children. She wants to know whose fault it is. She will send a physician to examine you, and a midwife will visit Her Highness. And, oh yes—Her Majesty permits you to postpone your fasting and your confession because you assure her that taking a bath at this time would injure your health."

In the days and weeks to come, Catherine noticed that at the receptions and other functions when the Crown Prince kissed his aunt's hand, the Empress, contrary to her custom, did not reciprocate. Years later, Catherine wrote, "I understood that this change was the demonstration by the Empress that more than ever before she was displeased with him."

But for now, Peter seemed happy. He felt he had won a signal victory over the meddlesome Choglokova and perhaps even over his terrifying aunt.

No physician was sent to examine him. Quite possibly the Empress had by then heard some disagreeable, if unsubstantiated, rumors about her nephew's penis and couldn't face the truth. What if the examiner returned to her and said that the defect was incurable? She probably decided to let the situation ride for a while.

Meanwhile, one evening during that eventful Holy Week, as though to celebrate his triumph, Peter sallied out to visit his cronies and perhaps a pretty lady-in-waiting or two. He knew he couldn't do anything about bedding the latter, but he was restless; he felt the need at least for feminine companionship.

The evening was not disappointing. He ran into Anna, the Duchess of Courland. She was the daughter of the ferocious Ernst Biron, so feared and hated in his time throughout the empire. During the blood-soaked reign of the late Empress Anna Ivanovna (Elizabeth's aunt), he had been the power behind the throne and his sovereign's sole lover. The young Anna was a favorite of Elizabeth's and had been elevated to head of the ladies-in-waiting.

Duchess Anna's contemporaries said that although not especially pretty, she had extraordinarily beautiful eyes. Everyone at both courts—Elizabeth's and the Grand Ducal pair's—was aware that young Peter, even if practically impotent, liked to flirt with the Duchess of Courland, mainly because, like himself, she spoke good German but very broken Russian.

A certain Praskovya Vladislavova, a courtier with a penchant for keyhole-peeking, at once ran to Catherine with a report of her husband's scandalous behavior during Holy Week. The evening of Praskovya's visit, Catherine, suffering from a severe headache, had left the dinner table early for her bedroom. She was undressing for the night when the tattletale arrived with her report.

"What poor taste His Highness is displaying!" she exclaimed. "How badly he treats Your Highness!"

Catherine writes, "She spewed out [about him] all sorts of unflattering epithets. She praised my many sterling qualities.

Her outpourings moved me to tears: she spoke of her pity for me, and I could never bear it when anyone pitied me."

No sooner had the busybody left and Catherine had at last fallen asleep, when Peter arrived, drunk and in high mettle. He woke his wife and began to praise the incomparable beauty of the Duchess of Courland. Catherine writes, "I pretended to be asleep but he shouted even more loudly. Seeing that I still did not react, he jabbed me twice and perhaps three times with his fist, hitting me violently on the ribs and cursing me for what he took to be my deep slumber. But at long last he turned his back to me and fell asleep. That night I lay long awake, shedding bitter tears over his behavior, because I felt the pain of his blows, and most of all out of awareness of my wretched situation."

The next day, Peter said nothing about the scene, and Catherine also kept her silence. Holy Week fasting continued, but now not a word was uttered to the Crown Prince by Maria or anyone else about his odor and the need for a bath.

On Easter Saturday, to be ready for the traditional midnight mass, Catherine went to bed at five o'clock in the afternoon. But she was not to have her sleep: Peter rushed in to announce in great excitement that his favorite oysters had just arrived from Kiel.

"Get up, get dressed! We'll eat them while they're fresh!"

Exhausted though she was after all the vigils she had endured, Catherine had to obey. The oysters were already on the table: "I ate a dozen or so of them," she writes, "whereupon he allowed me to return to my room and bed, leaving to him the rest of the oysters, for which he had a truly terrifying appetite."

Catherine desperately needed a lover, and in time the Empress probably realized this. Sometime in the early 1750s, Elizabeth's courtiers must have finally dared to tell her about her nephew's foreskin. But either out of ignorance or self-interest they neglected to inform her that a simple operation, circumcision, would restore Peter's deficient manhood. A learned Polish rabbi, a mullah imported from Kazan, or any capable surgeon at court could have performed the operation. But none of Elizabeth's male entourage would bring up the matter. Quite possibly each of them was hoping to be named by Her Imperial Majesty as Peter's deputy in Catherine's bed, if only long enough to impregnate the young and attractive Crown Princess and give the empire an heir.

The Empress hesitated; she thought long and hard, for the field was large and her decision would be momentous. Catherine's choice was one of the Chernyshevs, at first Andrew, then Zakhar.

Her relationship with Andrew had bizarre overtones, for the Grand Duke was also interested in the several Chernyshev males at both courts. All were handsome and likable, rich and distinguished. Both Catherine and her husband were especially drawn to Andrew, and between Peter and Andrew the mutual attraction may have gone beyond friendship.

Catherine was awed and fascinated when she learned on good authority that the progenitor of the Chernyshevs' was an illegitimate son of Peter the Great himself. Her flirtation with Andrew at one point threatened to become serious. Early in her wretched marriage to Peter, her intimacy with Andrew, exaggerated by gossip or not, placed her in peril. The Empress herself was investigating the rumors of this affair, and only the timely and clever intercession of a father confessor trusted by Elizabeth disentangled the web of intrigue that threatened to entrap and destroy the Crown Princess. Soon afterward, Catherine was not surprised, but Peter was astonished, that by a sudden ukase, three Chernyshevs—two brothers and a cousin, Andrew among them—were transferred from St. Petersburg's elite Guards to drab garrison duty in the distant Eastern provinces. Plainly, at that time the Empress disapproved of any of the trio as a likely choice for Catherine.

But in 1751, Andrew's dashing cousin, Count Zakhar Chernyshev, was permitted to return to the capital for a short stay. Whether or not Zakhar had also heard of Peter's incapacity, he at once proceeded to lay siege to Catherine.

That autumn, at one of the court's resplendent balls, he

made bold to say to her, "I find you even more beautiful than when I saw you last, at my departure."

Catherine writes, "This was the first time in my life that I heard such a compliment from anyone. I liked it very much, the more so since I sincerely believed that he spoke without guile."

At each ensuing ball or other court festivity Zakhar repeated his flattery, inventing new and ingenious variations and embellishments. Once, her favorite lady-in-waiting, Princess Gagarina, brought her a letter from him. Catherine writes, "On opening it, I noticed that someone apparently had already unsealed it, then resealed it." The effulgent ballroom was, of course, aswarm with spies. "As usual, the letter was in printed characters, not handwritten ones, and this time the missive consisted of two verses, both very tender, full of sentiment." In accord with the custom of the era, Catherine responded not by a letter but by a symbol she carefully drew, a drawing of an orange. She sent it to Zakhar through Princess Gagarina.

Another letter, not hand-printed but written, came from him the next day. Catherine acknowledged it, and a regular correspondence followed. Soon, at a masquerade, while dancing with Catherine, the young Guardsman said, "There are a thousand things I wish to share with you. But I do not dare to express them in a letter or by a symbol. Princess Gagarina may lose it en route to you, or at least it may become torn in her pocket. Do receive me in your chambers or any other place of your choice."

Primly she replied, "Entirely impossible. All my chambers are closed to outsiders, and I myself cannot steal away."

He pleaded: "I will disguise myself as a servant to come to your chambers."

"No, categorically no!"

From then on, it was only a teasing sort of correspondence between the pair, by symbols more than letters, and even this ceased when Princess Gagarina, realizing how far the affair might go, and having definite instructions from the Empress, became angry with Catherine, who sadly notes in her memoirs, "She refused to receive and deliver any more envelopes. Thus ended the year 1751 and began 1752."

Since Zakhar's leave was up, and it was not extended by Imperial order, he had to rejoin his regiment in the far-off steppes. Catherine was in no less despair than her handsome suitor, and a few days before his departure she fell ill. A physician was summoned to her bedside, and he bled her, so as, he pompously explained, "to relieve the nervous strain suffered by Her Highness." It was a most difficult winter.

By the spring of 1752, Catherine was ready for her first real lover, most likely selected by Elizabeth herself. Still, in the years to come, she frequently thought of her exiled Zakhar Chernyshev and was vaguely sorry that it had not been he.

เอ

Thus, Sergei Saltykov, the good-looking, virile, but not especially intelligent son of a distinguished battlefield general, entered the scene.

It is almost certain that the assignment for Sergei to "uncork" Catherine (as the colorful Russian folk expression puts it) issued from the Empress herself. There is reason to believe that Elizabeth had personally tried out Sergei first, and having judged his performance satisfactory, thought that under his fiery and experienced ministrations Catherine would deliver an heir for the Romanov dynasty.

The Choglokovs were entrusted with the delicate mission of coupling Sergei and Catherine. They agreed to this project with enthusiasm, although there is evidence that Nicholas Choglokov harbored the thought of himself becoming Catherine's lover. Should Sergei prove a dud as Peter's substitute, Nicholas was quite willing to step in as the deputy's deputy.

In accordance with Elizabeth's instructions, the Choglokovs now guarded the young Grand Ducal court with Cerberus-like ferocity. No one could come within whispering distance of Catherine, and sometimes Peter as well, without a Choglokov say-so. Moreover, knowing her husband's amorous interest in the Crown Princess, Maria zealously watched him. In short, Sergei Saltykov had a clear field.

Some thirty years later, in her remarkably candid memoirs, Catherine describes him as a young man of middle height, with well-developed muscles, a swarthy face, and an exceptionally passionate nature, but neither subtle nor dependable: "He was as beautiful as the dawn. In this he had no equal either at the court of the Empress or at our court. He was sufficiently clever and possessed that special knowledge—the ability to comport oneself with tact—that a person acquires by contact with the highest levels of society, and in particular with the court. He was twenty-six years old. He was a brilliant cavalier by his origins and his many excellent qualities."

Yet, at a distance, she could be more detached and critical: "He had the ability to conceal his deficiencies, most outstanding among them his inclination for intrigue and his lack of principles, but at the time I simply failed to notice this."

Saltykov was a fickle and notorious skirt-chaser, whose good looks and aggressiveness brought him a string of conquests among the ladies of both courts. He thought of himself as being irresistible, and more often than not he was just that. He gained a reputation for his amorous techniques and for his extraordinary stamina. He mentally undressed every likely female he encountered, and imagined how well her buttocks would fit into his eager, skillful hands. He pursued his prey with tireless patience and rarely gave up before she was bedded—but never wedded.

One day in 1750, two years prior to his conquest of Catherine, a lady-in-waiting demurely but firmly resisted his advances and extreme measures were called for. She was Matryona Balk, not especially pretty, but shapely, and from the Empress' immediate entourage. Sergei was frantic with desire for her—when he first saw the girl disporting herself on a garden swing, he almost fell on his face like a love-struck adolescent.

The desperate strategy he adopted when Matryona refused him was to propose marriage. The girl accepted with alacrity. Thus, by the time the Empress selected Sergei to deflower Catherine, he was already a married man. This of course did not faze Elizabeth, for she and everyone at court knew that

Sergei was unfaithful to Matryona from the beginning of their union.

Sergei came from a famous aristocratic family, one of the most ancient in Russia. Through one of its branches it was related to the Romanov dynasty.

Catherine had met Sergei's father long before she saw the young man. General Vasily Saltykov (1675–1755) had traveled to Riga the winter of 1744 as one of the high-level delegation sent by Elizabeth to greet the fourteen-year-old Sophie Augusta and her mother upon their arrival on Russian soil. Elizabeth favored the Saltykov family, gratefully remembering the important services General Vasily's wife (Sergei's mother), née Maria Golitsyna, had rendered her in seizing the throne in 1741: Maria was influential with officers and soldiers of the Guards and had agitated among them secretly and skillfully for Elizabeth and her coup d'état.

The Saltykovs, Vasily and Maria, had two sons. Peter, the elder, was practically a monstrosity, a sharp contrast to his brother in looks and cleverness. In Catherine's description: "Peter was a fool in the complete sense of this word, and his was the stupidest face I have ever seen in my life: large eyes the color of lead; a small, upturned nose; an ever half-open mouth. To this I must add that he was a horrible gossip, and this last endeared him to the Choglokov couple, who, however, fully realized that he was a freak."

The Choglokovs instilled into Peter Saltykov the idea that marriage with Anna, Duchess of Courland, might be advantageous to him. He agreed, proposed, and was accepted. This was an unpleasant surprise to the Crown Prince, who liked to spend hours with Anna, chatting in their beloved German.

But the Choglokovs' principal mission was to couple Catherine and Sergei. For a time there was some confusion about Elizabeth's instructions: Sergei came to the Choglokovs' quarters not alone but invariably with his friend Lev Naryshkin, who was also in Elizabeth's high graces. Maria Choglokova was puzzled—did Elizabeth mean Lev as a kind of backup paramour for Sergei?

To be on the safe side, Maria issued invitations to both young men to come to her house as often as they wished. Formally, they all belonged to the same youthful court, the Choglokovs as chaperones, Sergei as the Crown Prince's Chamberlain, and Lev attached to Catherine's entourage, also with the rank of chamberlain.

Maria began her campaign as early as the summer of 1751. Almost daily she sent invitations to Catherine to come visit her in her apartments. Maria pretended to be bored and in dire need of Catherine's company. Catherine went to see Maria to escape her husband.

Her life was tolerable when Peter was cavorting with his Holsteiners and other idlers: she could stay in her room and read. But when he inflicted his presence on her—and that summer such annoyances were frequent—he was in the habit of pacing the floor in front of his exasperated spouse, jabbering about subjects of interest to him and none whatsoever to her. Sometimes he ordered her to leave her armchair and accompany him, taking long steps as he usually did, and she had to listen, listen, listen: "These promenades took place several times a day, and lasted an hour or two. I had to keep pace with him until I was exhausted, heeding attentively all he was saying, and to respond to his questions, even though his words usually made no sense and were merely the product of his imagination. When he would at last leave, the dullest book was a charming entertainment for me."

Maria Choglokova's invitations were more than welcome.

The spring of 1752 proved to be decisive. Sergei and Lev Naryshkin came increasingly often to the Summer Palace, where the small court now resided, complete with the Choglokov pair as Catherine's guardians. Princess Gagarina also visited, although she plainly showed her disapproval of Saltykov. Catherine loved Gagarina and trusted her judgment, but the unhappy young woman was frustrated and more and more sought Sergei's company. Lev, bafflingly, also seemed in the running. His conversation was witty; he was generally regarded as an original personality, yet without malice or guile.

Maria was pregnant again and demanded amusement at her

home. When there were no concerts or plays at either court, the understanding was that the little group was to gather at Maria's. She disliked music anyway, and was usually late to the court concerts or missed them altogether.

But Nicholas loved music, particularly songs, and Sergei was quick to encourage him, if only to keep the host busy and to steer him away from his campaign to seduce the Crown Princess. Nicholas would delude himself to the end: if Catherine needed a good stud, why not he—wasn't he proving his potency by keeping Maria ever *enceinte*? Catherine writes, "I noticed that, rather suddenly, Choglokov grew very amiable toward all, but especially toward me. At once I realized that he had resolved to court me, which was unacceptable to me in every possible way. I was repelled by this man, so grossly stout, so full of fat both mentally and physically. His hair, his eyelashes and eyebrows white, almost colorless, he reminded me of a horrid toad. Everyone hated him. His wife was jealous."

This last detail was used by Catherine adroitly. She not only smoothly evaded all the attentions of Maria's husband, taking care not to offend him too openly, but also made a point of telling Maria, in a jesting but pointed phrase or two, of her husband's foolish amorous pretensions. This was of course no news to Maria, but now she took measures with dispatch. Her tongue-lashing in the privacy of their alcove one evening after the guests had gone so frightened Nicholas that he literally crawled into the farthest corner of the apartment. No more lectures by Maria were needed.

It was high time for a tête-à-tête with Catherine, as well. Making certain that they were alone, Maria said to the Crown Princess, "Hear me out, please. I must say something to you very sincerely."

Catherine recalls, "As was my way, I opened my eyes and ears wide."

Maria proceeded: "As surely you know, I am not devoid of mental ability or of loyalty to my husband, and I firmly believe in the sanctity of my marriage vows. I know what to do and what to avoid. But!" She lowered her voice and slowed her speech solemnly: "But there are higher interests, those of the state, of the fatherland, which make for an exception to the general principle."

Catherine waited; she would not interrupt. Maria took a deep breath: "You will yet see how much I love my fatherland, and how sincere I am with you. I don't doubt that by now you favor someone. But who is it? I ask you to choose between Sergei Saltykov and Lev Naryshkin. If I am not mistaken, it is the latter."

"No, no!" Catherine protested. "Absolutely not!"

Maria nodded with satisfaction and went on: "Well, all right, if not he, then of course it's Sergei!"

Which she had known all along. But she wanted to hurry things up.

Catherine said nothing. Maria talked and talked: "You will see that I will cause you no difficulties at all." She repeated this phrase again and again, in weeks to come, but, "I played a fool who did not understand her at all," Catherine writes, and Maria reacted in anger, chiding Catherine at every opportunity throughout much of that spring.

Meantime Saltykov stepped up his plan. Praising Choglokov's singing, he urged him to compose poems, these to be set to music, naturally, by Naryshkin. The poems of Nicholas Choglokov turned out to be awful doggerel, which Lev dutifully put to music. Everyone present had to sing them—Nicholas insisted on it. This entertainment was soon ostensibly the reason why Sergei kept coming to this house, always in company with Lev. The purpose of the visits was of course to seduce Catherine, who with every evening at the Choglokovs' seemed willing, yet plainly needed more time to make up her mind.

Initially, the entire assemblage was to sing, but soon only Nicholas and Lev sang in their corner by the stove, while the rest of the company chatted in pairs and groups elsewhere in the room, paying no heed to the music. Thus, noise of the duet by the stove proved to be a handy cover for those who wished to plot or flirt without being overheard.

Sergei was quick to take advantage of this convenient state of affairs and drew Catherine aside to tell her of his burning love! "At first I would answer nothing, but he spoke of his love repeatedly, untiringly, so I questioned him what precisely he expected of me. He then began to create a jolly and passionate vision of happiness awaiting us."

This went on for days on end, before and after the company sat down to play cards; before and after supper. Catherine was weakening. At last she asked Sergei, "And your wife, whom you married for love only two short years ago, and whom everyone says you still love, and who is crazy about you—what will she say to all this?"

He was never at a loss for words: "Alas, all is not gold that glitters. I have paid a high price for my momentary blindness."

Catherine replied that he was wrong, entirely wrong, and soon she even tried to convince him that she was returning him to his senses: "I was very sorry for him."

She also remembers: "I held fast to my firm refusal all through the spring and part of that summer, although we met daily, but always in the presence of others of our court."

On one occasion she declared to Sergei, "You may not know this, but my heart is taken by another."

He did not believe her, of course, and he was right. Nor did they ever mention the Crown Prince, her husband.

As the summer of 1752 set in, the Grand Ducal pair moved from the city to the charming suburban Peterhof palace, where the Empress had given Peter and Catherine a separate pavilion all to themselves and their small court. In imitation of Versailles, the pavilion was named Mon Plaisir. One part of it was made into apartments for the Choglokovs, and once again, as in their winter quarters at the capital, the same little company spent hours with Maria and Nicholas.

But the Choglokovs also had an estate, a gift from the Empress, on a large island in the Neva delta. One day Nicholas had a grand idea: they would go there on a barge and hunt rabbits. Horses, hounds, and servants were at once sent to the island, and the merrymakers followed.

Catherine loved riding but not hunting. She mounted her horse and waited for everyone else to gallop away after the dogs and the hares. Sergei stayed by her side. When all were gone, Catherine and Sergei rode slowly in another direction, their saddles and legs now and then brushing together.

Sergei resumed the attack: "Happiness is destined for those who dare to take it. We will make it a secret."

She was silent.

"I love you deeply," he insisted. "I hope you believe me, and that you, too, are not indifferent to me."

"You are free to imagine anything you like," she responded, trying to retain her composure. "I can't stop you."

He began to compare himself, his looks, to those of other young men at court.

"Compared with the others, you may indeed merit preference," Catherine admitted.

"Ah, you *do* prefer me!"

This went on for an hour and a half. Catherine tried to laugh off Sergei's ardent protestations, but inwardly she conceded that she liked him. At last she reined in her horse and said, "Leave me. Such a lengthy conversation between the two of us may appear suspicious to the others."

"I will not leave until you tell me that you like me."

"Yes, yes, only go!"

"So you *did* say yes!"

"No, no!"

"Yes, yes!" he shouted in jubilation and spurred his horse.

The hunt was over; the party had returned to the villa for supper. But the meal was suddenly interrupted by a storm. The wind was so violent that the Neva waters rose to the staircase of the shaking house. The island was flooded.

The group was marooned in the pavilion. No one slept. It was three o'clock in the overcast morning before preparations could be made to reboard the barge.

From the storm's beginning Sergei stayed close to Catherine, whispering time and again, "Heaven itself has sent me this opportunity to be near you, to feast my eyes upon you."

At long last, after snuffing out his candle, Sergei led Catherine into the dark privacy of one of the rooms. "A thousand alarming thoughts swirled in my head," she writes. Then and there Sergei pulled down her riding breeches and took her for the first time.

𝄞

The Crown Princess and Sergei Saltykov became steady lovers. Frightened and somewhat repentant at first, Catherine soon loved Sergei and was happy with him. They devised secret ways to meet. That first, enchanting summer they frequently rode out of Mon Plaisir, separately so as not to attract attention, and met in the woods. Occasionally they didn't bother to take this precaution. A carefully chosen meadow became their bed.

The Choglokovs knew, of course. So did the Empress. No one said anything to Catherine about it, except once, when Elizabeth, visiting Mon Plaisir and noticing Catherine's riding habit, rebuked her niece: "It does not become you to wear this male costume. Change into a lady's riding clothes at once!"

And to Maria Choglokova, to be relayed to the Crown Princess: "Her male habit is the main cause why Her Highness cannot get pregnant. The extreme tightness of the male riding habit surely has a constraining, harmful effect on her insides. Myself, you know, I love to don male attire now and then, but never when I ride. My saddle is for females, too, not for males."

Catherine obeyed at once, though she disliked the sidesaddle intensely. But she had been an excellent horsewoman since her childhood, and continued her rides well into her first pregnancy.

Sergei did his duty competently, and Catherine was pregnant by him twice. Alas, both of these pregnancies resulted in miscarriages—in mid-December 1752 and on June 30, 1753.

In December 1752, she was traveling from St. Petersburg to Moscow with but slight discomfort. However, at the last post station before Moscow, she was laid low by sudden, sharp aches in her stomach—her first miscarriage. Catherine reached Moscow miserably sick but recovered quickly.

The following June the Crown Princess was staying with her husband in one of his personal domains, the village of Lyubertsy. This estate lacked even a decent house, much less a proper palace or villa, so the Grand Ducal pair lived in a tent, which nevertheless seemed comfortable enough.

To keep up the appearance of love and harmony, Catherine took part in her husband's long rides and even hunts. On June 29, 1753, St. Peter's Day, the Crown Prince's name day, she put on her best holiday gown, attended the special church service in Peter's honor, ate at the festive table, and danced at the ball until a late hour.

The very next day came another miscarriage. The first fifteen days of her sickness, Catherine was near death. She remained in bed for six weeks, until at last her health and strength returned.

What was the cause of these miscarriages? It is quite possible that Sergei was syphilitic either by inheritance or by one of his countless mistresses. Whatever the reason, Elizabeth's carefully contrived scheme for the Imperial succession, and Catherine's first love, had ended wretchedly.

Sergei Saltykov was unaccustomed to bedding just one woman or of remaining faithful to her. His ego was satisfied: he had deflowered the Crown Princess. But now he craved other young females, many of whom were quite willing to surrender their charms to him. Although everyone was aware that he was still Catherine's lover, he left no doubt that he was still available. His dark curls invited any eager woman's loving fingers, and his smile, which revealed dazzling white teeth, beckoned. His exotic swarthiness was as romantic as ever. Sergei made good use of his court uniform—white in its upper part, light green for the rest, and covered with silver galloons which set off his dark complexion. "In this white and silver uniform I am like a fly swimming in milk," he once jested. But he realized how devastatingly effective this contrast was, and his renewed triumphs with the court ladies were many.

Catherine knew; she was intensely jealous. She made scenes, but to no avail, and her possessiveness drove her lover on to new conquests. He had found her lovemaking too passionate, too aggressive. He preferred Russian women in bed because they were more passive, more submissive, and more easily satisfied—or so it seemed to him. They certainly were not as demanding as this love-starved, demanding German!

So he tried to avoid the Crown Princess, particularly during her two pregnancies, and especially in the course of the illness that followed her second miscarriage. Even when she was well and longed for him, he was not around, pleading sundry court assignments. When the court temporarily moved from St. Petersburg to Moscow, he came to her infrequently, explaining lamely that the distances in that ancient city were so great that it was a chore to get through its convoluted streets and alleys from one mansion to another.

Once he was away for several weeks. The reason was viable: his mother was seriously ill, dying, and he had to be by her bedside. When Maria Golitsyna Saltykova died, mourning presented a valid excuse not to hasten back to the court and to the Crown Princess.

Time dragged for Catherine in melancholy, jealousy, and ennui. She went riding by herself, with a book in her pocket. Now and then she dismounted, tied her horse to a tree, and read, lying in the grass and flowers for hours, morosely trying to concentrate and occasionally succeeding.

Did the Crown Prince know of his wife's infidelity?

He did, and yet he tried to believe that it wasn't so.

On one occasion he remarked to his French valet and confidant, Bressan, "Sergei Saltykov and my wife only tease the Choglokovs, make them believe anything they wish, and then laugh at them."

At times, however, Peter's suspicions were more definite. He began to guess the real role of the Choglokovs, especially of Maria, in what was happening. Saltykov now feared for his position at court, for his career.

Seeing this, Catherine went to Bestuzhev-Ryumin, her old foe, and begged his protection for Sergei. Astonished and pleased at what almost resembled humility, the wily statesman saw long-range advantages for himself in what promised to be an alliance with his former enemy—the proud Crown Princess, a woman of ambition who would go far. He assured Catherine's intermediaries and then herself personally that he would protect Sergei Saltykov's career.

But Sergei was far from grateful. Catherine later said he was "becoming less insistent" on lovemaking, was "at times ab-

sentminded, pretentious, arrogant, inattentive," and full of
unnecessary precautions. "I was displeased and talked to him
about this. He gave me his flimsy excuses. He pretended that I
understood nothing in his allegedly prudent conduct with
me."

She soon categorized Sergei as "a foxy intriguer," and she
was right.

He decided to break off the affair, and to do it boldly.

Aware that Peter was still pretending that he was seducing
various ladies-in-waiting, Sergei asked for a private audience
with the Empress.

Gathering all his courage, he said, "Your Majesty, your
nephew the Crown Prince has phimosis and this is why he has
never consummated his marriage with the Crown Princess."

Elizabeth, after a weighty pause, responded calmly, "This I
know."

Sergei went on: "But the persons at court whom you trust
have never told you the full truth? That phimosis can be removed for good by a simple surgical operation? Have they?"

The Empress was startled. "No, nobody has told me this. Go
on."

"There is not much more to say. What any rabbi or mullah
does to any babe of his faith, any skillful Christian physician
can do for His Highness just as easily."

"You are sure?"

"Absolutely certain, Your Majesty."

The Empress gave her orders. A decisive transformation in
Peter's life occurred only a little more than two months after
Catherine's second miscarriage: in early September 1753 he
was rid of his phimosis.

Preparing the Crown Prince was a ticklish matter. For some
time now, his drinking companions had been telling him that
women were a source of delight, and that a very minor operation would lead him to this source of bliss. But fearful and
suspicious, the Grand Duke rejected the suggestion out of
hand.

One evening Peter invited a few courtiers to dinner. It
would be an all-male gathering, and for some reason Sergei
Saltykov was among the guests. Eating and drinking, the com-

pany got into high spirits, and boasts about successes with women were many and shrill. Peter alone sat silent and morose.

His friends poked him merrily with their elbows. "Why so sad?"

They egged him on, until—possibly for the first time in his life—he spoke frankly of his phimosis.

"This can be easily remedied!" they told him. "A trivial, thoroughly safe operation, as we have already told you so many times. But you wouldn't listen!"

*"Nyet!"* The exasperated Peter once again refused any acquaintance with the surgeon's scalpel.

But everything had been carefully worked out ahead of time for the Imperial drama that was to unfold on that vinous September day. Saltykov raised his voice in entreaty, and the Crown Prince's drinking companions dropped to their knees before him, begging him to listen to Sergei. Peter was taken aback; hesitated. He muttered something they thought was "Yes, do it, dammit!"

A signal was given and a court physician accompanied by a surgeon stepped from behind their place of concealment. The surgeon, carrying his awe-inspiring satchel, was the renowned Abraham Kaan-Boerhaave, a native of The Hague, member of the Imperial Academy of Sciences in St. Petersburg, where he had been professor of anatomy and physiology since 1747. In all of Europe, no finer hand could have been found to remove the offending foreskin from the royal glans.

Several of Peter's friends held his arms and legs in an unbreakable grip, while one of them jerked down his breeches. The surgeon bent down and with one deft motion neatly sliced off the prepuce.

When the incision had healed, Peter's trusted valet, Bressan, arranged, with the aid of Maria Choglokova, a trial run with an accommodating lady who moved on the outer fringes of the court. She was Madame Groot, the widow of an artist. Peter mounted as he was told, and to his amazement and delight experienced the joys of love for the first time.

But he soon recalled that he was, after all, Catherine's husband, so he proceeded to claim his conjugal rights. His wife submitted with utter aversion. The future Emperor Paul I was conceived in late 1753 or early 1754. This time there was no miscarriage, and the baby was born on September 20, 1754.

The Empress promptly took him away from the convalescing mother. The sovereign herself, in her own apartments, would see to the care, safety, and upbringing of the heir.

For over a century it was believed that Paul was the son of Sergei Saltykov, Catherine's first lover. This was based on Catherine's own testimony, particularly in her celebrated memoirs.

But this was not so; she made the false assertion because had she conceded that Paul was Peter III's legitimate son, the baby would have been the rightful future Tsar and Emperor, a great-grandson of Peter the Great's, a genuine Romanov. In which case the best Catherine could have claimed, after removing Peter III from the throne and then seeing him dead (which came to pass), was to be Paul's regent—not the ruling Empress she became when she overthrew her husband in 1762.

Elizabeth had no further use for Saltykov at court, and sent him off on a mission to Sweden—to proclaim to Stockholm that Russia's Crown Prince and the Romanov dynasty now had a male heir. It must have appealed to Elizabeth's sense of humor to choose Sergei as a messenger.

Catherine missed him and begged him to return. But although in time he did come back, he did not rejoin her, and soon left Russia on another diplomatic errand to Hamburg.

At last the Empress was content. There was now a male heir to her throne, to succeed the half-demented Peter and perhaps even to precede both Catherine and Peter under a proper regency, should Elizabeth, in one of her attacks of bile, decide to eliminate the Grand Ducal pair from the chain of succession. Best of all, the specter of a coup d'état by Ivan VI, now a thirteen-year-old political prisoner, was laid to rest.

On the day of Paul's baptism, one of Elizabeth's aides stepped into Catherine's bedroom and solemnly presented the new mother with an Imperial envelope on a gold platter. The envelope contained the Empress' ukase to her cabinet to bestow upon the Crown Princess 100,000 gold rubles. There was also an etui which Catherine opened after the aide's departure. In her memoirs Catherine tells what her reaction was to these rewards for motherhood: "The money came in handy, for at the time I had not a penny and was in horrible debt. But the case made no special impression upon me. It contained a small, poor *collier* with earrings and two miserable rings. Not a single stone in the case was worth more than one hundred rubles, all of the contents of mediocre taste and inferior workmanship. I would have been ashamed to favor even my chambermaids with such gifts."

As she grew well enough to leave her bed and dress to go out, Peter appeared. He wanted his marital rights, he announced. Catherine hated the sight and, literally, the smell of her husband, but he insisted. Finally, in no uncertain terms, she sent him away. No longer would she give herself to him. From then on they had separate quarters.

The Crown Prince did not press the matter, but practiced his newfound virility with a mistress who ended up a permanent acquisition. The affair began in the fall of 1754 and lasted until his brutal murder in the summer of 1762.

She was a noblewoman who in looks, character, and behavior was anything but noble. Countess Elizabeth Vorontsova, a niece of Count Michael Vorontsov's, second in command to Bestuzhev-Ryumin, issued from a talented and distinguished family. Her young sister Catherine was celebrated (perhaps excessively), both before and after her marriage to Prince Michael Dashkov, as a linguistic and scientific prodigy and an expert in court intrigue. But Elizabeth Vorontsova was adept only at plotting, and her manners were as coarse as those of her sister were gracious.

Elizabeth Vorontsova's contemporaries described her as fat, slightly lame, slump-shouldered, and almost hunchbacked. Nature had treated her face as unkindly as her body. Her skin, like Peter's, was pitted with smallpox scars, her teeth were decayed, and her eyes crossed. She exuded a fetid odor. Her command of profanity was the equal of any dockworker on the piers of the Neva.

Elizabeth Vorontsova could down her liquor as well as Peter

or any of his male cronies in their orgies in the Oranienbaum palace. The curious pair cursed each other constantly, even in public, and she was reported to enjoy slapping the face of the Crown Prince, who seemed to derive equal pleasure from the blows.

Peter deliberately flaunted his carryings-on with this harpy. He seemed to be saying to the world, "I am ugly—and so is my Elizabeth Vorontsova. We are the opposite of my wife's beauty and refined ways, and we are proud of it. We defy her—and the devil with you all!"

The Empress was as restless as ever. Balls, theatricals, grand receptions, endless dinners, and masquerades couldn't satisfy her. Sometimes she would invent bizarre entertainments such as a transvestite masked ball in which every courtier was commanded to appear in the attire of the opposite sex.

The extremes of splendor and sordidness persisted. Catherine was to note that, in St. Petersburg, in frequent movings between palaces or to Moscow,

the court proved to be so lacking in furniture and furnishings that the very same mirrors, beds, armchairs, tables and chests of drawers that we used in the Winter Palace traveled with us to the Summer Palace, and from there to Peterhof and even followed us to Moscow. Much of this was broken in such moves, and in this sorry state it was handed over to us for our use. Since it was impossible for us to live with such junk, and the Empress was inaccessible for discussion of this matter, I disregarded the rule that to buy each new piece of furniture her personal permission was necessary. With my own money I purchased tables, chests of drawers and other urgently needed furniture for my apartments in both the Winter Palace and the Summer Palace. Seeing this, the Crown Prince did the same for his own apartments.

Catherine particularly disliked the court's frequent visits to Moscow. She despised the Muscovite aristocrats:

The nobles of Moscow were most reluctant to join the court in St. Petersburg. In Moscow this nobility's principal occupation was wallowing in idleness and sloth. Often in Moscow I saw how an aristocratic lady would ride out in her carriage from her enormous courtyard, which was full of mud and refuse, and in the center of which there stood a barn made of rotten logs. The lady was dressed sumptuously, her person adorned with jewels. Her carriage was costly and beautiful, but the six horses drawing it were old hacks in antiquated and dirty harness. Her valets and outriders wore the richest liveries possible, but their hair was badly combed and their manners were atrocious.

Her verdict on the upper classes of Moscow was devastating:

In general, both men and women in that enormous city cannot help but deteriorate, for all they see about them is vacuity, and they occupy themselves solely with trivialities. This atmosphere can transform even an exceptionally gifted person into a mediocrity. Heeding naught but their whims and obsessions, they either evade the laws entirely or obey them badly, and are thus unsuitable for governing anything whatsoever, and turn into tyrants. This inclination to tyranny is cultivated in Moscow more than anywhere else in our land. It is instilled here from the earliest age, when children see the cruel treatment of servants by their parents, and there is not a single household in Moscow without handcuffs and shackles, chains, knouts and other devices to punish the least fault of those whom Nature has placed in the lower classes.

At times Catherine felt a strange fascination with the barbarism that surrounded her, and was forced to remind herself that she was no mere observer, but a participant. For Russia was her country, and some day she would rule over it.

She sometimes seemed to be surrounded by chaos and destruction. Fires were frequent occurrences in both St. Petersburg and Moscow, particularly in the fateful years of 1753 and 1754, when thousands of the Empress' legendary dresses were burned.

One such conflagration provided a note of humor. Peter's servants were ordered to carry his heavy chests of drawers down the marble stairs of the palace, out of the path of the flames. Catherine watched as the chests slipped and fell to the foot of the stairs and were smashed. Bottles of liquor, which Peter liked to hide in the drawers, spilled over the floor. But Catherine's delight turned to horror as the parade of groaning servants was followed by hordes of rats and mice that seemed to be vacating the burning palace with every sign of orderliness and aplomb.

Some vermin did not escape so easily:

One day, as I entered the apartment of His Imperial Highness, I beheld a large rat which he had ordered to be hanged in accordance with all the regulations of an execution. . . . I asked, "What is this?" He replied that the rat had committed a crime which by military law was punishable by the supreme penalty: the rat had climbed over the wall of the cardboard fortress on the table and had eaten two sentries, made of starch, at one of the bastions. One of his dogs, who had been napping nearby, woke up in time to catch the rat. Peter held a court-martial and condemned the criminal, who had been hanged at once, as I could see, and would remain hanging for three days, to be observed by the public and for their edification. Seeing this madness, I could not help but laugh; however, he did not at all approve of my levity, for he attached great importance to this event. I gave in; I tried to excuse myself that, being a woman, I simply did not know military law, but for a long time afterward he bristled with his displeasure with me for laughing. I could have said that the rat was hanged without first being given a chance to speak up in his own defense.

❧

Late in 1754 and early in 1755, Catherine was frequently

depressed. She yearned for Sergei, but he was irretrievably gone.

True, she now had her baby son, Paul. But for months after the birth, the Empress would not allow Catherine near her baby. Only later, in slow stages, was the young mother accorded visiting rights to the cradle and a modest influence over her child.

Soon it was noticed by all those who came in contact with little Paul that the boy was growing up with a terrible temper—just like Peter's—certainly not in the least like Sergei's easy-going disposition.

Now that Catherine had at last done her duty by producing a male heir, the Empress left her very much alone. Peter was too busy with Elizabeth Vorontsova to bother about his wife. Catherine's enemies at the Imperial court—and she had many—also ignored her. They apparently thought that now that she was permitted by the Empress to be with Paul, the Crown Princess was less of a threat to their plans. Her new alliance with Bestuzhev-Ryumin endured and provided her with protection.

Free again, Catherine's spirits soared—she could look for a lover to replace Saltykov. Only this time things would be different. This time she would choose her bedmate and not have one foisted on her by the Empress or the clique that happened to be in ascendancy at Elizabeth's court.

The opportunity presented itself, and Catherine's choice was made in the summer of 1755.

# Stanislas Poniatowski:
## The Gallant

In July 1755, the Austrian Ambassador to St. Petersburg, Count Nikolaus Joseph Esterhazy, was giving a gala ball in the Russian capital. The invitations had been sent, and Empress Elizabeth's principal court and Peter and Catherine's young court had graciously accepted. Vienna's finest craftsmen and caterers had been imported to clean the silk draperies and the gold-encrusted ceilings of the embassy, to regild the massive frames of the paintings that graced its imposing walls, to fit hundreds of elegant candles into the crystal chandeliers, and to reupholster the plush furniture. The work went on in the sort of organized chaos probably unique to Russia. Apprentices and other stalwart locals were on hand to work under the supervision of the Austrians. Everything was ready on time.

On the appointed evening, for a full hour, splendid vehicles carried the court aristocracy to the embassy. The envoy and his spouse stood on the principal landing, greeting the guests as they arrived.

At last there was a stir followed by sudden stillness. The Ambassador's majordomo rushed in to report that the Tsarina's carriage had just driven up. Elizabeth of Russia had arrived to honor the representative of Maria Theresa of Austria.

The Esterhazys hastened down the marble stairs to meet Her Majesty. On the balcony off the landing a string orchestra struck up a sonata composed in Elizabeth's praise. (At the time there were no national hymns to hail sovereigns.)

With her most gracious smile, Elizabeth acknowledged the homage of the hosts and the guests—the low bows of the gentlemen, the deep curtsies of the ladies. Immediately behind her came the Heirs Apparent, Peter and Catherine.

Young Count Stanislas Augustus Poniatowski, the newly arrived secretary and rumored lover of the British Ambassador, Sir Charles Hanbury Williams, stood by his chief's side, watching the glittering scene. He noted the charm of the Grand Duchess. Many years later, in his memoirs, he wrote, "She was twenty-five.* Only a short time earlier she had recovered from her difficult childbirth and was in the bloom of her beauty. . . . Her very dark hair, her skin lit by its unusual whiteness, her blue eyes full of life and her most expressive long eyebrows, her fine nose and those lips as if awaiting a kiss. . . . She was a little taller than the average height for a woman. Her waist was slim; her step was light, yet full of majestic quality. Her voice was pleasant, and her laughter as merry as her temperament."

That evening Catherine wore a silk ball gown, silvery white, with a red rose on her shoulder, and her diamond necklace was matched by a diamond-set diadem on her proud head.

The young Pole was in love with her the first moment he saw her, or so he claims in his memoirs. Catherine was at once attracted to the stranger. She asked her chamberlain, the

*In July 1755, Catherine was some two months beyond twenty-six.

shrewd and all-knowing Lev Naryshkin, "Who is that young
man in a Parisian dress-coat who is conversing with the British
Ambassador?"

"Ah, Your Highness, you've already noticed him! He is
Count Poniatowski, who is supposed to be the Britisher's
nephew and is officially his secretary."

"Introduce him to me," she quietly ordered. As Naryshkin
seemed to hesitate, she said impatiently, "Go on, then!"

Catherine walked over to the pair and began chatting with
Williams. The young man retreated slightly so the Grand
Duchess and his chief could talk privately. Interrupting her
conversation with the Englishman, ignoring court etiquette,
she demanded of Sir Charles: "But why don't you introduce
your nephew to me?"

Without explaining that Stanislas was not his nephew, Williams said, "My secretary, Count Stanislas Augustus
Poniatowski." Bowing with due respect to Her Highness, he
added, "The Count has just arrived in St. Petersburg. In Paris
he was frequently received by Madame Geoffrin." His mention of this salon, he knew, was a high recommendation.

"And how do you like our St. Petersburg? Aren't you bored
here in the North after Paris?" Catherine demanded.

A low bow accompanied the young man's response: "Your
Highness, the roses of the North can be yet more charming
than those of Paris."

She blushed and extended her hand to him. Just then the
orchestra launched into a spirited polka, in which the custom
was for the ladies to invite the gentlemen. Catherine placed
her hand on his shoulder and they joined the dancers.

And it was while they danced that on her bold and calm
initiative they agreed on their first night together. This was to
be very soon after the ball, no more than two or three days.

"Naryshkin will let you know," she said casually as they
parted.

Meanwhile, Sir Charles was comfortably seated in an armchair, chatting with Chancellor Bestuzhev-Ryumin and trying
to keep his eye on Catherine and the young Pole. He was per-
plexed by their sudden friendship, and, worldly though he
was, misconstrued the true import of their encounter and its

consequences. Sir Charles, a vigorous, intelligent, and life-loving man of forty-seven, had heard all about the adventures of Elizabeth and Catherine even before being posted to St. Petersburg. That his protégé should steal a march on him was a source of both jealousy and an odd sort of pride and satisfaction.

*ઢ*

On the morning of the chosen day Lev Naryshkin pretended to be bringing some state papers to Sir Charles. Finding a moment alone with the young secretary, he whispered, "Visit me on Thursday. The Grand Duchess will await you at six o'clock. Come to the Summer Palace, the western entrance. You will see me there, at the door. . . ."

In his memoirs Poniatowski thus recalls his first night with Catherine: "She wore a white dress, with feather-light lace and rose-colored ribbons—her only ornaments that evening. It seemed that she could not believe that there I was, in her room."

Catherine was living and sleeping in a palace apartment separate from Peter's, and cherishing this distance from him after all the years of forced and disagreeable closeness. Peter did not seem to care, and passed many nights in his outlying properties with Elizabeth Vorontsova.

Nonetheless, his principal quarters in the St. Petersburg palace were next to Catherine's, and the corridors between the two royal apartments were heavily guarded. Some of the guards were friendly toward Catherine; some were not. Peter's Holsteiners were among the latter.

When challenged, Stanislas would coolly continue on his way while calling out, as Catherine had instructed him, "A musician of His Highness!"

At first the dashing Pole hardly believed his luck: "I frequently marveled how in those days I walked through the swarms of palace guards and all sorts of sentries so easily, and on so many occasions, as if wrapped in a cloud rendering me invisible—walked into the intimate chambers of the Grand Duchess, of which I would not ordinarily dream."

Catherine and Stanislas were congenial both sexually and

intellectually. It was the first time Catherine had passed her nights with an educated and considerate partner. Poniatowski was blessed with an exquisite, sophisticated mind and a graceful body. He was a suave, elegant, European *gentilhomme,* in sharp contrast to the German or Russian barbarians Catherine was accustomed to. The couple shared literary interests, and were as free in discussing their opinions of Voltaire and Montesquieu as they were in analyzing their erotic tastes. The young Pole recited passages from Molière, Racine, and Corneille. Some passages they both knew by heart, and would declaim in unison. Occasionally Catherine would quote the first line and he would recite the rest of the passage.

Catherine was awed by the fact that her new lover had actually met Montesquieu and other *philosophes* of the Enlightenment. He had spent *soirées* at Madame Geoffrin's and had supped with the great minds of the age—the thinkers and writers she had worshiped since her girlhood in provincial Germany.

≈

Count Stanislas Augustus Poniatowski was born into a distinguished family on January 17, 1732, at Wolczyn in the Palatinate of Brzesc in Lithuania, then part of Poland (later called Brest-Litovsk, now Brest in the Soviet Union). He was thus nearly three years Catherine's junior.

Taller than the average eighteenth-century European aristocrat, slim and muscular, he was dark, not blond as one might expect of a Pole. And for this there was a reason: a prominent ancestor of the Poniatowski clan's was an Italian, a Count Torelli, who in the fifteenth century left his native Lombardy for Krakow to enter the service of the King of Poland.

In his process of Polonization, the immigrant adopted the name Ciolek. Later, however, Stanislas' grandfather, upon marrying a Poniatowski girl, adopted her name, discarding Ciolek altogether.

The remote Italian strain turned up in Stanislas. His high forehead was framed by thick, wavy black hair; his eyes were dark brown, eyebrows long, as if painted onto his smooth skin.

His nose was slightly aquiline; his lips sensual. His teeth were splendidly white and his chin was described by contemporaries as "well-bred Roman."

In late January 1728, Frederick of Prussia, then his country's frivolous Crown Prince, while on a visit to Dresden, capital of the united Saxony and Poland, in a letter to his sister Wilhelmine wrote of Count Poniatowski as "one of the nicest men at court." (Frederick had little to say that was flattering about the rest of the courtiers.) He was speaking of Stanislas' father. Unfortunately Frederick included not a word about Stanislas' future mother, the willful, ambition-driven Constanzia Poniatowska, Prince Adam Czartoryski's celebrated sister. Prince Adam's descendant Count Adam was destined to be still more famous as a close adviser to Tsar Alexander I, Catherine's grandson and Napoleon's nemesis.

The Poniatowskis and the Czartoryskis, at the apex of their power in Poland, even in the dissolute and brilliant court of Dresden, were zealous Roman Catholics who yet believed in secular education. As a child and adolescent, Stanislas had the best teachers available. Constanzia loved her son passionately, possessively, and saw to it that his schooling progressed freely within the limits of traditional piety.

By the age of eighteen, Stanislas' career was ready to be launched. His first patron was the renowned Count Maurice de Saxe. An illegitimate son of Augustus the Strong, Elector of Saxony and King of Poland, by one of that sovereign's many mistresses, Countess Koenigsmark, the Marshal was one of the outstanding soldiers of the eighteenth century. In the senseless and largely incomprehensible War of the Austrian Succession, Maurice de Saxe led the French army to its victory over the British and their Austrian and other allies at the battle of Fontenoy in Belgium in 1745. Appointed by the French King to be Governor of the Netherlands, he established his headquarters at Maastricht in Flanders. Stanislas' father was among Count Maurice's close friends. So in 1750, early in the interval between the War of the Austrian Succession and the Seven Years' War, the young Pole arrived at Maastricht to be on the illustrious Governor's staff. Count Maurice cheerfully promised Stanislas' father that he would personally teach the youth the art and science of war.

A certain Koenigsfels, a German who had previously served in the Russian army with the rank of major, was assigned as Stanislas' immediate superior. At Maastricht one more friend of his father's appeared, Count Ulrich de Lowendal, a French marshal of Danish descent, and like Count Maurice a victor in the battles of Flanders. Both soldiers treated their Polish friend's son with utmost warmth. They decided that since there was no war going on, the talented and handsome youth really belonged in Paris.

They supplied Stanislas with letters of recommendation so glowing that Louis XV himself received him in audience. By Louis' royal side stood Queen Marie, who, born daughter of King Stanislas Leszczinski of Poland, was naturally enough an old friend of the Poniatowski-Czartoryski elite.

Maurice Quentin de la Tour, a much-esteemed painter, was summoned to immortalize, in pastel colors, the scene of an audience granted to Stanislas at Versailles by Queen Marie, surrounded by her daughters and favorite courtiers. (The King's mistress, Madame de Pompadour, understandably enough was not included in the painting.) From then on, all doors in French society were opened to young Count Poniatowski.

There followed several years of dazzling social success, and by 1753 he was the darling of the capital.

Madame la Duchesse de Brancas was a relic from the age of Louis XIV and had been an intimate of the powerful Madame Maintenon. She had managed to hold on to her position as Lady of the Bedchamber and had officially presented Stanislas to Queen Marie at Versailles. In December 1753 she wrote to the Countess de Bruhl, wife of the Prime Minister to King Augustus II at Dresden and close friend of Constanzia Poniatowska's, "This handsome youth has set the heads whirling of all the young girls and even of my nieces. . . . This Stanislas Augustus is brilliantly educated, knows the history of France, our customs and even anecdotes pertaining to our kings. He speaks an excellent French and holds his own in conversations with cabinet ministers, writers, artists. . . ."

No longer was Major Koenigsfels retained to monitor the young Pole's activities. Stanislas sent him packing eastward at the dawn of his Parisian triumphs on the logical grounds that the officer knew German and Russian but no French. The young Count was on his own.

In those giddy years 1753 and 1754, his success reached its culmination in the fabled salon of Marie Thérèse Geoffrin. Madame Geoffrin was born a commoner, but money and wit had made her salon the goal of every aspiring intellectual of the age. The fifty-year-old widow of Pierre François Geoffrin, she knew how to use for civilized purposes the fortune amassed by her late husband in the manufacture of crystal mirrors. Madame Geoffrin even partially subsidized the writing and publication of the *Encyclopédie,* which contained the finest writings of the Enlightenment. With her money and connections, she supported the elite of literati, philosophers, and artists, and scintillating evenings elevated her luxurious town house in the rue Saint-Honoré to the talk of the nation.

On Monday evenings, France's most famous painters were received. In addition to de la Tour, there were Jacques-Germain Soufflot, primarily an architect, builder of the Paris Pantheon; François Boucher; Claude-Joseph Vernet; Jean-Louis-François Lagrenée; and the brothers Vanloo, Jean-Baptiste and Charles-André, called Carle. On Wednesdays, mathematicians and other scientists were invited, together with philosophers and writers. There were Jean le Rond d'Alembert, originator of D'Alembert's Principle of Dynamics and co-editor of Diderot's *Encyclopédie,* for which he wrote its epoch-making "Preliminary Discourse"; Charles de Secondat, Baron de la Brède and de Montesquieu, then in the last years of his life. Each evening opened with a reception followed by an elegant supper.

This was where Stanislas rubbed shoulders with thinkers and novelists, ambassadors and ministers, princes, courtiers, and relatives of the King. In spite of the frequent conservative guests, the atmosphere was tolerant of new ideas, and conversation was often critical of the official Bourbon policy of backing Austria against Prussia. For the *philosophes* disliked the repressiveness of the Austrian regime and mistrusted or detested Maria Theresa. They admired the skeptical Frederick, a man of letters who openly ridiculed organized religion and professed a brand of liberalism singular for a crowned head.

Stanislas was occasionally invited to informal evenings. He stayed late, talking with his hostess earnestly, listening avidly to the woman he affectionately called *maman*. It was an education to be envied.

The impressionable young man sympathized with her troubles, for even this wealthy and famous friend of the great had her share. Her daughter, the Marquise de la Ferté-Imbault, was a straitlaced bigot who was horrified by the liberal ambience of her mother's salon. The Marquise even made nasty scenes, demanding that her mother close her house to these freethinkers and subversives.

Stanislas remembered some amusing episodes, such as his conversation with that master of scientific popularization, Bernard le Bovier de Fontenelle, then ninety-seven, who even in the summer was provided by Madame Geoffrin with a large pan filled with smoldering coals placed by his armchair to keep him warm, and who once asked the youth benevolently, "Do you speak Polish as well as you speak French?"

ॐ

Madame Geoffrin wrote of Stanislas, "He is like a beautiful cloudless sky of the best climes which, however, now and then is suddenly covered by black clouds and breaks into a storm of most immoderate extremes." She was referring to his intermittent lapses into debauchery. For periodically he indulged in days and nights of behavior decidedly different from the primly stimulating evenings at Madame Geoffrin's.

He whored and gambled, bought luxuries beyond his means, drank, and indulged in love affairs that cost him money he did not have. His pious mother had pumped his sensitive mind full of notions of sin and hellfire, and Stanislas seemed to be getting his revenge on her, bursting out of his cage.

In the eighteenth century, it was considered *comme il faut* for members of the upper classes, both men and women, to pay for their erotic pleasures, and a well-bred gentleman might

have, in addition to his wife and mistresses, one or more favorite bordellos.

Even Casanova, who had no trouble in finding willing ladies
of his own class, married or otherwise, visited brothels. In
Paris in 1750, he left us a description of one of the finest of
these establishments: Madame Justine's ("Justine Paris") chic
Hôtel du Roule, at Chaillot. Here, a gracious house was surrounded by a lovely garden which in good weather served as a
place of amorous delights for those who preferred lovemaking
*alfresco*. A friend took Casanova to the hotel:

> The gate was shut, but a big *commissionaire* with a great
> beard came out to open the gate and we drove inside. A
> one-eyed lady about fifty, who still had traces of beauty in
> her face, spoke to us and respectfully bade us wel-
> come. . . . She led us into a large, beautiful room where
> we saw fourteen young girls, all beautiful and dressed
> alike in muslin. They rose and greeted us very gracefully.
> They were all of practically the same age, some blonde,
> others brunette or tawny haired, others again had black
> hair. Every taste could be complied with here. We spoke a
> few words with all of them and made our choices.
>
> The two chosen ones uttered loud shouts of joy and
> embraced us so voluptuously that an amateur would have
> called it lovingly, and we walked out into the garden. . . .
> The garden was very large and laid out to give oppor-
> tunities for the delights of love. . . . In the midst of the
> sweetest occupations we were called in for the meal. We
> were excellently served; the meal aroused new desires in
> us. . . .

In their unoccupied time Madame Justine's girls were given
regular lessons in music and dancing. A physician examined
them every other day, for Madame knew the importance of
such precautions—she had syphilis and was destined to die of
it. A chronicler of the era observed that her girls were "taken
care of so well that Justine Paris' brothel had the reputation of
being an exclusive place which only the very richest rakes and
foreigners could frequent. Justine understood the importance

of having the right friends. Besides the most eminent officials in the police, the foreign guests were her favorites."

Another, more singular, house was owned by Madame Richard, who in her youth was popular among the capital's clergymen. Now, as the proprietress of her own brothel, she specialized in serving the needs of priests and monks, who could slink into her house and choose her girls in complete safety.

An even more celebrated brothel belonged to Madame Gourdan. It was described as "*the* fashionable erotic resort of the court and the world of rank and fashion . . . very smart, sophisticated, elegant and equipped for every erotic activity," with a special room where in preparation for their clients "the girls were made delicious and alluring . . . bathed, perfumed and powdered."

Madame Gourdan arranged with her next-door neighbor, a merchant, to connect their houses with a secret door that opened into a dressing room. Here, ambassadors, court officials, bishops, and other important persons who had to remain incognito could change into different clothes and otherwise disguise themselves. They then stepped into a brilliantly lit salon where the girls awaited them.

Daring ladies from the aristocracy sometimes passed through the door into the dressing room, where they discarded their silks for peasant attire, then entered the great salon to offer themselves to clients.

Beds in Madame Gourdan's alcoves were fitted with exquisite black sheets, and mirrors adorned the ceilings as well as the walls. There was a room for impotent men. Its walls were covered with spicy engravings to stimulate the imagination, and lewd statues and the latest and best in pornographic books were there to arouse them. Those beyond help could rent an armchair before a peephole and observe the pleasures of their more lusty fellows. Whips soaked in precious scents were at the service of masochists.

Some of Madame Gourdan's protégées became famous. "At Madame Gourdan's the best mistresses of the elegant world were educated; the most famous pupil from this institution was the Countess Du Barry," wrote a chronicler.

This milieu was a vital part of young Stanislas' education.

Decades later, having rather despite himself attained the throne of Poland, he tried to deny the profligacies of his youth. In his memoirs he would make the absurd claim that he had remained a virgin until, at the age of twenty-three and a half, he met Catherine, and that prior to going to Russia he had been virtuous as well as frugal: "I received 3,500 florins from my father, 1,000 florins from my grandmother, Princess Czartoryska, and 500 ducats from the Duke of the Palatinate. With this money for fifteen months I traveled in Austria, Saxony, Holland, France, and England . . . spending nothing on drink, nor on gambling at cards, nor on visiting bordellos; in a word, not surrendering to what is called the excesses of youth. I even bought and paid for all my uniforms and equipment in Paris."

Yet this was the epoch in which many who knew him said that his indebtedness in the French capital had reached the impressive total of 100,000 livres. Claude de Rulhière, in his *History of Polish Anarchy,* writes that, apparently in 1754, "Poniatowski was compelled, by the pressure of public opinion and the persecution from his creditors, to leave Paris and even to know the inside of a jail."

Which prison was it? De Rulhière does not say. Had there been any such confinement, the author, who hated Poniatowski and who was generally quite well informed, would have known it. Madame Geoffrin's daughter, the Marquise de la Ferté-Imbault, also a bitter enemy of the Pole's (she suspected him of being too *intime* with her mother), wrote that Stanislas was incarcerated in the Bastille. Then she contradicted herself by saying that he was only "threatened" by his creditors with this fate. Dufort de Chaverny, another contemporary, specified the Petit Châtelet as Poniatowski's prison. This establishment was known for its harsh treatment of debtors. However, de Chaverny hastened to say that "He stayed there not even an hour." And Louis Petit de Bachaumont declared in 1766 that Poniatowski was imprisoned in Fort-l'Evêque.

All we know for certain is that the diplomat Sir Charles Hanbury Williams, having encountered the young man first in

Berlin and then in Madame Geoffrin's salon, and having been captivated by his charm and intelligence, joined forces with *maman* to rescue Stanislas from his voracious creditors, using connections and money. They may have paid off the creditors and then used their influence to expunge from the records any unsavory details of the case.

It is a safe assumption that in the years to follow, Catherine, first as Russia's Crown Princess and then as Empress, ordered her secret agents to find and destroy any documents that compromised her lover.

Whatever the truth of the matter, Stanislas had to leave France, and not of his own free will. Even the favor he enjoyed at the Bourbon court couldn't shelter him from the wrath of his creditors or from the enmity of the police.

At this point Sir Charles entered the picture, engaging Stanislas as his secretary and taking him to the Saxon-Polish capital of Dresden.

Here Sir Charles was struck by a disorder that eventually was to finish him. It was a baffling illness in which long periods of excellent health would be interrupted by spells in which the diplomat took to his bed in a state of acute depression. Poniatowski's descriptions point to a form of schizophrenia. In any case, the young man cared for his protector with a love and solicitude that was practically filial.

In 1755, London announced that Sir Charles was to undertake a new mission as soon as he was well; he was named His Britannic Majesty's envoy to Elizabeth, Empress of Russia. He at once requested permission to take along Stanislas Poniatowski. While the request was under consideration, the young man visited his parents in Poland, where a solemnly convened Poniatowski-Czartoryski family council weighed their heir's new opportunity and agreed to it.

In early June 1755, Sir Charles arrived in St. Petersburg. On June 12 he was received by the Empress. Poniatowski joined him before the end of the month.

ॐ

Sir Charles Hanbury Williams was born in 1708, a descendant of an ancient and prominent Worcestershire family, part of England's squirearchy. His father, Major John Hanbury of Pontypool, Monmouthshire, died when Charles was twenty-six and already making his mark in the world. Monmouthshire was regarded by some as part of Wales and many of its inhabitants spoke Welsh.

From the county's hills and the low, fertile land of its Wye Valley, young Charles was sent to Eton, where he was a close friend of Henry Fielding's, the future author of *Tom Jones*. Both began their careers as satirists, but while Fielding attacked the government of Sir Robert Walpole, Hanbury, a Whig, was a staunch supporter of the Prime Minister.

He also made friends with William Pitt, who later considered both Fielding and Hanbury his political associates.

As a young man, Hanbury went to London, where he became a member of an obstreperous and debauched club of aristocrats known as the Dilettantes. He wrote and published several pamphlets lampooning the puritanism of the English upper and middle classes. His family was outraged, and he broke with them, publicly ridiculing his elder brother, a prominent London banker.

But luck was with Charles. A wealthy man named Williams was his godfather, and willed him a large estate, including mining properties. Charles Hanbury promptly added Williams to his name.

Hanbury Williams' money and talent gave him access to Walpole, who eventually became his friend, and for whom he wrote political satires. Sir Robert reciprocated by seeing that Charles was given a seat in the House of Commons from Monmouthshire, which Charles represented from 1734 to 1747. And it was Walpole who obtained from the King a baronetcy for his clever adherent.

In 1746, another prominent friend of Eton days, William Pitt, was appointed Joint Vice-Treasurer of Ireland and within two months became Paymaster of the armed forces. Pitt's acceptance of the latter post, widely known as the fondest dream of fortune hunters, was bitterly resented by many, including his friends. When Pitt reversed his long-held opposition to England's use of Hanoverian troops, rumor spread that he was unprincipled and for sale. Hanbury Williams supported this view in these widely circulated doggerel verses:

> While Balaam was poor, he was full of renown;
> But now that he's rich, he's the jest of the town.
> Then let all men learn by his present disgrace,
> That honesty's better by far than a place.

Yet he and the other critics were wrong—through all nine of his years as Paymaster, Pitt remained honest.

Pitt's criticism of the British role in the War of the Austrian Succession led to Walpole's resignation in 1742. Pitt remained in opposition, and finally, in November 1756, formed a ministry.

It didn't take long for Hanbury Williams to become bored with domestic politics. He wanted to shine on the European stage and would have loved an embassy in one of the sunny little Italian kingdoms, or possibly in Spain or France. But these were not areas in which Europe's destiny was being decided: it would be necessary for him to go to North, Central, or Eastern Europe. Hanbury Williams' superiors in the foreign service considered him to be the right man to serve his country in one of the colder but more politically important capitals.

In 1746 he was sent to Dresden. In 1750, through the influence of Henry Fox, the first Lord Holland, an ally of Pitt's while still in the House of Commons, Sir Charles became King George II's envoy to Berlin.

His much-admired reputation as the wit of Walpole's coterie had preceded him to the Prussian capital, and Frederick was delighted to have him as a member of his Sans Souci group of writers, artists, savants, philosophers, and diplomats. Frederick was fond of extolling his retreat as "l'Abbaye de Sans Souci" and its inhabitants or habitués as the "monastic brothers" in a mythical church whose task was to "declare holy all that was condemned by Rome and impious all that Rome enjoined."

Sir Charles was glad to humor the Prussian monarch and his entourage with his scintillating repartee and verses. But

Frederick, himself a satirist, soon ceased to find the caustic Englishman amusing and brusquely requested London to recall him.

In 1751 Sir Charles found himself in Dresden for the second time, now as Britain's Ambassador. In 1753 he was transferred to Vienna in the same capacity, then in 1754 once more to Dresden. That year, briefly back home, he ran for Parliament again, now from Leominster. He won, and held the seat until his death in 1759.

However, his second term in the House of Commons was a nominal one. He remained a diplomat, and in 1755 was sent to St. Petersburg.

It was on his initial mission to Dresden that Sir Charles was first introduced to the Poniatowski-Czartoryski clan, becoming close with Kazimir, Stanislas' elder brother. Subsequently, in 1750, at a dinner in Berlin, Sir Charles met Stanislas, then just past eighteen. Both brothers were remarkably good-looking, but without hesitation the Englishman chose the younger as worthy of his intimacy. Already then, in 1750, Sir Charles wrote to the Duke of Newcastle, the mighty tower of Britain's foreign policy, "The young Poniatowski is a young man with an exceptionally gifted mind. In the future he will doubtless be a great man in Poland."

A few years later, the Englishman was delighted to encounter Stanislas in Madame Geoffrin's salon. His hostess noticed that at the end of each evening Sir Charles made a point of sitting next to Stanislas and offering to take the young man home in his ambassadorial carriage. And so, when in 1755 Sir Charles was sent to his last, most crucial, and most difficult post, St. Petersburg, he would see to it that the handsome Pole joined him in that fabled Venice of the North, the city of canals, and of Europe's most intricate and treacherous diplomacy.

The young man and his patron were fated to be together four eventful years. Whatever Stanislas had learned from his tutors or at salons before casting his lot with Sir Charles was insignificant compared to the education he received from this sophisticated, hardened, and knowledgeable British diplomat. His horizons expanded, Stanislas—thanks to Sir Charles—

plunged into the polite but deadly game of international relations.

Separated from time to time and finally torn asunder during the last days of Sir Charles' life, the pair corresponded in code. These letters are more than expressions of personal tenderness—they have considerable historical value.

In his ciphered messages Stanislas addresses his mentor as "my beloved friend and spiritual father." And in his memoirs written while King of Poland, he characterizes the years spent with Sir Charles as his "happiest and most productive" time. Until his death, the King of Poland cherished a large oil painting of the man he called his "closest and most prominent friend."

That summer day in 1755, when a carriage brought Stanislas to the steps of the waterside Samoilovsky Palace, which housed the British embassy, Sir Charles rushed down the marble staircase to welcome his secretary.

Neither man dreamed of the heights to which the young Pole would rise in this incomprehensible land; Sir Charles could only rejoice at seeing his friend again.

But after his conquest of Catherine, there was a months-long cooling in the affection between the older man and his protégé, for when he at last heard the story through a certain Mr. Swallow, an English busybody who lived in St. Petersburg, Sir Charles was livid with rage. There was a terrible scene that culminated with Stanislas' attempt to kill himself by jumping out the window of the embassy. Moving quickly, Hanbury Williams seized and calmed him.

Sir Charles had hoped to deliver England's gold subsidies and his personal erotic talents to the royal boudoirs. Now Mr. Swallow's revelations and his friend's tearful confessions had brought the sobering realization that he hadn't a chance with Elizabeth, and that Catherine, without prompting, had selected Stanislas. His feelings of defeat must have turned to pride and gratitude when he realized that the Grand Duchess had chosen, if not himself, then a representative of Great Britain for this promising service.

Promising, because in 1755 and 1756, the lot of a British

diplomat in Russia was extraordinarily difficult. Charles' initial assignment was to cement an alliance between England, Russia, and Austria, principally against Frederick's military machine. George II, who was also Elector of Hanover, thought he needed the Russians' help in the defense of his German possessions. Sir Charles completed his mission rather swiftly. On September 19 (by Western style the thirtieth) of that year, a treaty was signed by which Russia, in return for an annual subsidy of 500,000 pounds sterling, undertook to equip and send 55,000 troops for the defense of Hanover.

All seemed to be going well for Hanbury Williams when, within a few months, his superiors in London executed an about-face, much to the diplomat's embarrassment and anguish. On January 16, 1756, the Treaty of Westminster was signed whereby George II and Frederick II gave each other a mutual guarantee of their possessions, with a reciprocal arrangement to defend their territories in Germany against Austria and France. No longer was Elizabeth's help required in the delicate matter of Hanover.

That next year, 1756, the Seven Years' War would explode. It was in effect a continuation of the War of the Austrian Succession, which, beginning in 1740 and ending in 1748 with the treaties of Dresden and Aix-la-Chapelle, had been but half-settled, if at all.

In 1755 and 1756, on the eve of the Seven Years' War, the powers of Europe, great and small, were aligning themselves. England and France were the two principal antagonists in the New World, while the center of Continental European enmities was the alliance of Russia with France and Austria against Prussia.

The Franco-English colonial rivalry in America (and, to a lesser degree, in India) had as its counterpart the struggle for supremacy in the Germanies between Frederick of Prussia and Maria Theresa of Austria. But where did Russia come in?

Elizabeth feared Frederick's ambitions which (she thought) would before long prompt him to attack her Baltic provinces, won from the Swedes decades earlier by her father, Peter the Great. Above all, she hated Germans, who, under her cousin Empress Anna, and under her other cousin, the Regent Anna, had ruled Russia so despotically. Moreover, she personally loathed Frederick, who, in his correspondence and conversations, repeatedly called her a slut.

Frederick had nothing but contempt for the three women who in his time dominated so much of Europe: Elizabeth in Russia, Maria Theresa in Austria, and Madame Pompadour in Louis XV's France. He told outrageously obscene tales about all three, making sure that with their astounding details these were echoed and reechoed all over Europe, particularly at the courts of his targets. Some historians explain his bile by his impotence. As Nathan Ausubel in his *Superman, the Life of Frederick the Great* puts it, "He felt a compulsive need to demonstrate the superiority of his insufficient masculinity over their rich femininity. It galled him to be at their mercy. He was possessed of too great an ego to permit mere women to lord it over him. Down with the Sacred Cows!"

In her memoirs Catherine recalls Elizabeth's reaction: "In her presence one was not allowed to speak of the King of Prussia, Voltaire, illnesses, of the dead, of beautiful women, of French customs, or of the sciences."

It is to be noted that Frederick headed this list.

The mercurial Prussian, as if opposing the Triple Alliance were not enough, had waged a campaign against Hanover, that tempting hereditary property belonging to his uncle, George II. This pleased Louis XV, who hoped that British concern over Hanover would make George more amenable to peace in North America, where things were going badly for the French.

But British diplomacy was shrewd. London was impressed by the Prussian military machine and by the need to contain it. The Treaty of Westminster was aimed at inducing Frederick to keep his hands off Hanover, and at protecting Hanover against Russian or Austrian aggression. So, for the moment Hanbury Williams' work at St. Petersburg was for naught.

ॐ

In the mid-1750s Elizabeth's principal lover was the young and virile Ivan Shuvalov, whose uncle, Alexander Shuvalov, ran the all-powerful Secret Chancery, Russia's secret police, which punished dissent with arrest, torture, and exile. Catherine was revolted both by his grip on the nation and by his perpetual grimace, which turned her stomach. The Shuvalov party at Elizabeth's court, with all its adherents and influence, zealously supported Russia's alliance with France and Austria against Prussia. The Shuvalovs were opposed, as stealthily as possible, by Bestuzhev-Ryumin, that Russian nobleman of remote English ancestry and Elizabeth's favorite statesman, who, with his followers, pressed for an understanding with England and Prussia.

For years the British diplomats in St. Petersburg had encouraged Russian military action against Frederick with generous gold subsidies delivered directly to Elizabeth's bedside. But the radical turnabout of January 1756 involving the inviolability of Hanover changed the situation.

Sir Charles had his new instructions: prevent the Empress from acting against Prussia—a delicate and unpleasant mission, but a vital one. Sir Charles was confident he would succeed, especially if he could enlist the help of Stanislas.

To work clandestinely for, not against, the Prussian King! British gold would, as before, on the strength of prior agreements, be delivered to Elizabeth, but with little expectation of converting her to a pro-Frederick policy. The Grand Duchess, however, was another story—she was clearly a new force in Russian politics. His Britannic Majesty's revised foreign policy could be furthered if Stanislas showered Catherine with gold pieces, especially since Sir Charles strongly suspected that the Crown Princess was a secret admirer of Frederick's.

The King of Prussia's many virtues were practically the only subject on which Catherine and Peter agreed. The difference was that she would act in Frederick's behalf, keeping her hand cleverly concealed, while Peter was outspoken in his praise but did nothing about it.

಼

Lev Naryshkin brought Stanislas to Catherine two or three times a week, each time standing guard outside the bedroom door. Afterward, he guided the young man home.

Then, perhaps to add spice to their lovemaking, the couple

transferred their liaisons from the palace to Naryshkin's house at the other end of the city.

Catherine would undress for the night, and her most trusted chambermaid would light a candle on the windowsill, a signal to the waiting Naryshkin. He would miaow outside the window; Catherine would jump from her bed, don male attire, and leave the palace. Naryshkin, in a modest hired drozhky, would drive her to his house without arousing anyone's undue interest. There Stanislas waited.

Occasionally Stanislas watched for her approach outside the house, sitting in an ordinary drozhky, concealing his identity in heavy fur wraps and with a fur hat pulled down to his eyebrows. One wintry night the rendezvous nearly ended in disaster. As Poniatowski was to describe it in his memoirs:

> An officer of a lower rank began to circle around me and even ask me questions. I pretended I was a servant taking a nap while awaiting his master. Let me confess that despite the evening's horrible frost I suddenly felt hot all over. At last this suspicious interrogator went away. The Grand Duchess arrived. But the night was not without further adventures: her sled, on nearing my drozhky, hit a large stone so violently that she was thrown out. I leaped out and found her lying in the snow, face downward. She was motionless, and fear seized me that she was dead. But when I bent over her I saw that she was alive, with no more than a few bruises. Nor was it all for that night: when we came to the room of our delights we saw, in despair, that her chambermaid through an error had locked the door and had gone away with the key. Fortunately someone else with a key came along to unlock the door.

Alarmed by this chain of mishaps, the lovers decided to meet only in Catherine's bedroom.

The affair continued through the exceptionally severe winter of 1755–1756, as though defying the ice and snow.

Meanwhile, Sir Charles was getting nowhere. Elizabeth, infuriated by the Treaty of Westminster, turned her back on offers of friendship by King George, and went so far as to refuse installments of British gold due her—her anger triumphed over her usual greed.

The English diplomat pleaded with her cabinet ministers to use their influence vis-à-vis the Empress, but she was unmoved. Hanbury Williams found himself excluded from the main court, where the Shuvalovs and their pro-French party dominated. He turned his energies to the Germans of the small court, where Bestuzhev-Ryumin, with his opposition to the Shuvalovs, was a power. But by then it was a diminishing power.

Within the minor court the old split persisted and even widened: Peter against Catherine. The amount of intrigue was appalling.

Clouds were gathering around Catherine and her Polish lover. As battle lines were drawn, it was decided, possibly by Sir Charles and Bestuzhev-Ryumin, to remove Stanislas from Russia, for a while at least. In August 1756, he left for Warsaw, for a brief stay with his parents—or so the inconsolable Grand Duchess was assured.

Months passed, and the couple exchanged passionate letters through trusted intermediaries. But Stanislas did not return.

Catherine then had a happy inspiration: she would bring Poniatowski back to St. Petersburg as the new Saxon-Polish Ambassador. She began to put the daring scheme into action, enlisting the aid of both Bestuzhev-Ryumin and Sir Charles, showering favors upon both, and even—slyly, shamelessly—holding out to the Englishman a hint of a promise of her bed.

She skillfully set the two allies against each other to see who would best carry out her plan. Bestuzhev-Ryumin won. He induced Dresden to appoint Count Stanislas Poniatowski as its new Ambassador to Elizabeth's court. But the Chancellor stipulated one condition: the new envoy was not to live in Sir Charles' mansion, even temporarily. Quite logically he was to be installed in his own embassy.

And still the Count did not return. Catherine demanded to know the cause of the delay. He finally explained in a frank letter: "This is how it is: by dint of questioning me with all the tenderness and adroitness possible, my mother understands clearly what it is that makes me so ardently wish to come back to you."

Countess Poniatowska had doubtless heard rumors of the liaison but possibly had not until then realized how serious it was—that the two considered themselves practically husband and wife. Even if, upon Elizabeth's death, Catherine succeeded in overthrowing Peter and becoming the next sovereign of all the Russias (as some shrewd Western Europeans were beginning to anticipate and hope), even if she married Stanislas and Russia and Poland became one, Constanzia Poniatowska's devout and unbending Roman Catholicism would demand that Catherine—and Russia—abandon the Eastern Orthodox Church and convert to Rome. But she knew that this would never happen. Her son must not return to Russia, to Catherine, to all those wild impossibilities and dire perils.

"I pressed her more strongly to consent formally to my return," Stanislas' letter to Catherine continued, "but she said with tears in her eyes that she foresaw with grief that this affair was going to cause her to lose my affection, on which she depended for all the happiness in her life, that it was hard to refuse some things but in the end she was determined not to consent."

Despondent, the son threw himself at his mother's feet. She, crying copiously, mourned, "This is just what I expected."

She went away, after pressing Stanislas' hand, leaving him "in the most horrible dilemma I have ever experienced in my life."

In his letter he desperately implored Catherine, calling her *Poutres,* one of his fond and curious nicknames for her (French for "wooden beams," "supports"), to tell *Bonn,* a code name for Sir Charles, the entire sad story of his mother's fierce opposition, and to urge the Englishman to write at once to Stanislas' father "to send me back over there because I am necessary to him."

Among other points in his quarrel with his mother was her stubborn refusal to believe that Stanislas' presence in St. Petersburg was crucial to the English diplomat.

However, at long last, one of his uncles, a Czartoryski uniquely influential with Constanzia, interceded—and, miracle of miracles, the Countess gave in and the couple were reunited on January 3, 1757. Their joys were to last some eighteen months.

Just as before, Peter suspected what was going on, but the hideous Elizabeth Vorontsova and his drinking bouts kept him too occupied to care. Sometimes, under the prodding of his sinister mistress, he seemed to be on the verge of doing away with both his wife and her lover. But he chose to bide his time, waiting for the death of his aunt, which everyone knew was approaching swiftly.

In the spring or summer of 1757, Catherine was pregnant.

ప

Their affair continued, but not without its anxious moments. A hair's-breadth escape occurred one white night in June 1757.

That summer, Catherine was staying in the outlying Oranienbaum palace. Stanislas had a special key to a small door that opened onto the park. Beyond the door a short flight of circular iron stairs led to Catherine's bedroom suite. Again her gallant utilized the services of an ordinary drozhky which he hired in St. Petersburg. Wearing a light-colored wig and a wide-brimmed hat, bundled up in a dark cloak, he would direct the coachman to Oranienbaum. Once in the park, he would tell the coachman to stop in a nearby lane and wait until morning, after paying him generously.

On that evening Stanislas took a considerable risk: one of his servants from the embassy was in the back of the drozhky, and instead of leaving the driver with his vehicle in a dark lane, he ordered the man to take him close to the palace.

The drozhky was proceeding along the wide approach road when they heard the sound of hooves. A group of riders appeared, all Guards officers from the minor court. The cavalcade was headed by a man on a white horse whom Poniatowski with a skip of his heart recognized as Grand Duke Peter. By his side rode Countess Vorontsova. They were chatting merrily, swaying in their saddles, apparently half-drunk.

At first they paid no heed to the drozhky, but suddenly the Crown Prince reined in his horse.

"Who is your passenger?" he called out to the driver.

"How should I know?" the cabman grumbled, not realizing that it was Grand Duke Peter who was addressing him.

Stanislas' quick-witted servant rose from his perch behind his master's seat: "The tailor of Her Highness, the Grand Duchess!"

"Pass on," Peter responded indifferently.

But Vorontsova knew better.

"The tailor of Her Highness, indeed!" she mocked. She turned on Peter furiously. "You fool! Some tailor he is! Don't you see this is Poniatowski, who has just arrived to spend the night with her?"

They rode on, yet this virago would not relent: "Question him, make him confess!" she stormed at him. "This way you will get your divorce and send her off to a nunnery!"

Peter tried to argue with his formidable mistress, but, weak-willed as usual, he gave in to her nagging. He would set a trap for his wife's lover when he left her bed that night: Elizabeth Vorontsova was right, here was the perfect opportunity to get rid of Catherine once and for all.

He ordered his officers to ride back, conceal themselves, and wait for Poniatowski.

It was nearly three in the morning when Catherine's lover left her bedroom and walked onto the wide road where the drozhky waited. He had barely taken a few steps when three mounted men sprang at him from ambush, brandishing their sabers. Dismounting, they seized him and tore off his disguise. The Grand Duke appeared. Staring at the captive, he exclaimed, "Oh, so this is the tailor! The Saxon-Polish Ambassador himself, Count Poniatowski!"

The cabman and the servant were also arrested. Peter ordered the three prisoners and his officers to follow him along a path that led toward the Gulf of Finland shore.

In his memoirs Poniatowski concedes that this was one of the most desperate moments of his adventurous life. He expected the worst, certain that to avoid a high-level scandal, the Grand Duke would have him immediately executed. The guards would throw his body into the sea, weights attached to it. A like fate awaited his servant and the innocent cabman—dead men tell no tales. Catherine's memoirs assert that von Brocktorff, the Holsteiner whom she had dubbed the Pelican, was among Peter's companions that night and urged her husband to murder Poniatowski.

They arrived at a house in a grove by the sea. Here, soldiers who had violated orders were sometimes imprisoned pending trial. The house was vacant. At the door, Peter's Holstein retainers untied Stanislas' hands and escorted him to the upper story. The Grand Duke led this grim procession.

Peter appeared to be very nervous. He entered a room and indicated that Poniatowski be brought in. An officer closed the door behind them, and Catherine's lover and her husband stood face to face. The Grand Duke planted himself squarely in front of his enemy. Their eyes met. "Now, admit it. You were with her . . . Well, speak!" Peter said in a choking voice.

Poniatowski resolved to die rather than admit the truth. He began to speak. Stubbornly he denied that which had been common knowledge for two years.

The interrogation went on for several hours, yielding no results. Suddenly Poniatowski had an idea. He pretended to cave in. "All right, I will tell you the truth. I will tell you why I visited the Grand Duchess."

Joyfully Peter rubbed his slender hands together, anticipating victory: "Go on, out with it!"

"All right," Poniatowski said, recalling the admiration the Grand Duke felt for the King of Prussia. "I visited Her Highness to receive from her certain information which Sir Charles had asked me to obtain from the Grand Duchess before his imminent departure for Western Europe—the information he was to relay to King Frederick."

For a second Peter stood motionless, as if thunderstruck. "My God! What have I done! Why didn't you tell me right away? What an idiot I am!"

In the ecstasy of his relief Peter embraced his wife's paramour. Then, to Stanislas' astonishment he said, "However, I now give you my permission. We are friends from now on. If you indeed sleep with her, and if this is of value to our common cause, I will not oppose you."

Meanwhile, day had broken and news of Poniatowski's ambush and imprisonment had been brought to the Empress. Appalled and angered by what she considered to be her nephew's most colossal piece of stupidity ever, she summoned the head of the secret police, Alexander Shuvalov, and ordered him to the scene. He was to quash the scandal before it grew worse.

A very apprehensive Shuvalov was driven posthaste to the little house in the grove—to be greeted by smiles. To his amazement he beheld the cuckolded Crown Prince and the handsome Polish aristocrat sharing a bottle and chatting amiably.

The police chief hastened back to his sovereign to assure Her Majesty that the Heir Apparent had meant no harm, that he had been drinking through the night—the reason for all the commotion. But all was quiet now.

It was, in fact, over. The Grand Duke was in raptures—his faithless wife's influence was now being enlisted on the side of his idol, Frederick! Capital, splendid! Much to Countess Elizabeth's disgust, he released the prisoner—and the servant and the cabman. All St. Petersburg soon hummed with fanciful versions of the affair.

The other, mightier, Elizabeth was having second thoughts. Her niece's romance with the fetching Pole had gone far enough. She would ask the sovereign at Dresden to recall his all-too-successful envoy.

And then again she hesitated. Would the request cause a diplomatic brouhaha after all? Would the wicked tongues of Europe wag even more busily?

No one knew just what the Empress would do, least of all Elizabeth herself. Late in June (by the Russian calendar), two days after the bizarre events, the court was to celebrate St. Peter's Day. Ever since the reign of Peter the Great, and particularly from the time of the ascension of his daughter Elizabeth, this was an important holiday in Russia. The Grand Duke was flattered by the identical name. Actually, that day two saints were to be honored, St. Paul only secondarily to St.

Peter. And the little son of the Grand Ducal pair, then a few months short of three years of age, was baptized Paul. A grand day, in sum.

The principal ball was to be held at the Peterhof palace, near Oranienbaum. Two weeks earlier Ambassador Poniatowski had received an invitation. He was to come with Jan Clement Branicki, a Polish magnate, Governor of Krakow, then visiting St. Petersburg. The guest, moreover, was a close kinsman of the Ambassador's, having married Stanislas' sister. Would the two invitations now be canceled? Poniatowski and his guest wondered till the very last hour.

But no, there was no cancellation, polite or otherwise. Stanislas and his brother-in-law, in a splendid equipage, drove to Peterhof.

In his exquisitely cut Parisian frock coat, with a lacy *jabot* around his neck and continuing down to the middle of his shirt, the Polish Order of the White Eagle crossing his powerful shoulders, the Ambassador, with his portly brother-in-law in tow, bowed low before the Russian Empress.

All eyes were on them. Breathlessly the aristocratic crowd waited for Her Imperial Majesty's words. Smiling graciously, she extended her plump hand to Poniatowski and cheerfully acknowledged his greeting and his introduction of Branicki. There seemed to be a collective sigh, half relief, half disappointment. The storm had not broken, at least for the moment. Catherine had been spared; Elizabeth Vorontsova was cheated of her prey. Peter's mistress knew that prudence dictated that she feign defeat.

Later, during the ball, in another of the palace rooms, Peter and Catherine were chatting gaily with their courtiers. All fell silent when Poniatowski entered. With an easy and dignified bow he rendered his respects to the Crown Prince, kissed Catherine's proffered hand, and for a few minutes conversed with both, seemingly at ease. But then, he was a cool and consummate actor.

The French envoy, the Marquis de l'Hôpital, watched this scene closely. He was surprised, though naturally did not reveal it, by the calm, even benevolent attitude of the Heir Apparent and the unruffled poise of the Pole. At this point the

Marquis even began to doubt the veracity of what he had heard about that curious night at Oranienbaum.

He was even more astonished when he saw Poniatowski approach the Grand Duke's repulsive mistress and ask her to join him in a minuet. Filled with her recent resolve not to show her bitterness over the failure of her scheme, she accepted Stanislas' arm with a smile of pretended pleasure. Despite her misshapen body, Elizabeth Vorontsova danced well.

Stanislas found a moment to whisper, "You could make a certain person happy."

His partner, not at all taken aback, replied, also in a whisper, "Done," and added gently, "Come tonight at one o'clock to the Mon Plaisir pavilion, the entrance to the lower park."

The victorious Stanislas pressed her hand, then raised it to his lips.

At one o'clock, at the appointed place, Vorontsova met him. "Wait here," she instructed. "The Grand Duke has guests. Let them finish their pipes."

When at last Peter was alone in his suite she brought the Ambassador in.

"Ah," exclaimed Peter, at once returning to the subject last touched upon in the little house by the seashore, "how stupid it was of you not to have warned me beforehand! We would have avoided that foolish incident."

Speaking in French, the Crown Prince for the first time addressed his rival with the familiar *tu*.

Stanislas responded with some effusive words of admiration for the military skill with which the Grand Duke had captured him. Peter smirked. Flattered, he patted Stanislas' shoulder, then exclaimed, "It seems to me that someone is missing here!"

With this he half-ran to Catherine's bedroom and found her already retired for the night. Rousing her with a giggle, giving her just time enough to pull on her stockings, thrust her feet into a pair of slippers, and get into a light silken robe, he led her into the room where his mistress and his wife's lover were amiably exchanging small talk.

"Well, here she is!" Peter cried, immensely pleased with himself. "I hope that now you are satisfied with my behavior!"

Recovering from her surprise, Catherine managed to say, "Now everything must be done not to let them recall the Ambassador back to Dresden."

Readily agreeing, Peter forthwith sat down to write to Bestuzhev-Ryumin his firm request that Count Poniatowski not be recalled.

Soon, summoned despite the late hour, Lev Naryshkin and Poniatowski's brother-in-law joined the curious foursome and they all talked, jested, and drank till dawn.

In his memoirs, Stanislas Poniatowski leaves us this brief sketch of Peter: "Nature created him a coward and a glutton, and he was so comical in all respects that anyone seeing him could not help but think, 'Here is a clown who painfully claims to be a prince.'"

He quotes the Grand Duke as saying to him in one of Peter's frequent spells of opening his heart to his new friend, "You see how unfortunate I am! I so longed to serve the King of Prussia. In such service I would have invested all my zeal and all my capabilities, and I am confident that by now I would have commanded a regiment for him and would have been a lieutenant general and even perhaps a major general. But alas, no! They brought me here to be the Grand Duke in this accursed country."

Poniatowski recalls how angrily Peter ridiculed the Russian people, using his customary vulgar and inflated language, which, the Count adds, was not always displeasing, for he concedes that Peter, although demented, had at least some remnants of cleverness.

He tells of Peter's incessant smoking, his thin and sickly frame, always clad in a Holstein officer's uniform. Only infrequently would the Crown Prince wear civilian clothes, and these of such comical bad taste that "he rather resembled an arrogant braggart from an Italian comedy."

To cement this curious and abrupt friendship, Peter invited his wife's lover to be his personal guest at Oranienbaum for two days. With the Pole, a Swedish visitor in Russia, Count Von Horn, was asked to come. Later, with a chuckle, Stanislas describes how the Swede must have guessed (or was confirmed in his knowledge of) his intimacy with Catherine. As the two entered her boudoir, Catherine's little dog met Von Horn with its unfriendly bark, but leaped joyfully at Stanislas, thus betraying the animal's long acquaintance with this "close friend of the Grand Ducal family."

&

In mid-1757 the Seven Years' War was at one of its critical junctures.

In May, Frederick shattered a sizable Austrian army at Prague. Alarmed, Maria Theresa pressed her ally Elizabeth for immediate help. An emergency audience with Elizabeth was arranged for Ambassador Esterhazy by Alexander Shuvalov. The envoy brought with him a bank draft for 500,000 gold rubles, Austria's second installment of the payment for Russia's participation in the anti-Frederick coalition. Handing over the draft, the Ambassador reminded this powerful daughter of Peter the Great's about the Versailles Treaty, which she had signed with Austria and France. Pleased with the gold, Elizabeth assured the Austrian that she had ordered her Field Marshal Stephen Apraxin to attack Frederick from two sides, using two Russian armies then standing ready in Poland.

The campaign began shortly. Frederick had excellent troops, as always, but they were too few for this multifront war. That June the Austrians went on the offensive. Defeating Frederick at Kolin in Bohemia, they invaded Silesia, the main bone of contention between Austria and Prussia. The French simultaneously occupied Hanover, much to the horror of George II.

On July 15, Apraxin's armies crossed the Prussian border and took Memel and Koenigsberg. Pushing on through East Prussia, Russia's 80,000 soldiers badly trounced the Prussians in the battle of Grossjaegersdorf, in which 4,500 enemy troops were killed and many more wounded, captured, or missing.

In St. Petersburg, Elizabeth ordered a series of triumphant Te Deums, and one day, as she was leaving the cathedral, enthusiastic crowds shouted, "To Berlin! To Berlin!"

The road to Berlin, in fact, appeared to be wide open.

While the Heir Apparent, Frederick's admirer, walked

around openly glum and dejected, Catherine cleverly concealed her sadness. She attended all the Te Deums and was discreet during jubilant conversations about Frederick's plight.

From Hanbury Williams, through Stanislas, she had by then received several English subsidies, in gold, each of 100,000 florins. She had kept up her secret correspondence with Sir Charles, but had ordered that all her documents be returned to her. Sir Charles complied—after first sending copies to London. And some papers in their original were never given back to the Grand Duchess—Sir Charles conveniently forgot about them. (They are still in the archives of the British Foreign Office.)

But now that the British policy in St. Petersburg appeared to be a failure, particularly since Hanover was occupied by Elizabeth's French allies, Sir Charles was recalled to London. Not only had the Foreign Office decided on this, but the Shuvalovs' French party had in its triumph also insisted on it.

Sir Charles was reluctant to leave; he would not concede his diplomatic bankruptcy. He postponed his departure again and again. By this time, there being no earthly chance for him to visit Catherine safely, he could maintain a perilous contact with her only through Stanislas. Nor could Hanbury Williams see his friend Bestuzhev-Ryumin, who kept a low profile in these uncertain times, and whose assistant, Count Michael Vorontsov (the uncle of Peter's mistress), watched his every step in hopes of getting his job. A personal friend of Alexander Shuvalov's, Vorontsov reported to the secret police chief whatever went on in the Chancellery.

Why did Sir Charles delay? Quite possibly he was waiting for what he believed to be Elizabeth's imminent death. He expected that Peter on his ascension would reverse Russia's policy, would favor Frederick with all his newly begotten power. If overthrown by Catherine, his alliance with Prussia and England would naturally be continued by his wife (most likely, his widow), who would rule the empire either by herself or as the regent of her little son, Paul.

But Elizabeth, although continuing her nonstop drinking and dissolute habits, clung to life, and, with the backing of the Shuvalovs, held firmly to her anti-Prussian course.

Sir Charles had to go. He left for what he said would be his Scandinavian route homeward, but in the fall of 1757 unexpectedly returned from Finland, loudly complaining that the horses given him were patently unsuitable for such a long and difficult journey.

He announced that he would sail for England on a British ship due to depart from Kronstadt. But now good horses were promised him for a trip via Finland and Sweden, so he procrastinated, waiting for fateful news from the Empress' doctors. No news came, and, late in October, refusing the fresh horses, he took a berth on a ship from Kronstadt for Finland, thence to Stockholm, Copenhagen, and Hamburg. He purposely chose this roundabout route, hoping the events in St. Petersburg would interrupt him, would bring him back to the Imperial court.

Instead, Hanbury Williams had to be carried off the ship at Hamburg, gravely ill. The local physicians said he had gone mad. He was brought home to England, where he did not even recognize his kin and friends.

The diplomat was confined to his luxurious but somber mansion at Monmouthshire. A year passed. Toward the end of 1758, he seemed to be recovering. Yet the realization of his failure in St. Petersburg was too great a burden for him. He lived one more year, and on November 2, 1759, in a new bout of insanity, killed himself.

Sir Charles Hanbury Williams was buried at Westminster Abbey.

In England, connoisseurs of belles lettres remembered him for years to come. In 1763, a collection of his light verse was published; in 1822 his *Works* appeared.

In 1757, since that adventure-filled June night at Oranienbaum, the liaison between Catherine and Stanislas was almost in the open, having been sanctioned, as it were, by the cuckolded husband and his mistress.

As Catherine's pregnancy neared its term, she told Stanislas how pleased she was to bear his child. She, like Hanbury Williams, at the time was anticipating her aunt's death and the inevitable changes that would follow—perhaps even an amicable divorce from Peter and marriage with Stanislas, then a different, peaceful existence.

On the morning of the ninth of December 1757, Catherine gave birth to a baby girl. The Empress chose the name Anna for the child—in memory of Elizabeth's late sister, Anna Petrovna, mother of the Heir Apparent Peter—even though she knew that the baby's father was not her nephew, Peter Holstein Romanov, but Count Stanislas Poniatowski of Poland and Saxony.

The baby was given the title of Grand Duchess, and her mother was granted an Imperial reward in gold for her fertility. Whether Peter received or even demanded a grant for himself as the supposed father, similar to the gold he had received when Paul was born, is not recorded.

Candidly and jeeringly he told all and sundry that he was not the father, and named Poniatowski. He joked: "God alone knows precisely who is responsible for my wife's pregnancies. I am not sure that this baby is mine or that I must officially acknowledge her as mine."

Learning of such talk, Catherine sent Lev Naryshkin to Peter: "Tell him from me to write an oath that the baby is not his daughter."

Peter took fright, for some reason imagining that the Empress herself wished such a document from him so as to declare him insane and choose another Heir Apparent.

As Catherine had hoped, he shouted at Naryshkin: "Go to the devil and never again utter such stupidities to me!"

Elizabeth's health steadily, though not as yet catastrophically, worsened, and she stayed in her bed for long periods. Only the Shuvalovs and occasionally Bestuzhev-Ryumin could see her. The French party was in an ever-increasing ascendancy, and the Shuvalovs were even thicker with Michael Vorontsov. Cunningly, the Grand Duke grew friendly with these men, especially with the uncle of his mistress.

Catherine knew what they were planning. After Elizabeth's death they would do away with her somehow or other, then marry Peter to his mistress and divide power in the empire between the Shuvalovs and the Vorontsovs.

Catherine and Stanislas decided to be more circumspect.

Once again their nights together were to be arranged discreetly; once again he wore wigs and cloaks and was escorted to their place of lovemaking with due precautions, now by Naryshkin, now by Catherine's most trusted chambermaid.

She had a set of complicated screens installed in her boudoir, behind which Stanislas was to hide in case of unexpected visits by her enemies.

Once there was a knock on the door, and Stanislas ducked behind the screens. Alexander Shuvalov entered with a message from the Empress. Looking around the bedroom, he asked, "And what do you have behind the screens?"

Catherine smiled at the secret police chief and replied, "That is where I keep my portable toilet."

Shuvalov left with no further questions.

In late 1757, now that Sir Charles was gone, Bestuzhev-Ryumin was the only man of influence she could truly depend on. The Chancellor, once her enemy, was now not only a friend—he was a co-conspirator. Shrewdly, he believed in both her brains and her luck. And so it came to pass that together the two succeeded in drawing Field Marshal Apraxin to their side.

Secret instructions from Bestuzhev-Ryumin and Catherine reached the Field Marshal amid his victories in Prussia: go easy on Frederick. So, instead of advancing on Berlin, Apraxin suddenly retreated to the Russian frontier, as far as Narva.

Europe's capitals, most of all St. Petersburg, were astonished. Soon word got around that Apraxin's retreat was masterminded by Bestuzhev-Ryumin and Catherine. The Shuvalovs presented to the Empress whatever meager evidence they could scrape up, to substantiate a plot against her own Imperial person. The French and Austrian envoys rushed to the court with their indignation over Apraxin's strange conduct.

The Crown Prince, in fear and trembling, hastened to his aunt's bedside to swear he was innocent and to point his finger at Catherine and the Chancellor. Aware not only of his pro-Frederick sentiments but also of his cowardice, Elizabeth believed him. To her, his assurances were in a way one more confirmation of the machinations of Bestuzhev-Ryumin, Apraxin, and Catherine against her.

The Empress ordered an immediate investigation.

The Shuvalovs demanded that she dismiss Bestuzhev-Ryumin at once and appoint Michael Vorontsov in his place. Elizabeth declined, for she valued her Chancellor's many years of service to her. But by January 1758, it was clear to her that he was indeed involved.

Alexander Shuvalov and Michael Vorontsov had learned much of the Chancellor's and Catherine's connection with the British. Indeed, through much of 1757, if with increasing discretion, the Grand Duchess had continued her contacts with Hanbury Williams. Knowing that he would be forced to leave soon, she had used their last opportunities to work behind the scenes together on Frederick's behalf. In the process, till the very end of Sir Charles' diplomatic posting, she had eagerly sought from him—as well as from Poniatowski—details of British politics at home and abroad. She was learning about life in England as assiduously as in her girlhood she had imbibed French literature and culture from her governess, Mademoiselle Babette Cardel.

All the while Catherine knew that rough waters lay ahead. In her memoirs she was to write of this period, these weighty years 1757–1758, "Now I was fated either to perish because of him [her husband] or with him; or rescue myself, my children and perhaps the state itself from that perdition which everything presaged for the future, judging by the psychological and physical state of the Grand Duke."

In despair she thought and secretly wrote of various plans to save herself. Yet all such schemes were predicated on Elizabeth's early demise. But the tough old despot refused to die, not then. With what appeared to be her last strength, she was to move against her niece's alliance with the Chancellor and the Field Marshal.

෫෧

In February 1758, Lev Naryshkin was to be married. On a Sunday early that month he held a sumptuous wedding reception at which Catherine was the principal guest of honor. Just as the assemblage was preparing to sit down at the festive tables, Naryshkin quietly approached the Grand Duchess with a note in his hand. "From Count Poniatowski," he whispered. "You are to read the message at once."

Catherine walked into a bedroom and unfolded the note. She read it in horror: her lover was informing her that the night before, Bestuzhev-Ryumin had been arrested, and with him three others—Bernardi, her jeweler, who had often in the past brought letters from Sir Charles to her; Adadurov, her Russian teacher; and Yelagin, a member of her court.

Feverishly she searched her memory. Yes, Bestuzhev-Ryumin must have preserved her letters to him, including the one in which she outlined a project of succession to the throne, and, above all, the ones in which she had insisted that the Russian advance in Prussia be halted. If the Shuvalov-Vorontsov clique got hold of those papers, she was doomed.

But she made a supreme effort to look calm and even cheerful as she reentered the main hall of the house. A ball followed the supper. In a pause between the dances she walked over to Prince Nikita Trubetskoy, a member of the secret police, who was aiding Alexander Shuvalov in the investigation ordered by her aunt.

"Well now, how are things in your office? More crimes than criminals or more criminals than crimes?" she asked casually.

Trubetskoy was laconic: "We do our duty as ordered. As for crimes, we haven't uncovered them yet. The investigation is continuing."

A few minutes later she strolled over to Count Alexander Buturlin, another important adherent of the French-Austrian party at the principal court. She repeated her question in the same bantering tone. The Count proved to be a bit more open. He sighed. "Bestuzhev-Ryumin is under arrest, but we don't know why."

Controlling her apprehensions, Catherine bade a leisurely farewell to the Naryshkins and their guests and rode home to her palace apartments. First of all she carefully inspected her furniture and furnishings, her desk drawers, her chests and closets. No, nothing had been disturbed. Apparently, as yet no search of her quarters had been ordered and carried out.

Then she methodically went through her papers, keeping her fireplace ablaze with stacks of diaries, receipts, drafts of letters, books, and even an autobiographical sketch of herself at fifteen—much to the sorrow of future biographers.

In the morning Stambke was announced. He was the Holstein envoy to the Empress; he was expected to be loyal to Peter but was devoted to Catherine instead. He reported to her that he had managed to penetrate Bestuzhev-Ryumin's mansion, where the Chancellor was under house arrest, that despite the alertness of the soldiers guarding the prisoner he had succeeded in seeing the Chancellor, and was now bringing a note from him to the Grand Duchess. In trepidation she opened the message and read, "Do not worry, I had time to burn everything."

Relief enveloped Catherine.

She now remembered that at the height of his power and of their intrigues together, the Chancellor had advised her to write to him and to Apraxin several run-of-the-mill birthday greetings and anniversary congratulations, and, most importantly, a letter to the Field Marshal urging him to press on with his offensive in Prussia. The wily Chancellor must have kept and allowed the searchers to find these innocuous papers while burning everything incriminating on the very eve of his arrest. Now, Catherine hoped, the noncompromising letter would be in the hands of the Empress, proving her lack of involvement in Apraxin's retreat.

But had Apraxin thought in time to burn whatever proof of their conspiracy might have been in his files? Or were these now in the hands of Alexander Shuvalov and the Empress?

In the following days and weeks, the arrests and grillings of high-level suspects continued, and the news of the uproar spread over Europe. In Germany, her former lover, Sergei Saltykov, was upset by it. Sent by the Empress as her envoy to Hamburg and other non-Prussian cities, he had helped Catherine from afar by secretly relaying her correspondence with her mother. Would his role be uncovered by Alexander Shuvalov's snoopers?

The old, infirm Field Marshal Apraxin was under strict guard at Narva, on the border. Like Bestuzhev-Ryumin, he was questioned brutally if not actually tortured. The old soldier swore there was no conspiracy, that he had retreated amid his victories over Frederick because he had run out of supplies for his large army and money to pay his troops. Alexander Suvorov, the future military genius of Russia, then a young supply officer in Apraxin's army, must have smiled sardonically at this, for it was common knowledge that a conquering army can always find food, money, and even munitions in captured territory, especially in such a prosperous land as King Frederick's Prussia. Apraxin also maintained that he had never acted on his own initiative, but had sought the advice of his Military Council and his Chief of Staff, General Vilim (William) Fermor, the able son of an English immigrant in Russian service.

All evidence in Narva and St. Petersburg led Alexander Shuvalov to Catherine's concealed hand, yet apparently not a single incriminating document was found in Apraxin's papers from either Bestuzhev-Ryumin or the Grand Duchess. Shuvalov ground his teeth in rage.

He himself was questioning and threatening Apraxin, but to no avail. Suddenly, during one such session, the Field Marshal keeled over—he was dead of heart failure.

He died without breaking. Elizabeth's investigator came back to her with empty hands and in acute embarrassment. He could not very well conceal from the Empress the circumstances of Apraxin's demise. She either knew or could have guessed that torture had been used on him. Perhaps the thought even bothered her a little.

Now she began to suspect that possibly she could let up on Catherine. When Esterhazy called on the Empress, she defended her niece, showing him Catherine's letter to Bestuzhev-Ryumin with its insistence that the Russian advance in Prussia be maintained. The skeptical Austrian responded that he knew of this and other such letters, for Bestuzhev-Ryumin had taken care to display them to the military attaché on Esterhazy's staff, but that this letter and others like it were proof of Catherine's slyness, her precautions in the midst of her complicity.

On the evening of February 21, 1758, the Empress convened a council of her cabinet ministers, to which Bestuzhev-Ryumin was brought. Prince Nikita Trubetskoy, Alexander Shuvalov's aide, with a snarl tore from the prisoner's chest the Order of St. Andrew ribbon and a diamond star, his rewards for many years of service. Results of the interrogation achieved so far were made known.

These were not conclusive. The investigation was to be continued, as before assigned to the troika of Shuvalov and his assistants Trubetskoy and Buturlin. Elizabeth announced, more for the record than for actual observance, her decree that no torture be used.

No evidence of treason, particularly any that would ensnare the Grand Duchess, was presented or even uncovered. But it was officially announced that for years Bestuzhev-Ryumin had used his high position for personal profit. The accused, per the custom of that era, demanded to be allowed the procedure of a church confession. This was denied, for his persecutors were certain he would lie under the sacred oath as he did under the state oath when he professed his innocence. They asked Elizabeth to permit them to apply torture. She refused, obstinately. But what was done in fact, as in Apraxin's case, may have been another matter.

At long last the Empress issued her sentence. Stripped of all his posts and honors, Bestuzhev-Ryumin was to be exiled to one of his provincial estates. The other defendants were also treated leniently.

They had managed to destroy the evidence in the nick of time, and the tired, sick Empress was not feeling vindictive. For even though she rallied from time to time, she knew she had only a few years left and that she would soon have to answer to her Maker for any excesses. Elizabeth altogether avoided dealing with Catherine.

It was now the pre-Lenten carnival season, Russia's period of joyous abandon that Christianity had adapted from pagan times. For weeks, Poniatowski had been stressing to Catherine the importance of attending all such festivals, so as to prove by showing herself in public that she was not under arrest. Now, among other events, a play was scheduled in the palace theater. She planned to be there.

Just before curtain time she had visitors. Her husband came, accompanied by his mistress and Alexander Shuvalov. The Grand Duke decreed that his wife was to stay home. "Otherwise," he explained, "my friend the Countess would have to escort you as your official lady-in-waiting, and I would be without her company all evening long."

Catherine balked. Peter, incensed, yelled at her, seemingly half deranged, and Shuvalov, wearing his habitual rictus, backed him. The secret police chief said angrily that he would see to it that her carriage was withheld from her.

Catherine flared up: "I will walk to the theater! And I shall at once write to Her Majesty about this horrible treatment of me by my husband, and I shall petition to be returned to my mother in Germany!"

This had its effect. Subdued by the threat of scandal, the trio left hurriedly. But in a few minutes Shuvalov returned, his face flaming with hatred. Catherine had her brief letter written and sealed.

"Deliver this to Her Majesty at once."

Bristling, he took the letter—and at the same time informed her that her equipage was ready. With all the dignity she could summon, she walked toward the exit. In the vestibule her husband and his mistress were deep in a card game. On seeing her, both rose and with mocking pretense at respect bowed to her.

This was a victory. Yet to her letter to the Empress there was no reply.

As was her pious habit, during the third week of Lent Elizabeth took her confession to Father Dubyansky, the uncle of one of the young women at her court who was truly devoted to her. The priest was the spiritual adviser and confessor to the Empress herself. Catherine felt he was one of the few persons close to her aunt who could intercede for her. He had done so in the past; he might do it again.

Catherine recited her troubles to the priest, who couldn't believe she would really go back to Germany: "Her Majesty will never agree to your leaving."

But he promised to speak to the Empress, to try to prevail upon her to grant Catherine an audience.

Within a few days, Alexander Shuvalov arrived to announce that Her Majesty would receive Her Highness on the night of April 13. Increasingly, Elizabeth slept during the day and conducted at night whatever affairs of the court and the state she could still deal with.

On April 13, 1758, at ten o'clock in the evening, Catherine dressed and sat down in her boudoir to wait. Drained, fatigued, she fell asleep in her armchair. At one-thirty her favorite chambermaid awakened her: Alexander Shuvalov was in attendance, ready to take her to the Empress.

Through a reception hall, Catherine was ushered into her aunt's bedroom. Elizabeth, sitting in an armchair, seemed to the Grand Duchess a burned-out woman. On the windowsills several candles burned in crystal candelabra, and between them two small golden basins were placed, filled with papers. Catherine guessed that these were her letters to Bestuzhev-Ryumin and Apraxin. She made an effort not to lose her composure.

Two men stood flanking Elizabeth, who was seated in her armchair—Grand Duke Peter and Alexander Shuvalov. Both stared at Catherine with undisguised hostility and with an air of malicious anticipation. A screen extended along one wall of the room, and Catherine surmised that other persons, probably her enemies, were concealed behind it—possibly including Ivan Shuvalov, the wily Alexander's nephew and the lover of the ailing Empress. (It was later confirmed that Ivan was indeed present.)

Catherine approached the Empress, fell to her knees, and started to weep. Through her tears she declared that she had no more strength left to bear her burdens, that no one loved her, that the Empress herself, who had earlier been so gracious to her, had turned away from her, allowing all to witness her disgrace . . .

Elizabeth listened, betraying signs of agitation, looking at

Catherine with what appeared to be a modicum of sympathy. At one point she dropped a tear or two herself. She asked, "How can you request that I send you back to Germany? What about your children?"

"They cannot remain in better hands than those of Your Majesty."

"But what will people say, and what reason will we give for your departure?"

"Your Majesty will say that which she will consider appropriate. She will give the reason for which your disfavor has fallen upon me and for which the Grand Duke hates me so."

Repeatedly the Empress bade her visitor rise, but Catherine remained on her knees, as though she had not heard. Tears streamed down her cheeks.

"How will you live?" the Empress continued. "And besides, your father is dead and your mother was compelled to flee and is now an émigrée in Paris."

"I know," Catherine told her. "The King of Prussia suspects that she is too loyal to Russia, and that is why he persecuted her."

Apparently Elizabeth had not expected this display of meekness and supplicating words from her haughty niece. Although her father confessor, Dubyansky, had forewarned her that Catherine might adopt this tactic, the Empress was moved to pity. Again tears welled in her eyes, and she stretched out her arms toward her niece, helped her to rise, and said excitedly, "God is my witness how much I have loved you, how I wept when you were ill and on the edge of death. Would I have left you to die? Ah, but there is my love for you! But you are terribly proud. I remember how once, in the Summer Palace, you barely nodded your head while greeting me, and I even asked you, 'Does your neck hurt so that you do not even bow to me?' The trouble is that you fancy yourself the cleverest creature in the world."

By Elizabeth's side, Peter, seeing a reconciliation in the making, whispered a few words to Shuvalov and then shouted at the top of his voice, "She is horribly malicious and stubborn!"

Catherine kept her calm as she addressed her husband: "If you are referring to me, well, I am prepared to admit in the presence of Her Majesty that I am angry with those who cause you to be unjust. It is true that I have grown stubborn from the time I realized that by giving in to you in everything I earned nothing but your hatred."

The Empress became sterner: "You interfere in matters that are not your concern. Myself, during the reign of Empress Anna, I would never have had the audacity to behave the way you do. How dared you, for example, issue orders to Field Marshal Apraxin?"

"I never even considered doing such a thing."

"You dare deny it? And what about these letters?" She pointed to one of the gold basins containing crumpled papers.

"I wrote to him only about what was being said concerning his conduct of the war." Catherine presented her long-prepared alibi, the camouflage letter in which she had suggested to the Field Marshal that he continue to advance in Prussia. "And another letter is my New Year's greeting to him. The third letter contains my best wishes for the birthday of his son. Such were my 'orders' to Apraxin—"

Elizabeth interrupted: "Bestuzhev-Ryumin says there were many other letters."

"If that is what he says, he is lying."

"Well, then," the Empress said in a tone meant to conclude the scene, "if he is slandering you, I will order him put to torture."

Peter, watching his battle being lost, began to shout and curse. The Empress gave him a look of supreme contempt and with one gesture silenced him. Then, rising from her armchair and approaching Catherine, she said in a quiet, even voice of conciliation, "There is much more I would like to say to you, but I am afraid it might rekindle your quarrel"— meaning the rift between Peter and Catherine.

Catherine replied, maintaining her tone of humble submission, "I also cannot speak here, no matter how much I wish to open my entire soul, my entire heart to you."

Again tears flooded Elizabeth's eyes. Then, with a wave of her hand, she terminated the interrogation.

Shuvalov and Peter strode out of the audience hall in a rage. Neither seemed to understand that no matter what

Catherine did, the Empress would not harm her, for doing so would open the path to the throne to the detested Elizabeth Vorontsova as Peter's future Imperial consort. During the last few years of her life, more dead than alive, the Empress was still sufficiently lucid to stand in the way of this development. Catherine would remain in Russia, unpunished and unmolested.

Calm, almost joyous, the Grand Duchess returned to her suite. As her chambermaids were disrobing her for bed, there was a knock on the door. Shuvalov entered, smiling ingratiatingly, his habitual grimace suppressed. "A message from Her Majesty. She promises to see you soon, tête-à-tête."

It was nearly four in the morning when Catherine finally fell asleep, her first untroubled rest after so many weeks and months of alarums.

But she knew there would be more months, perhaps years, of hardship and self-abnegation before the fruits of victory would fall to her.

The next day she wrote a long, tender letter to Stanislas, her beloved, her dear and only friend. It was a *billet-doux* filled with bright, rainbow-hued hopes for their life ahead together.

Soon Catherine was stunned by a reliable report from her faithful adherents that a note from Poniatowski had been found among Bestuzhev-Ryumin's papers. Its tone was bland and noncommittal, and in normal times would not have aroused suspicion. But this brief document revealed that the year before, it was Bestuzhev-Ryumin who, by exceeding his authority and not asking permission from the Empress, had arranged the Pole's return to Russia as the Saxon-Polish envoy to the Imperial court. Michael Vorontsov, the new Chancellor, immediately demanded that the King of Saxony-Poland recall Poniatowski.

After several delays, in October 1758, Catherine's lover departed for Warsaw and Dresden. Both were desolate.

A special courier from St. Petersburg caught up with him almost at the frontier. The Empress had a special parting gift for the disgraced envoy—a golden snuffbox. Inside was a note in her hand: "The cat knows whose milk he has lapped."

In St. Petersburg, as autumn darkened into winter, the

bleak Russian horizon seemed to close in around Catherine. She knew full well that her many enemies were continuing to plot against her. Sir Charles was gone, Bestuzhev-Ryumin under arrest, and now, in the cruelest blow of all, they had taken Stanislas from her. Her isolation was increasing.

Then, to add one more misery, the little Grand Duchess Anna became ill and, a few weeks after her lover's departure, died. Catherine writes, "It was a good thing [that all of her short life] she had been under the care of the Empress. Otherwise I would have been accused of neglecting her. . . . They did not see my tears."

In Western Europe, the despairing Poniatowski sensed that it would be a long time before he would see his mistress again. He brooded. In his memoirs he asserts that for two and a half years after his last tryst with Catherine, he abstained from making love.

The news of their daughter's death reached him months after the event, and he at once wrote to Catherine telling of his grief.

He also said that he wanted to return, soon.

However, two women were doing their utmost to dissuade Poniatowski. Catherine, the realist, wrote to him that there was no immediate possibility, and his mother was once again up in arms at the very mention of his going to Russia.

Countess Poniatowska was horrified when she realized that her son's passion showed no sign of abating. But she had a plan, and carried it out forthwith.

In a solemn ceremony to take place in the family chapel, while receiving Holy Communion, Stanislas was to confess his repentance for the sinful affair and to swear by everything sacred to him and his mother that he would renew the liaison with Catherine only if she became widowed, in which case he would marry her in none other than a Roman Catholic rite. Stanislas submitted, and in 1759, Constanzia Poniatowska died, her ambitions partially fulfilled.

Stanislas told Catherine about the oath, and this news must

have strengthened her new resolve to have nothing further to do with Stanislas, the best of her lovers. She regretted the loss, but saw the necessity of the sacrifice.

Besides, in 1759 a new, extremely satisfying man was enjoying her favors. Satisfying and more politically promising than the gallant young Pole who had dropped out of her life.

Catherine the Great.   COURTESY OF THE NEW YORK PUBLIC LIBRARY PICTURE
COLLECTION.

Johanna Elizabeth, mother of Catherine the Great. COLLECTION OF VSEVOLOD
A. NIKOLAEV.

Catherine as a young
woman. THE BETTMANN
ARCHIVE.

Elizabeth, Empress of Russia. A forceful woman in her own right, she was the daughter of Peter the Great and the aunt of Peter III. THE BETTMANN ARCHIVE.

Catherine's young husband, Peter III, as a boy. He was seventeen and a half years old when they were married; she was sixteen.

Later portrait of Peter III by Antropov. COURTESY OF THE NEW YORK PUBLIC LIBRARY PICTURE COLLECTION.

Grand Duke Paul (the future Emperor Paul I) at the age of sixteen. According to Catherine's memoirs, Paul's real father was not her husband Peter III, but her first lover, Sergei Saltykov. This assertion does not accord with the facts.

Stanislas-Augustus Poniatowski, Catherine's second lover and, later, the King of Poland. Original lithograph printed in England, 1797.

Gregory Orlov, Catherine's third lover, at age 28. Portrait by F. Rokotov. COURTESY OF THE NEW YORK PUBLIC LIBRARY, SLOVONIC DIVISION; ASTOR, LENOX AND TILDEN FOUNDATIONS.

Hanging by the rib and burying alive were two of the old-time Russian punishments. Women thus buried were commonly those who had been condemned for murdering their husbands. From an engraving of the eighteenth century; artist unknown.

Hung by the rib, the Pugachev rebels were sent floating down the river to impress the populace. From an engraving of the eighteenth century; artist unknown.

Catherine the Great early in her reign. COURTESY OF THE LIBRARY OF CONGRESS.

A view of the old Winter Palace, before its reconstruction. An engraving of the eighteenth century, artist unknown. REPRODUCED FROM STOLITSA I USAD'BA, PETROGRAD, SEPTEMBER 15, 1916.

# Gregory Orlov:
# The Conspirator

He was Gregory Orlov, a handsome young officer in an elite artillery unit. Gregory was one of five brothers, all of them officers in the Guards or in other privileged regiments stationed in St. Petersburg. All five were merry giants, tough, scrappy, and daring.

Catherine wanted Gregory not only for her bed, so desolate after Stanislas' departure; she needed him—and his fearless brothers and his friends—because by the end of the 1750s she was ready to gamble for the highest stakes. This man and loyal praetorians like him would be of incalculable aid.

For Catherine always remembered her pledge to herself when she first set eyes on Russia's vastness, first met Peter, first realized how inherently superior she was to him and to the other mediocrities at court: "Someday I will rule this land."

There had been many setbacks and some very dangerous
escapes; nonetheless Catherine's goal seemed to grow nearer
with each passing year. But she needed help. And she knew
that Gregory and his brothers would gladly serve as stepping-
stones to the throne.

Unlike her husband, so pigheaded in his German ways and
his Lutheranism, she continued to speak her accented Russian
at every opportunity, and carefully observed the numerous
holidays, feasts, and fasts of the Orthodox Church. She knew
all its dogmas, rituals, and pageants by heart, even the least of
them.

Hers would be no run-of-the-mill palace revolution. Catherine would rise to power on the crest of the mighty wave of the
Russian people. She would be one of them and they would be
one with her.

                                  *≈*

In the summer of 1698, the twenty-six-year-old Tsar Peter I
was visiting Vienna and planning to journey to Venice when a
breathless courier from Moscow brought him alarming news.
In his absence the *streltsy* had once again risen against him.

These men were sharpshooters, then numbering some
50,000, whose regiments were the sturdy yet pampered back-
bone of Muscovy's army. Formed by Ivan the Terrible in
1550, the *streltsy* were Russia's first troops to carry and use fire-
arms, not just halberds, pikes, and sabers. Recruited from
commoners of all social levels, for over a century they lived
with their families in their own settlements, their shops at
their elbows, where they profitably engaged in crafts and com-
merce in addition to their military duties.

In 1682, after Peter as a ten-year-old boy was proclaimed
Tsar and his mother Regent, his elder half-sister, Sophie, had
prevailed on the more than willing *streltsy* to proclaim her
mentally retarded brother, Ivan, as Russia's Tsar, reducing
Peter to second, or lesser Tsar, while making herself the new
Regent. In 1696, she had tried to foment a new revolt of the
*streltsy* to seize all power for herself, but Peter, by then a confident young man of twenty-four, had easily thwarted her plot
and locked her up in a nunnery.

Now, two years later, in 1698, the sharpshooters were at it again, with wily Sophie most likely the cause, despite the convent walls.

Quitting Vienna, Tsar Peter rode eastward day and night until in late August he reached Moscow. Here, to his relief, he saw that his loyal adherents had not been idle. The chief conspirators had already been seized, and many of them executed. Peter took over.

He forced Sophie to don her final veil; she was to die a nun in 1704. Meanwhile, under the personal supervision of the enraged Tsar, hundreds of the *streltsy* were hanged, hundreds burned at the stake, and yet others had their heads chopped off in Moscow's principal square, Peter himself sometimes swinging the bloody ax.

The grandfather of the Orlov brothers had been selected for beheading, and Peter was approaching one more doomed *strelets* on the gore-bespattered scaffold. The victim was a huge man who faced the Tsar coolly. The soldier turned slightly, kicked aside with his boot tip the severed head of a fellow insurgent, and, looking at the head, requested, "Well, friend, clear the spot for me!"

Peter halted and lowered his ax. The fellow's sangfroid impressed him.

"What is your name?"

"Ivan Orlov, son of Gregory." (*Oryol* in Russian means Eagle; Orlov means Son of Eagle.)

"An eagle you are indeed!" exclaimed the Tsar, and pardoned him on the spot.

Once again in Peter the Great's army, soon to be modernized along Western standards, Ivan Orlov served well, garnering numerous rewards for battlefield exploits. In 1741, his son Gregory was Vice-Governor of Novgorod. Gregory married late, and his wife, less than half his age, bore him nine sons, of whom by the late 1750s five survived.

Gregory, the second-eldest, was born in 1734, and was thus five years Catherine's junior. He was the best-looking and the most charming of the quintet. Alexis, the third brother, born in 1737, was the most intelligent and the least principled. The fourth and the fifth, Fyodor and Vladimir, were rather mediocre compared to Gregory and Alexis, but were always ready to be of service to them.

After their father's death, Ivan, as the eldest, assumed the family's unquestioned leadership. The other four paid him homage, calling him Little Father, and handed over their regimental salaries and other monies to him. They all loved high living, sharing with one another everything except women.

Catherine writes, "They lived in unity as no brothers had ever lived before." The British envoy reported to London, "In a most brotherly way the Orlovs share their income; they have just one purse, out of which their expenditures are also done in common."

Their St. Petersburg mansion was renowned for its open hospitality, and the golden youth of the capital flocked there day and night. Not only were the five brothers popular in their own regiments, they were heartily welcomed in the mess-halls of the other elite units.

The brothers occasionally carried their jolly games into the streets of the outlying districts of the capital. There, they organized bloody *kulachnyie boi*—free-for-alls involving men and youths in which one neighborhood was pitted against another. Artisans, butchers, apprentices, and other commoners fought in brawls that often ended with serious injuries or even deaths.

The Saxon diplomat Georg Helbig paints an unattractive picture of the Orlovs in his memoirs. The brothers "had sold their father's rather substantial estate and lived on this capital, always revolving in a merry but unselective society, gambling at cards and by their excesses causing talk about themselves both at court and in the city. Their money was gone; in its place there appeared debts. Since they soon lost credit, the brothers' situation was quite perilous, but they were always saved by their cleverness and their luck at cards."

Subsequent to their successes, it was said that, having received a good education in the empire's finest military schools, all five Orlovs spoke German and French. This was not the case. Foreign diplomats, and Catherine herself, complained that Gregory neither spoke nor understood any foreign language, and certainly not French, so important at court, and which she vainly tried to teach him.

Like many of his contemporaries, Helbig marveled at the astuteness with which Gregory Orlov, that "handsomest man of the North," used his looks to secure the position of aide-de-camp with no less a person than General Peter Shuvalov. Soon enough, however, Gregory overreached himself when he seduced the mistress of his chief, Princess Helen Kurakina. Shuvalov was infuriated by this betrayal of trust and fully intended to avenge himself on the seducer and on his mistress. It was at that moment that Catherine invited Gregory to her bed, an event which might not have shielded him from Shuvalov's wrath had not the latter died of a timely stroke.

Catherine chose Gregory Orlov perhaps on an impulse, after one more nasty quarrel with her husband. On coming out of the chamber where the spat had just taken place, she noticed a gallant-looking officer in the corridor. He was on duty, escorting a high-born Prussian prisoner recently brought to St. Petersburg from the front of the Seven Years' War.

Gregory distinguished himself, first as a lieutenant, and since 1758 a captain, in an artillery unit commanded by Count Vilim Fermor against the troops of King Frederick. On August 25, 1758, in the battle of Zorndorf, which ended in heavy losses for both sides but was judged to be a Prussian victory, Gregory Orlov was wounded three times, but each time refused to leave the battlefield and was rewarded accordingly.

Among other German captives the thirty-year-old Count Wilhelm Friedrich Karl von Schwerin was taken—a fine catch indeed. The young Colonel, son of the King's famous Field Marshal and Chief of Staff, himself happened to be one of Frederick's favorite aides-de-camp.

The Russians lost some high-level staff to the Prussians. Among these was Nikita Beketov, destined to spend two years in captivity. Did it wound Empress Elizabeth to learn that one of her former lovers was now a prisoner of the hated Prussian? Quite possibly it did. But above all, the Empress was in-

trigued by the news of von Schwerin's capture, and wished to
see him.

In the spring of 1759, as his reward for bravery under fire,
Orlov was given the honor of escorting the Prussian prisoner
to St. Petersburg. And this was why Gregory was on duty in
the palace corridor, awaiting the emergence of his charge.

(Among the countless legends concerning Catherine's amorous intrigues, one long persisted that she first beheld Gregory not in the corridor but when she happened to glance out
the palace window. She saw the handsome officer walking
across the courtyard and, the story goes, ordered him to come
up and present himself.)

Ever since his arrival in the Russian capital in early April
1759, von Schwerin had been treated more like a visiting diplomat than a prisoner of war, and was quartered in a sumptuous private house not far from the Winter Palace. Peter took
him on a tour of the military academy, and, drawing him
aside, began to praise King Frederick, saying, "It would have
been glory and honor for me to serve in a campaign under the
leadership of the King of Prussia," adding, "Had I been this
country's sovereign, you would never have been a prisoner."

But for Gregory Orlov, guarding this pampered and titled
"captive" was an excellent opportunity to visit the Imperial
palaces almost daily.

For Catherine the young officer's presence was welcome.
She was at once drawn to him. She thought she still loved the
exiled Stanislas, she continued to write tender replies to his
love letters, but she needed a man by her side. Her hunger
was unbearable—she was only thirty—and she didn't care that
Gregory had no intellect since they were a good physical
match.

Catherine's choice of young Orlov for a bed-companion
may not have been the chance result of an encounter following a marital dispute. She must have heard by way of court
gossip about the Orlov brothers, their reputations as
daredevils, and, more significantly, about their influence
among both officers and common soldiers of the Guards regiments. She recalled that it was the praetorians of the Guards
who in 1741 had elevated Elizabeth to the throne; at a crucial

moment in the future they could again help to shape the destiny of Russia. And it would be politic to take a lover of Russian, not Polish or other foreign stock.

The liaison was arranged easily and quickly, for Gregory was more than willing. He was obviously flattered that the Grand Duchess herself had opened her bedroom and her arms to him. Manly in physique, limited in intellect, he soon fell under Catherine's astute sway.

Gregory lost no time in boasting of his exalted connection to his comrades, but he ran little risk in doing so, for the affair was no secret. Even Peter knew about it, for by 1759 Catherine's indifferent husband took it for granted that she had a stable of lovers. To Elizabeth Vorontsova and others in his entourage he swore that he would make short shrift of his wife when the moment was ripe. He was certain that his aunt was about to die and that he would then mount the throne as the only legitimate heir of the Empress. At that point he would bid Catherine a bloody *adieu*.

Even Stanislas, exiled in Western Europe, had heard of his darling's new lover. In one of his plaintive letters he gently chides her for installing Gregory in a suite next to hers.

ﻥ

The Russian Christmas of 1761 was approaching. In St. Petersburg, the Imperial court was gripped with apprehension: the Empress was dying, only fifty-two but all burned out by excesses of the table and the bed. No longer would she lovingly choose from her wardrobe of 15,000 dresses. No longer would she enjoy masked balls or her beloved French plays; her Italian and Ukrainian musicians would no longer enchant her ears. No more would she personally dress her chambermaids for their weddings and then, through a crack in the door, spy delightedly on her serfs at their nuptial festivities.

She, who had once savored the subtleties of Russian folk cuisine, turned her head from her favorite dishes brought to her bedside. The German *Kaffeeschenk*, who years before had been hired because of his art in brewing that exotic drink, and who had always accompanied her on her voyages with his pots and cups, was not required now that her last journey was approaching.

๛

Two women named Catherine were by then close friends: the future Empress Catherine Romanova and Princess Catherine Vorontsova-Dashkova, the sister of Peter's mistress.

The two Vorontsova sisters grew up in different households and hated each other. Catherine Vorontsova-Dashkova idealized the Crown Princess; she admired her intellect and daydreamed of the glorious future when her friend would be Russia's sovereign. Early in her life she firmly resolved to help the Crown Princess seize the throne.

Meanwhile the two talked earnestly of literature and art. In years to come the Princess wrote about the latter 1750s, when they first met in the house of her uncle, Michael Vorontsov, "At that time it could emphatically be said that in the entire empire there were no other two women who, like the Grand Duchess and myself, were engaged in serious reading."

Their acquaintanceship began in late 1758, although even before their meeting the Grand Duchess had heard Vorontsov's niece described as a prodigy. Only fifteen, she was reported to be an assiduous lover of learning. The Crown Princess was curious.

Michael Vorontsov's brother Roman lost his wife when Catherine Vorontsova was two years old. The family was then scattered: the two eldest girls, Maria and Elizabeth, were taken to the court to become ladies-in-waiting (their late mother was an intimate friend of the Empress'; as a young, spendthrift princess, Elizabeth had often needed money, and her friend had never failed to supply her with rubles). The elder of the two boys, Alexander, remained with Papa Roman in St. Petersburg; the younger, Simon, lived with his grandfather on a country estate. Catherine was brought to her uncle, at that time Bestuzhev-Ryumin's Vice-Chancellor. She grew up in his house as a companion to his daughter Anna.

The two girl cousins were given a very good education; teachers were engaged to tutor them at home. By her early teens Catherine Vorontsova knew four languages—her native

Russian, French, German, and Italian. On her own she read Voltaire, Montesquieu, and other Western authors.

In later decades her doting biographers echoed her self-serving memoirs in praising her as a multifaceted near-genius: a connoisseur of art, a teacher, a published writer, an editor, a surgeon, a natural historian, and even a composer. In her memoirs she slyly boasts how a work of sacred music that she wrote was performed in a church in Dublin before a large audience who were eager to hear a composition by "this Russian bear."

Some of her compatriots spoke admiringly of the young Catherine as a pretty girl maturing into a captivating woman. But they, too, exaggerated. Although not positively ugly like her sister, she was not especially comely either. The respected historian Dmitry Ilovaisky, though highly partial to her, describes Catherine a century later: "Her clever, expressive face had features that were too manly, and her vivacious and somewhat abrupt mannerisms, owing to her small stature, were not at all graceful." Nonetheless, at least in her youth, Catherine possessed a little charm. Above all, she was a brilliant conversationalist, and knew how to display her wit and her learning. "In my character," she writes, "there was a considerable share of pride, combined with extraordinary tenderness, and I had the strong wish to be loved by all those surrounding me with the same ardor as I loved them."

The need to love and be loved, she writes, manifested itself after the age of thirteen, so that at the age of fifteen, when she met the Grand Duchess, then almost thirty, she attached herself to her august namesake with frank abandon.

Catherine Vorontsova married early, at sixteen, in 1759, becoming Princess Dashkova but known from then on as Vorontsova-Dashkova. Her union with the rich and important Prince Michael Dashkov was happy; she began to bear him children at once. But devoted to her young family though she was, her main passion remained Grand Duchess Catherine.

The two Catherines visited each other frequently and exchanged fond letters constantly. They seemed to hold no secrets from each other, but in fact the Grand Duchess did not confide in the Princess as deeply or as openly as the latter thought she did. In the Grand Duchess' letters there was more *politesse* and pretense of tenderness than real love; she did not really need a woman friend.

The Princess in her astonishing naiveté did not even at first comprehend the role of Gregory Orlov at her idol's side, and the Grand Duchess, amazingly, succeeded in keeping her ignorant of her pregnancy by Gregory. She trusted the Princess up to a point and no further. In her practical view, the girl was too volatile, too mercurial.

Peter noticed and resented his wife's new admirer and friend. He did not want the two Catherines to be together so much of the time. Not always the clown he was thought to be, or at least played at being, he correctly assessed the agile mind and perhaps also the burning ambition of this sister of his mistress. Once, in a serious moment, he said to Princess Vorontsova-Dashkova, "My child, it would not be amiss for you to remember that it is much safer to deal with honest simpletons like myself and your sister than with those mighty intellects who, after squeezing from a person all the juice as if from an orange, discard the skin."

But the Princess persisted in her course, for she believed in her friend and namesake; she had confidence in her own star. With her cleverness she would some day accomplish great things. She longed for action, for the chance to play the lead in a stirring drama.

During the ominous winter of 1761, the Princess feared with every fiber of her being Grand Duke Peter's imminent ascension to the throne, for she knew full well that he would name her worthless sister Tsarina-Empress while incarcerating her namesake, his wife, in a prison or a nunnery if not condemning her to death.

One night in mid-December, while the Princess was in bed with a heavy cold and a fever, news was brought to her from the house of her uncle, Michael Vorontsov: the Empress' doctors had just confidentially informed him that Elizabeth had only a few more days to live.

The Princess decided that she had to act immediately. It was close to midnight when she forced herself to leave her warm bed, put on a thick fur coat, and order the driver of her sleigh to take her through the freezing night to the wooden palace in the Moika area in the capital, the temporary residence of the Imperial family while the Winter Palace was being redecorated.

She entered the unfamiliar building through a back door and soon lost her way in the dark. She was wandering desperately through the pitch-black corridors when she stumbled against a woman—a lady-in-waiting who knew her and, reluctantly, led the Princess to the bedroom of the Crown Princess.

Peter's wife was then in her fifth month of pregnancy with Gregory Orlov's child. She had spent most of that evening by the fire, reading a French novel. Tiring of the book, she undressed and went to bed. She was just pulling up the covers when there was a knock on the door. Rising, the Grand Duchess opened the door cautiously, to see her frozen, sneezing, and highly agitated namesake. Behind her there hovered the lady-in-waiting, hissing her protest over the unseemly hour.

The Grand Duchess welcomed her friend gladly, though chiding her for a visit that would only worsen her cold. She made the Princess lie in bed next to her, wrapping the visitor's legs in a thick blanket, and only then asked, "What has brought you at such an hour despite your illness?"

The Princess spoke urgently in a voice punctuated by coughing: "Your Highness, the Empress has only a few days to live, perhaps only hours. I can't bear the uncertainty of your situation any longer. Isn't there any possibility of forestalling the danger, of dispersing the cloud hanging over your head? For heaven's sake trust me! I will prove I am worthy of your complete confidence. I beg you—tell me: do you have any plan at all? Have any precautionary measures been taken? Have you thought of your own safety? I beseech you—give me orders. What should I do? How can I be of use to you?"

The Grand Duchess pressed the young woman's hand to her heart and shed an obligatory tear or two, but kept her composure. She made a show of submitting to her fate, whatever it might be. In truth, she admitted to herself, she admired her charming nocturnal visitor, but she felt that with all her good intentions, the Princess was too young, too hotheaded.

In fact she did have a plan, but she needed time. She calculated that her husband, on becoming Peter III, would not move against her at once. Moreover, she had to wait for her baby to be born. Perhaps the Empress would not die for a few months more. Gregory Orlov and his brothers were stronger-nerved allies and conspirators than this brilliant but impulsive princess. The Grand Duchess would take her chances with the Orlovs, not with Princess Catherine.

"My darling little Princess," she sighed, "you can't even imagine how deeply I am touched by your concern for my destiny. But let me tell you: I have no plan whatsoever and I do not intend to undertake anything at all. The only thing I shall do is quietly meet whatever events take place, no matter what they may bring me. I give myself into the hands of the Almighty. My trust is in Him only."

She lifted her eyes heavenward.

"If so," persisted the Princess, "permit your friends to act on your behalf. I have enough zeal to inspire all of them to rise in your name!"

The Grand Duchess spoke more firmly: "For God's sake, I beg you, in your eagerness to help me, do not expose yourself to danger in vain. Please, please. There is no cure for my misfortunes."

And she hung her head.


On December 23, 1761, of the Russian calendar, the Empress suffered her last stroke. She lingered two days, and on Christmas morning was lucid enough to receive last rites and recite her final prayers in the presence of Peter and Catherine as well as numerous clergymen and courtiers. She asked their forgiveness in the traditional Russian Orthodox ritual and then expired publicly. Her death was announced to the nation and to the world on Christmas afternoon—in the West, January 6, 1762.

Grand Duke Peter of Gottorp-Holstein and Heir Apparent of all the Russias became Tsar-Emperor Peter III. For the moment there was no outward sign that he would dispatch Catherine to a nunnery or punish her in any other drastic way. Officially she was proclaimed his Imperial consort; the Grand Duchess was now Empress. But she was Empress with absolutely no power; she was, on the contrary, immediately subjected to numerous humiliations. Elizabeth Vorontsova was now living in the new Emperor's apartments, and courtiers treated her—not Catherine—as the rightful Empress.

The funeral of Empress Elizabeth was held soon afterward. It was made an occasion for display as well as mourning. The distance of a half mile from the palace to the cathedral, along the streets and across the frozen Neva, was made comfortable for the procession by wooden slats laid flat in order to form a sort of pavement. At ten in the morning the capital's church-bells rang out and troops lined up on both sides of the route.

Three hundred officers and soldiers of the Guards opened the procession, followed by more than that number of priests, in pairs, in their full vestments and chanting lugubriously. Important officials marched behind these, bearing crowns, medals, and other regalia on rich pillows. The catafalque, with its brocade-adorned coffin, was drawn by eight horses whose caparisons were of black velvet. The lofty canopy over the catafalque was supported by generals and senators.

Immediately behind the catafalque came the new Emperor, in a heavy black mantle whose long train was supported by twelve senior courtiers, each of whom held the hem in one hand and a lighted candle in the other. These were followed by Peter's closest Holstein relatives—the two uncles then residing in Russia, Prince George and Prince August Friedrich. Then came Empress Catherine, also in a black mantle, its train held up by her ladies-in-waiting. Catherine carried a lighted candle.

Three hundred grenadiers closed the procession.

Peter had behaved in a suitably decorous fashion when in the room in which his aunt lay in state, but during the funeral, in the cortège, and later in church, he played the buffoon. The new Emperor of all the Russias amused himself by jerking the train of his mantle from the hands of the dignified courtiers, running perilously close to the catafalque, and then suddenly stopping abruptly and laughing at the astonishment and discomfiture of the courtiers.

In the church, during the solemn service, he laughed and jested with the ladies and talked with his men at the top of his voice even as the priests trilled their soulful recitatives. He stuck his tongue out at the holy men; wagged his fingers as a derisive extension of his nose at them. Robert Keith, the new British Ambassador, said to a lady of the court, "Your Tsar must be insane to behave like this."

There should have been the usual period of mourning at court and throughout Russia, but Peter III would not hear of it. In his memoirs Count Jean Louis de Hordt, a Swede who served Frederick and was captured by the Russians but released at once after Elizabeth's death, writes that he was present at the funeral as an honored guest of Peter's, and notes, "That day everyone dined at home and spent the evening in solitude as a sign of general grief. But already on the next day there was not a word spoken about the late Empress."

On the contrary, Peter decreed that festive banquets and other entertainments be given, with black clothes forbidden. Ball dress was *de rigueur*.

Catherine refused to cooperate. The French envoy reported to Louis XV, "Empress Catherine impresses all with her proper behavior. No one performs the duty to the late sovereign prescribed by the Greek religion more faithfully than she does. The clergy and the people believe that she indeed deeply mourns the late Empress. All see how punctually she observes the rituals and fasts, which are so prized in this country, but toward which the Emperor displays such a frivolous attitude."

&

The most abrupt change that occurred after Elizabeth's death was in Russia's foreign policy. Peter III at once ordered a suspension of all hostilities toward Frederick of Prussia.

Throughout the Seven Years' War, Frederick had fared poorly against his opponents, particularly against the Russians. Time and again only his enemies' ineptitude following their victories saved the King.

A notable example was the battle fought at Kunesdorf near Frankfurt on the Oder on August 12, 1759. That day Frederick's courageous but woefully small army faced superior forces under the command of the Russian Field Marshal Count Peter Saltykov and the Austrian Field Marshal Count Leopold Joseph Marie von Daun. Fortune smiled on one side, then the other. At one point Frederick himself was nearly captured or killed. A Prussian captain had to drag him off the field, despite his protests.

In the end the Prussian defeat was complete. The King blamed some of his soldiers: "The victory was ours when suddenly my wretched infantry lost courage. The silly fear of being carried off to Siberia turned their heads and there was no stopping them."

But Saltykov and von Daun failed to take advantage of the Prussians' discomfiture. Instead of pressing their advantage all the way to Berlin, the victors engaged in what historians describe as a vodka-guzzling contest. When they at last sobered up, they blamed each other. After von Daun had chided him, Saltykov replied, "I have done enough this year. I have won two battles costing Russia 27,000 men. Before going into action again I will wait for a couple of Austrian victories. It is not right that the Russian troops should bear the brunt of all the fighting." And, leaving Frederick free to rebuild his forces, he summoned his comrades to resume their celebration.

In October 1760, a rather inept raid by the Russians on Berlin, during Frederick's absence, resulted in the brief capture of his capital. There were only five days of siege, a mere ten hours of artillery fire, and but three days of Russian occupation.

But by the end of 1761 Frederick was plagued by other and more serious reverses. He felt hopelessly cornered, and in despair spoke and wrote of suicide, actually making preparations for it and for a takeover of his beloved but battered Prussia by his younger brother Henry.

And now, in January 1762, Elizabeth, his bitterest enemy, was dead, and the new Emperor had, just in the nick of time to save Frederick, made a marvelous about-face, recalling his armies from German territory and allying himself with Frederick. The Russian troops were to be sent against Denmark, Frederick's enemy, for Peter wished to punish the Danes for invading his lovely Schleswig and to regain it for Holstein.

Frederick was beside himself with joy and wrote to his envoy in London of Elizabeth's death: *"Morte la bestia!"* To Peter III he wrote in a near-delirium, like a man sentenced to death but now granted not only his life but liberty and wealth, "Were I a heathen, I should erect a temple and altars for your Imperial Highness as a divine creature. You have given the world an example of virtue from which everyone, including kings and sovereigns, should learn much. . . . I wish I could express everything I feel about you in my heart. I wish I could express to you my desire to show my gratitude."

ॐ

In his domestic policy, much to the astonishment of many of his contemporaries and, later, historians, the new Emperor, in his very first edicts and regulations, proved himself to be far from the cretin he had been generally taken for. It is possible that much of Peter's clowning was an act; more likely that his advisers were wise and competent.

An epoch-making law was enacted early in Peter's brief reign decreeing that noblemen no longer owed service to the state. For centuries, all such males had been obligated to serve either in the armed forces or as administrators. Peter the Great had strictly enforced this tradition. Now the eccentric Holsteiner was proclaiming *vol'nost' dvorianstvu*—the unprecedented freedom for the nobility to serve or not; to go abroad or remain in their town mansions or country estates. Peter's sudden popularity with the ruling class was understandable.

Simultaneously, most if not all of the aristocrats exiled during previous regimes were recalled from Siberia and other far-flung provinces and given back their palaces, estates, serfs, titles, decorations, and even their court positions. Countess Maria Aurora Lestocq came to St. Petersburg to thank Peter III for bringing her and her husband, Elizabeth's former physician and lover, back to civilization: "Your Majesty is still the same gracious and humane sovereign that you always were.

Your magnanimous heart forgives your enemies. But, believe me, your goodness will ruin you. Many persons are known to be your enemies, and you must have them executed."

But the Emperor only smiled. "Ah, Countess, do have compassion for these unfortunate people. Am I not what I wanted to be—the Emperor of Russia? Must I begin my reign with bloodshed? Let them live! My good deeds will inspire them to behave better in the future."

Now, as friends of Peter's, high and low, were rewarded, his opponents were removed from their posts but were otherwise left unmolested, not even banished. Alexander Shuvalov's secret police agency was officially abolished, but its former chief, together with his nephew Ivan and the rest of the clan, remained high at court.

The common people were granted one noticeable reform: the state-controlled price of salt was reduced. But no other significant amelioration of their misery was decreed by Peter III. The institution of serfdom remained in force, and new restrictions were introduced, such as the prohibition for serfs to file complaints against their masters.

In the army and the navy, punishment by that dreadful instrument of leather and twisted rope, the cat-o'-nine-tails, was banned, but other cruelties remained.

The military class was unhappy from the start. Not only were the recent hard-won victories over Prussia annulled by the young Emperor's ukase that Russian troops and warships side with Frederick, but both officers and enlisted men were forced to wear the detested Prussian-style uniforms.

Nor did the army, the navy, and the Guards welcome the prospect of the incomprehensible war being readied by Peter against Denmark. Discontent among the Guards regiments stationed at St. Petersburg was audible. They had no heart for the forthcoming campaign; they "gritted their teeth," as one contemporary put it. Nonetheless, Peter obliviously and enthusiastically built up his forces at Narva, thence to strike at Denmark.

≈

For some six years, Catherine had been harboring a scheme

for a coup d'état when the Empress died. Like Elizabeth in 1741, she would utilize the Guards. In a letter of 1756 to Hanbury Williams, she wrote:

> Here is how I imagine it: The moment I hear that the Empress is dead and have determined that the report is true, I will . . . send a trusted messenger to inform five officers of the Guards who are loyal to me and are prepared to bring me fifty soldiers each. I will then summon the Chancellor, Apraxin, and Liven. I will go to the chamber where the Empress is lying and order the Guards captain on duty that day to remain by my side—not a step away. I would also consider it prudent that both Grand Dukes [Peter and her son] not leave my sight. I will then gather my supporters about me. Should I notice any unusual activity, I will order the Shuvalovs and the aide-de-camp on duty arrested by my men or those of the Guards captain. I believe, however, that the enlisted men and the Guards are loyal to me.

But now, in January 1762, with Empress Elizabeth dead and buried, Catherine made not a single move toward putting this scheme or any other into effect. The main reason was her pregnancy by Gregory Orlov, which she desperately tried to conceal even in its last few months by wearing voluminous gowns, which fortunately were in fashion, and by trying to appear at the principal court as little as possible, pleading a sprained foot.

Luckily, everyone at court was too busy dancing attendance on the new Emperor and Elizabeth Vorontsova. Those few of Catherine's friends and well-wishers who knew of her pregnancy went to heroic lengths to help her disguise what the Russian euphemism called her "interesting condition."

The open secret and general expectation was that Peter III was preparing to arrest Catherine, try her on charges of infidelity and high treason, and sentence her to Siberia or the scaffold, or, at the very least, dispatch her to a nunnery for life.

For the time being, he had to proceed cautiously. First of all there was the opposition of his trusted advisers. After his ascension to the throne, Peter made his uncle, Prince George of Holstein, Commander-in-Chief of the armed forces, promoted him to Field Marshal, and designated him as "the foremost prince of our blood." Backed by a group of Peter's more levelheaded German companions, Prince George informed his mercurial nephew that the crowned heads of Western Europe would be outraged if he harmed Catherine. Some of them might even take military or diplomatic action against Peter and Russia.

Also, there was increasing fear among influential Russians and Germans in Peter's entourage that the Guards regiments, so intensely nationalistic, might rise against the Emperor if he exiled, imprisoned, or executed his wife. The officers, under the influence of the Orlovs, considered Catherine to be, despite her German origins, a true Russian in spirit, their own *Matushka,* their Little Mother.

And from abroad, Frederick impressed upon Peter the folly of any rash action vis-à-vis Catherine. Peter should, the Prussian King counseled, before doing anything else get himself solemnly and officially crowned. Only then would the throne be secure.

But during the six months of his reign, Peter never got around to arranging his coronation. He could have done so even within this brief period, but there were factors other than mere negligence that deterred him.

Peter III detested the Russian Orthodox Church, and a coronation would have meant close and distasteful involvement with its representatives. A pious Lutheran by early upbringing, he had been officially converted to Orthodoxy because his late aunt Elizabeth had insisted the law of the land required it. Nevertheless, Peter's contempt for the Church remained open. Now that he was Tsar and Emperor, a solemn coronation by these barbarous clerics in their glittering robes would have been a dreadful imposition.

Peter rudely thrust aside the Orthodox prayer books held out to him and turned to his dog-eared Lutheran equivalent. He even had a Lutheran chapel built at his palace.

The new Emperor summoned Archbishop Dimitry of

Novgorod, who in 1757 had been appointed Chief Almoner to the Imperial court. Peter was sharp and peremptory with him and announced that all sacred icons were to be removed from churches and private homes and forthwith destroyed. Only images of Christ and the Virgin were to be spared. The priests were to cut off their beards and to shave their faces in the seemly manner of Western clergymen. Furthermore, they were to discard their long-skirted vestments and don short cassocks and long stockings.

The Emperor decreed his intention to confiscate for the benefit of the state the immense fortune consisting of precious stones, jewelry, and money held by the Church treasury, and of taking possession of, perhaps even emancipating, the serfs owned by the Church. Archbishop Dimitry argued back angrily and left the audience with Peter gloomily.

The rumor was making the rounds of the capital that, after ridding himself of Catherine, Peter would marry his mistress according to the Lutheran rite, and only then would crown himself and her—in a Lutheran ceremony, not an Orthodox one.

Frederick, who knew nothing of any such plan, continued his admonitions:

> I must confess to you my urgent wish that Your Imperial Majesty crown yourself. This ceremony awes people; they are used to seeing their sovereigns crowned. Any other nation would have blessed heaven for giving it a ruler of such exalted qualities as Your Imperial Majesty is gifted with. But these Russians—do they know how lucky they are? And the damnable bloodthirstiness of someone or other—will it not prompt him to seek his advantage in cooking up a plot or sowing mischief for the benefit of the princes of Braunschweig [Ivan VI and his kin]? Recall please, Your Imperial Majesty, what happened during the first absence of Peter I from his country, when his own sister fashioned a conspiracy against him! Suppose that some ambitious scoundrel or other starts, while you are away at war, an intrigue to restore Ivan to the throne, and with the help of foreign money weaves a plot to free Ivan

from his dungeon, incite some troops and other scoundrels like himself, who will be sure to join him: will you not then be compelled to abandon the battle against the Danes and hasten back to put out the flames in your own house?

Peter replied:

Your Majesty writes that in your opinion I should be crowned before departing for the war precisely on account of my people. But I must say to you that, since the war is nearly begun, I do not see an opportunity for a coronation exactly because of the people. The coronation by custom must be full of splendor, and I cannot make it splendid, since it is impossible to find here the necessary money for it in a hurry. As for Ivan, I keep him under strong guard, and had the Russians wished to do me evil they could have done it a long time ago, seeing that I take no precautions whatever, walking the streets as simply as I do. I can assure you that when one treats them right, one does not have to worry about them.

◆

Despite the show of bravado, the new Emperor began his reign by displaying considerable curiosity as well as precaution with regard to the young cousin locked up in the dungeon of the Schluesselburg Fortress. This grim fortress dated back to the fourteenth century and was situated on an island at the mouth of the Neva, practically at the doorstep of the Imperial capital.

On Russian New Year's Day of 1762, only one week after his aunt's demise and his ascension to the throne, Peter issued a decree, signed by his own hand, on the subject of the prisoner, then not yet twenty-two years old and a captive all his wretched life. Addressed to Prince Ivan Churmanteyev, a captain of the Preobrazhensky Guards Regiment, the order appointed the officer to take charge of "a certain important prisoner in the Schluesselburg Fortress" and stressed the extraordinary strictness to be exercised vis-à-vis the prisoner.

The order closed with these words: "Should anyone, against our expectations, try to take the prisoner away from you, you are to resist to your utmost and never to surrender the prisoner alive."

One more order to Prince Churmanteyev, again signed by the Emperor, was issued on January 11. This contained a warning not to honor any writ, even one signed by Peter, to remove the prisoner to any destination. Such a writ should be obeyed only if one of Peter's two aides, therein named, carried the authorization. Clearly Peter feared that the captive might be freed by someone with a forgery of his signature. On February 11 a third order was sent, confirming the exceptions for the two trusted aides.

Finally, in March, Peter decided to pay a visit to the Schluesselburg, to see the unfortunate deposed Emperor with his own eyes, to talk to him, and so find out for himself what sort of young man he was.

Why the visit? Was Peter playing with the idea of freeing Ivan and proclaiming him Heir Apparent in lieu of Grand Duke Paul, then seven years old, the son of his hated wife, Catherine, and possibly (or so suspected Peter) of her first lover, Saltykov?

If so, Peter was to be disappointed. On March 22, in the course of his visit to the dungeon, he found the prisoner half-insane and babbling in utter confusion, although Peter's first questions were answered fairly coherently and even correctly, the pathetic nonsense setting in later in the conversation.

Peter was incognito, pretending he was an officer sent on this errand by His Imperial Majesty. He asked the occupant of this dingy, dark cell, in which cobwebs hung from the ceiling, "Who are you?"

"I am Emperor Ivan."

"How did it enter your head that you are a Prince or an Emperor? How did you learn this?"

"I learned it from my parents, also from the soldiers guarding me."

"What do you know about your parents?"

"I remember them still."

From then on Ivan's speech became muddled. "Emperor

Ivan is not among the living anymore. But his spirit is reincarnated in me," he said.

After a few more pitiful exchanges, Peter left. Two days later, on March 24, he sent an inquiry to Churmanteyev as to what changes his visit might have effected "in the prisoner's conduct and speech." The next day the Prince responded, "In the wake of the visit nothing special is noticeable in the prisoner." On the thirty-first he reported to the Emperor again: "No falsehood from the prisoner has occurred, nothing new has been observed. He only keeps on laughing and muttering to himself, and, at that, in a low voice."

Peter was reassured. Even if freed by some desperate coup, the demented young man could never be dragged to the throne to replace him.

Soon enough, events in Russia showed how blind Peter was in his complacency. Though he was in no danger from adherents of Ivan, Peter was undone soon enough by his formidable wife. It took a few months, but once the machinery of destruction was set in motion, the Emperor's fate was sealed.

≈≈

Catherine could count on the Orlovs and their dashing comrades-at-arms in the Guards, as well as the clergy, which was deeply impressed by her scrupulous observance of the Orthodox rites while being appalled by Peter's clumsy iconoclasm. In addition, she could depend on an occasional farsighted courtier who believed that she had a chance to seize the throne in the near future. Among her allies were Count Cyril Razumovsky and Nikita Panin, who was entrusted with the care of her little Paul. Panin was an ambitious, calculating statesman, loyal to Catherine beyond any doubt, though not too openly at this early stage.

The anti-Catherine party had been strengthened by those surviving Germans whom Elizabeth, upon seizing the throne in 1741 or later in her reign, had exiled to the far corners of the Empire and who had been recalled to the capital and honored by Peter. Among them were Field Marshal Burkhard Christopher Minikh (Münnich); Ernst Johann Biron (Buehren), Empress Anna's lover and once virtual overlord of

Russia; and the two sons of another of Anna's favorites, the astute Westphalian Heinrich Johann Osterman, who died in Siberia in 1747. These pardoned exiles hated the Russians over whom they had once held dominion and whom they hoped to rule again. Catherine, so demonstrably pro-Russian, a traitress to her German blood, was most definitely in their way.

An uneasy truce prevailed during the first few months of 1762. Frederick, in his letters and by means of his agents, repeatedly implored Peter to act, but the Emperor turned a deaf ear. To the Prussian monarch he insisted that the war against Denmark took precedence. "My pride demands that I take revenge upon the Danes for all the insults they have heaped on me and my ancestors." The coronation could wait: "The ceremony would demand enormous expenditures; these monies would be better used in the war against Denmark." Frederick was not to worry about any danger stemming from Catherine and her partisans. "My soldiers call me their father. They themselves say they would rather obey a man than a woman. I am benevolent to everyone, I completely rely on God's will and fear nothing."

Frederick's representatives at court, von der Goltz and von Schwerin, were instructed by their King to dog Peter's footsteps, to constantly bring the conversation around to that of internal perils, not arising from poor Ivan, but from his treacherous and intelligent wife. To no avail; Peter merely laughed. Finally he became exasperated and thundered at the two diplomats, "If you wish to remain my friends, you are never again to bring up this hateful subject!"

The ambassadors were defeated. The historian Ilovaisky comments, "Thus there is no doubt that the success of Catherine's side was best aided by the Emperor himself."

As the winter of 1762 passed, Peter intensified his ill-conceived attacks on the Church, issuing controversial edicts that quickly became known to the clergy and the populace. His behavior, when it was absolutely necessary that he appear in church, scandalized priests and laymen alike. During services in the court's Orthodox chapel, Peter would receive foreign envoys, and, while conversing loudly with them, would pace back and forth across the sacred floor. On Holy Trinity Day, as worshipers knelt at the prescribed moment of the priests' chanting, the Emperor burst out laughing and left the church.

His subordinates took their time about enforcing his clerical reforms. Nonetheless, the priests and their pious flocks waited in horror for the effects to become evident. The one that probably caused the most consternation was the plan to confiscate most of the land and the serfs belonging to the Church and its monasteries. The property would be controlled by the state, which would pay modest salaries to the holy men and women affected.

It is possible that in other areas such as the abolition of state service by the nobility and of certain cruelties in the armed forces, Peter was carrying out the suggestions of his advisers and was in reality indifferent. But where it concerned curtailing the power of the Church, there is no doubt that he acted on his own volition.

૨ર

Although the plot was gathering momentum, Catherine's pregnancy hindered her: she refused to give the go-ahead signal to the conspirators.

Gregory Orlov is mentioned in some sources as the chief organizer, but Alexis appears to have played an equally daring and ingenious role. The other three brothers were less conspicuous, though they carried out their assignments in their Guards regiments quite ably.

Count Cyril Razumovsky, the younger brother of the Night Emperor who following the death of Empress Elizabeth was in retirement, soon occupied a prominent place in the conspiracy. Count Cyril, Commander of the Izmailovsky Regiment of the Guards, was wealthy and generous, and his officers loved him for his entertainments, loans, and gifts. He had been educated in the West—in Berlin, Paris, and Geneva—and spoke excellent German and French. He loathed the new Emperor and his boorish entourage, and placed his own officers and soldiers far above the uncouth Holsteiners.

There were rumors, perhaps based on reality, that one day without warning Peter would send his Holsteiners against the

Guards and disband them. The rank and file would be distributed among army units stationed in the provinces, or at Narva or in Frederick's Pomerania, preparatory to striking at Denmark. The Guards rebelled at the idea of a campaign against Denmark after being forced to renounce their conquests gained at the expense of Prussia. And they of course feared the prospect of losing their elite status, of being reduced to the condition of ordinary soldiers.

To make matters worse, most of Peter's German corporals and sergeants, with their hatred for all things Russian, were not even from Holstein—they were Prussians. In the words of Princess Vorontsova-Dashkova, they were "scum, sons of German cobblers."

Even though Catherine refused to encourage the Princess, the latter took it upon herself to advance the cause of her idol, and in her memoirs she claims that it was she who finally enticed Count Cyril to join them.

The Count loved a quiet life and preferred to shun politics, and was regarded too apathetic even for the petty intrigues of the court or the barracks, certainly unfit to participate in a coup d'état. But now that the new Emperor publicly, in front of the troops, kissed Frederick's portrait and knelt before it in his Prussian-style uniform, now that Peter compelled the Russian regiments to march incessantly and perform the intricate and wooden Prussian exercises, Cyril began to grumble.

However, despite his annoyance and temperamental dislike of change, Count Cyril bowed to the will of his sovereign, and his men were soon drilling Prussian-style, a fact that astonished and delighted Peter and won his admiration. In the gathering tension, in the dark whispers carried to Peter about the machinations of Catherine and the Orlovs, the Count remained above suspicion.

The plotters nonetheless learned of his disenchantment and approached him. Vorontsova-Dashkova and certain Guards officers and courtiers dropped hints that important changes were in the wind; they told him that his own regiment was unhappy with the new Emperor and his German retinue.

Finally they revealed all.

At first Count Cyril refused to listen, but the Princess and others argued, "Now that Your Excellency knows of the conspiracy, it means you are a part of it."

And, "Will you, now that you know, go to the Emperor?"

"Of course not!"

"Then join us!"

He did, and proved to be committed and extremely valuable.

Later, the Princess wrote that she enlisted Nikita Panin. Empress Elizabeth's former Ambassador to Sweden, Panin had been ordered back to Russia to take care of little Grand Duke Paul's education. He was known to admire the Swedish form of government, more enlightened than that of his fatherland; and in the St. Petersburg whirlpool of intrigue to value Catherine and to dislike Peter.

Yet, like Count Cyril, he loved an agreeable life and was not at all eager to risk it by taking part in chancey schemes. Immaculately dressed in accordance with the latest Paris fashions, he was pale, fragile, and sickly. Still, with all his fastidious aloofness, Panin was a figure of consequence, to be flattered and otherwise courted by the conspirators.

He was a distant kinsman of Vorontsova-Dashkova's, and this gave her the courage (if she needed any) to weave a net around him. Just how she eventually gained her end, her memoirs do not reveal. Her vagueness in time led some of her enemies to say that she had used her feminine charms on Panin, that, in Ilovaisky's rendering of this accusation, she, in her zeal on Catherine's behalf, "went so far as to disregard any and all inhibitions and to sacrifice herself for the success of her party." The Princess denounced this accusation as "black slander."

According to Ilovaisky, "Although in that era's society such sacrifices were the accepted thing, in this instance we willingly side with the Princess. We cannot accuse her on the strength of rumor alone, unsupported by any clear evidence."

Panin could be thorny, and it must have been a considerable undertaking to enlist his aid. As an example of his firmness of character, on one occasion, when the Emperor, pleased with the results of Paul's examination in the subjects Panin was teaching him, rewarded the tutor with the rank of general, but, apprised of this honor, Panin adamantly declined it, arguing that were he to accept, he would have to drill with the troops on the muddy fields near the capital—not advisable considering his age and precarious health. To the courtier who brought the message from Peter he declared, "If there is no other way to avoid this appointment, I will go back to Sweden."

When he heard this comment, Peter sputtered, "I always thought Panin was clever, but now I see my error. Don't ever mention his name in my presence again."

Reconsidering, Peter not only accepted the refusal, but even endowed Panin with the civil prerogatives equivalent to those of a general.

To Vorontsova-Dashkova's arguments that Peter had to be ousted for the good of the fatherland, the wily Panin responded with a lengthy and learned discourse on the quasi-legal ways in which this could be accomplished: the Senate could first be drawn into the enterprise and lend its authority to the dethronement; Catherine could be made not the sole ruler of the nation but only a regent during her son Paul's minority; or the Swedish constitution, which he revered, could be the model for a similar document for Russia under the child Emperor Paul.

But Panin gradually became one of the clique, first as a passive supporter, then taking the plunge and eventually becoming the equal of the Orlovs in the direction of the operation.

At the suggestion of an unimportant sympathizer, five leaders of the anti-Peter plot were selected to be specially safeguarded. Each person was always shadowed by an adherent to watch for signs indicating impending arrest or betrayal. The warning would be immediately communicated to the others so that steps could be taken.

The conspirators divided themselves into four major groups, each with its own leader. Meetings were not rigidly scheduled. The historian Klyuchesvky writes, "There was none of the usual conspiratorial ritual, formal meetings, or methodical agitation. There was no detailed plan of action; there was no need for it. The Guards had for so long been accustomed to the thought and the mechanics of palace coups that they required no special preparation. All they needed was a popular personality in whose name they could rise."

It was clear that Catherine was that person. On the eve of the coup, she could thus count on some forty officers and 10,000 soldiers.

On the surface, Catherine seemed to have been abandoned to her fate and to be living in constant fear. Elizabeth Vorontsova behaved, and was bowed to by the courtiers, as though she and not Catherine were already Empress. Peter abetted this ill-treatment by insulting his wife publicly.

In January 1762, Peter ordered Catherine to move from her suite in the central area of the Winter Palace to less comfortable lodgings at the rear of the building. Elizabeth gleefully moved into the vacated apartments. Secretly, Catherine did not mind; it was now easier to conceal her pregnancy.

A stinging personal humiliation followed. In February, Peter sent a courtier to his wife with this peremptory message: "You are to remove from your bosom and hand over, to be delivered to me, your diamond star and your ribbon of the Order of St. Catherine."

Catherine was appalled. She was to be deprived of the precious gift pinned on her by Empress Elizabeth herself on the occasion of Catherine's engagement to Peter. Now, drawing herself up unflinchingly, pale but with a haughty expression, she relinquished the award and it was handed to Peter.

What did he plan to do with it? Soon it was clear. On February 21, there was a birthday celebration at the Winter Palace. Catherine declined to come, pleading her sore foot, but the entire court and the diplomatic corps were present. In the midst of the merry hubbub, Peter rose, obviously tipsy. He pointed to his mistress, who now stood by his side. All could see that she was wearing the diamond star and the ribbon.

The hush at the festive tables deepened into shock, for court protocol limited this exalted decoration to either an empress or the Emperor's fiancée.

What sort of Empress would Vorontsova make? was the question that came to every mind.

In his shrewd dispatches to Louis XV, the French envoy,

Baron Louis-Auguste le Tonnelier de Breteuil, wrote at the time, "Elizabeth Vorontsova is totally stupid, and as for her appearance, one would be hard put to find anything worse. In all, she resembles a scrubwoman in a country inn."

And in his next letter: "Should Emperor Peter . . . give his mistress the opportunity to bear him a son, many believe he would then marry her and the boy would be proclaimed Heir Apparent. But when the two quarrel and curse each other, the epithets that Mlle Vorontsova showers upon him permit one, not without reason, to call in question his capabilities."

The envoy reported to the French Secretary of State and Foreign Affairs, Duke Etienne François de Choiseul, possibly echoing what Catherine herself had told him:

> The Empress is in an extremely difficult position, and the Emperor treats her disgracefully. . . . She tries to find consolation by reading philosophy, but this is not at all in her nature. . . . I have determined—and there is no doubt as to this—that she is barely able to tolerate the Emperor's attitude toward her and the arrogance of Mlle Vorontsova. . . . I am convinced that the Empress, whose boldness and courage I am acquainted with, will sooner or later think of taking extreme measures. I also know that she had friends who try to soothe her but who, if she were to ask it, would follow her in any adventure.

But weeks, then months passed, and Catherine did not act. Few were aware that her pregnancy was the principal reason. She stayed discreetly in her rooms at the rear of the palace, ceasing her court appearances still on the excuse of her lame foot.

At last, on the evening of April 22, she felt labor pains. To prevent the Emperor from learning about it and rushing over to her rooms in a fury with his long-brewing decision to get rid of her, Catherine's friends went to unusual lengths. Recalling that Peter loved fires and would dart out at the sound of an alarm to admire the smoke and flames, Catherine's trusted valet, Vasily Shkurin, set his own house on fire.

The house was close to the palace where Peter and his mistress were relaxing that night. Shouting joyously, the pair hastened to the fire, as did many of their coterie. With the possibility of detection thus minimized, Catherine was safely delivered.

It was a boy. He was secretly christened Aleksei Grigoryevich—Alexis, son of Gregory. His family name would be Bobrinsky. This was Catherine's humorous fancy as she glanced at the beaver-fur *shuba* in which the baby was wrapped, *bobr* being the Russian word for beaver. Spirited out of the palace successfully, the baby was adopted by Shkurin and his wife, who reared him in their own family. A few months after his birth, having defeated her husband and become Russia's sovereign, Catherine would openly acknowledge the boy as her son, elevating him to the rank of count. The Count Bobrinskys had distinguished careers through the subsequent 150 years of Imperial Russian history.

All through May Catherine recuperated while pondering her next move. Foreign envoys in St. Petersburg were soon reporting to their capitals that she was entirely well. The Austrian Ambassador, Count Claudius Florimand de Mercy d'Argenteau, wrote to Maria Theresa that, upon hearing his suave compliment on her beauty, Catherine replied, "You, my Count, cannot even imagine how much effort it costs a woman to be beautiful."

The fateful month of June arrived.

For Sunday, the ninth, Peter had decreed a solemn commemoration of the peace treaty officially concluded between him and Frederick on the preceding May 24. That morning, a Te Deum resounded through every church in the capital. Peter himself attended the service in the Kazansky Cathedral. Then came a parade of Guards regiments. When Peter greeted the troops with congratulations on the glorious treaty, officers and soldiers responded with the obligatory huzzahs rather unenthusiastically, apparently not thinking that the pact with their recent enemy was so glorious for Russia. Per custom, cannon and muskets were fired to honor the occasion.

Later that day the Emperor presided at a gala reception and banquet in the palace. Amid pomp and fanfare, 400 guests, consisting of the three highest categories at court as well as all of the resident foreign dignitaries, were invited to the tables.

Catherine seated herself at the center of the principal table, while Peter took his accustomed place at the head. On his right was the guest of honor, Baron von der Goltz, the Prussian Ambassador.

As the boom of cannon came from the nearby Peter and Paul Fortress, the Emperor, resplendent in the Prussian general's uniform he had donned for the occasion, proposed toasts. On his meager chest were displayed the star and ribbon of the Prussian Order of the Black Eagle—Frederick's appreciative gift.

There were three toasts: to the health of his Imperial family; to the health of His Royal Majesty, the King of Prussia; and to the happily concluded Russo-Prussian peace. The guests stood up, glasses in hand, but Emperor and his wife remained seated, as protocol decreed.

Before Catherine could lower her glass Peter, in a rage, sent a special messenger to her, Adjutant General Andrew Gudovich, who throughout the dinner had been standing in attendance behind the Emperor's chair. He brought Peter's angry question: "Why didn't Her Majesty rise when everyone drank to the reigning house?"

Gudovich carried back her answer: "As the Imperial family consists only of His Majesty, herself, and their son, she did not at all think that the Emperor would require her to rise."

Upon receiving this response, Peter sent his rejoinder: "There are only two members of the Imperial family here—my uncle the Duke of Holstein and myself. You are a fool."

As the General was quietly delivering his message, Peter, apparently concerned that Gudovich would tone it down, screamed across the table at his wife, *"Dura!"* —you are a fool!

A shocked silence fell across the room. Knives and forks were poised in midair; servants halted with their trays and wine bottles.

In her memoirs Catherine writes that never in her life had she been so insulted. Fighting back tears, making a heroic effort to smile, she turned to Count Alexander Stroganov, who stood in attendance behind her, and asked him to say something—anything—funny. The Count obligingly launched into a witty anecdote. De Breteuil and several other guests close to Catherine then joined in the conversation, trying to pretend that nothing had happened.

From the head of the table, the Emperor observed with increasing rage this attempt to console his wife, then ordered Gudovich to immediately confine Stroganov to his house and to place the Empress under arrest.

He repeated the arrest order to Prince Fyodor Baryatinsky. Four days later, on June 13, Peter signed a ukase decreeing that Catherine be confined in the Schluesselburg, where Ivan VI had lost his reason. It was with considerable difficulty that Prince George of Holstein, supported by von der Goltz, prevailed upon Peter not to put the decree into effect. To do so, they explained, might set off a rebellion among the Guards. He should first dispose of those who were trying to unseat him and only then punish Catherine. The Emperor recognized the validity of their arguments and reluctantly acquiesced. But he did not tear up the arrest warrant; he merely put it in a drawer. Yet he would not move against his enemies.

After the banquet, Catherine realized she could delay no longer. She needed money for those Guardsmen who would back her, and asked de Breteuil for 60,000 rubles—a modest sum considering the magnitude of the undertaking. The envoy wrote Paris for instructions. His superior, de Choiseul, wrote back without committing himself, and ordered de Breteuil to leave St. Petersburg for Warsaw and Vienna and to wait out the events.

It was the opinion of Louis XV and his counselors that the Russian nationalists at the St. Petersburg court would shortly rid themselves of both the Germans—Peter and Catherine— and would probably proclaim Paul as Emperor, with a Russian regent over him. Or perhaps they would restore Ivan VI to the throne. Certain Frenchmen disagreed with this analysis and prediction. Marshal Duke Victor François de Broglie, who commanded the French armies during the Seven Years' War, wrote to de Breteuil, "The Empress will never forgive you that at such a moment, so important to her, you turned your back on her."

Catherine then remembered her British friends. Sir Charles' successor, Ambassador Robert Keith, who was cautious yet capable of decisiveness at crucial moments, at once gave her 100,000 rubles. He had borrowed the sum from one of those ubiquitous English merchants ever present in the Russian capital. Keith believed Peter III to be insane; he admired Catherine and was confident of her eventual triumph. Upon receiving the British money, Catherine dispatched a brief note to the French embassy: "The purchase that we are contemplating will soon be made, and on much more advantageous terms, so that we have no need of any further monies."

By mid-June the Emperor was increasingly absorbed with his preparations to punish Denmark. He sent order after order readying his army for the first crushing blow against the Danes, all the while disregarding Frederick's warnings.

In all the warlike hustle and bustle Peter did not forget Catherine, and commanded her to quit the capital and move to the outlying Peterhof palace. Catherine taunted him by deliberately waiting a week before complying. Her faithful Nikita Panin advised her not to take her son with her, but to leave him in the St. Petersburg palace for safety. She agreed, and the Orlov brothers guarded the boy.

Peter, too, changed his base of operations. From June 12 on, he lived at the Oranienbaum palace, near Peterhof. He still had the arrest warrant for his wife, and seemed determined to have done with her before the end of the month.

This news was brought to her by her former sworn enemies, the Shuvalovs, who, having shrewdly appraised the situation, decided that since the Orlovs and the Guards regiments were solidly on her side, Catherine had a far better chance to win than Peter, and so cast their lot with her.

Councils of war with the Orlovs and Panin followed, first in the capital and then at Peterhof. Saturday, June 29, seemed to loom as the critical day. On that day, Peter informed his wife, he would pay her a visit. It was the Day of Saint Peter and

Saint Paul, the "Angel Day" of Peter and the little Crown Prince.

At Peterhof, Catherine set up her headquarters in one of the pavilions, not in the palace itself. The pavilion was on a hill, from where she and her entourage could see as far away as Oranienbaum and thus be warned in good time of whoever or whatever might be approaching. She told Shkurin to have a carriage at the ready for a sudden flight if necessary.

On the sixteenth, two Captains of the Preobrazhensky Guards, Sergei Bredikhin and Peter Passek, warned Vorontsova-Dashkova that their men were openly demanding to move decisively against the Germans at Oranienbaum and overthrow Peter. The Princess begged the Captains to restrain their troops for just a few more days. Panin, who knew Passek well, appointed him one of the four principal leaders of the impending coup.

On Thursday morning a Guards soldier came to Passek: "They say in the barracks that Little Mother Catherine is dead."

Passek calmed the man and promised that the plotters would strike any day now. Reassured, the soldier spread the good news, telling it, among others, to one of his officers whom he naively thought to be of the same mind as Passek.

This officer, however, immediately arrested the soldier and reported Passek's words and role to his immediate superiors, Major Fyodor Voyeikov and Captain Simon Vorontsov. Vorontsov, the younger brother of Countess Elizabeth and Princess Catherine, a nephew of Chancellor Michael Vorontsov, dispatched a messenger to Oranienbaum to alert the Emperor.

Peter ordered Passek's arrest. An interrogation of the prisoner was scheduled, but not right away—Peter and his mistress were too busy carousing with their friends. Politics could wait.

Meanwhile Peter continued relentlessly to pursue his favorite domestic project—the humiliation of the Russian Orthodox Church. On June 25 he issued a ukase to the Holy Synod that thenceforth all Christian beliefs were to be considered equal to

the Orthodox faith, thus undermining an ancient and privileged bulwark of the Russian state.

The ukase also confirmed that all serfs belonging to the
monasteries were to be state property. As an unintentionally
humorous non sequitur, the ukase also contained the provi-
sion that the Church was no longer to condemn violators of
the Seventh Commandment (Thou shalt not commit adul-
tery), "since Christ Himself did not condemn it."

This singular document concluded with the strict injunction
to the Synod to obey every order of Peter's without dispute.

The armed forces learned of this, and so did the populace.
A mad rumor swept St. Petersburg and its vicinity: all the
ladies of the court were to divorce their husbands and take
new mates of the Emperor's choosing. Thus would he justify
his own intention of divorcing Catherine in order to wed Elizabeth Vorontsova.

The shadow attached to Passek quickly notified the Orlovs
of the arrest. At noon on the twenty-seventh, Gregory Orlov
hurried to Princess Vorontsova-Dashkova's house in St. Petersburg, where Panin was visiting: "Captain Passek has been
arrested!"

They had to act immediately. Under torture Passek might
talk, and so might other Guards who would be arrested
momentarily.

The Princess was understandably alarmed. Panin tried to
calm her: "It was surely not in connection with our plans.
Some trifling violation of service regulations, no doubt."

But she would not be reassured. Sending both Panin and
Orlov away, she wrapped herself in a man's cloak, pushed a
man's hat down to her eyebrows, and hastened out of the
house—to reconnoiter, to seek further news, but exactly
where, she in her agitation did not know.

She saw a horseman approaching at a gallop a short distance from her house. Curiously, up to that day, of the five
Orlov brothers she had met only Gregory. But now she somehow guessed that the rider was Alexis.

"Alexis Orlov?" she called out to the man.

He reined in his horse. It was indeed Alexis. She identified herself.

"Princess," he said hurriedly, "I was on my way to let you know that Passek is being held on charges of high treason under heavy guard. One of my brothers is en route to tell Panin."

"No time to be lost!" she exclaimed. She named four of the Guardsmen involved in the plot. "Tell them to be at their posts in the Izmailovsky barracks and to await the Empress. Then you or one of your brothers go to Peterhof and implore Her Majesty to go at once to the barracks. Her friends will be waiting there to proclaim her as sovereign and take her to the capital."

The Princess ran back to her house. She remembered that her tailor was going to bring her a full male attire but was unaccountably late. She decided to wait for him.

Presently there was a knock at the door and a young Guards officer was admitted. "Princess, I am Vladimir Orlov. I have come to ask you whether it isn't premature to send for the Empress and bring her here to the capital."

The Princess blew up. At the top of her voice, not being overly polite in her language, she lashed Vladimir and his brothers for their procrastination. "You are wasting precious time! Instead of worrying about disturbing the Empress, you must fetch her at once! She must not be left at Peterhof in such peril. Can't you understand that she could find herself in prison, or perhaps even on the scaffold, along with the rest of us? Tell Alexis to proceed to Peterhof without any more delays and to take the Empress to the capital immediately. Otherwise we are lost!" Vladimir, his ears ringing, rode off.

The Princess stayed home, waiting for the tailor, who never did show up. She passed a terrible night, in which she seemed to see Catherine as a tragic, pale, and mangled form. The least sound terrified her. In her memoirs she recalls, "Never in my life have I suffered as I did that night."

&

Meanwhile the five brothers were engaged in their various missions.

Fyodor, the fourth Orlov, rushed into the presence of Cyril
Razumovsky, who sprang into action. The Count recalled that
in addition to being the Commander of the Izmailovsky
Guards, he was President of the Academy of Sciences, which
had the finest printery in Russia. He summoned Johann Cas-
par Tauber, director of the printery: "Here, have this set. Several hundred copies."

The Count handed the German the text of a manifesto he
had composed. It announced the overthrow of Peter III and
the elevation of his wife as Empress Catherine II.

The terrified Tauber refused. Count Cyril then said to him,
reasonably, "Well, since you know about this manifesto, your
head is already at stake. You had better print it."

And so the type was set by the trembling Herr Tauber himself, with the aid of just one helper. Soon several hundred
copies were ready.

In the past few days, the inhabitants of Peterhof had experienced all the extremes of hope and despair. A number of adherents had called on Catherine, each bearing some sort of
disquieting report. The most sinister rumor was that on June
29, at the Angel Day banquet, Peter III would declare her son
Paul illegitimate, and that one of the dishes served to her
would be laced with a poison selected for its ability to cause an
agonizing death.

At dawn on the twenty-eighth, Catherine's devoted
*Kammerfrau,* Maria Perekusikhina, burst into her mistress' bedroom to inform her that Alexis Orlov had just arrived from St.
Petersburg, secretly and in haste, having avoided the sentinels
en route. He had to see Catherine immediately.

Quickly wrapping herself in a bathrobe, Catherine sat on
the edge of her bed, her eyes wide with anticipation, as Alexis
briskly strode in without the usual court ceremony. "Passek is
under arrest," he announced. "There is not a single hour to
spare. All is ready in the capital. It is time for you to declare
yourself the sovereign Empress, the autocrat of all the
Russias."

For this occasion Catherine had laid by a long black dress
with a matching black mantle. She put these on as best she
could, but did not have time to comb her hair or even remove

her nightcap. Maria, still in her slippers, rushed out of the pavilion with Catherine, and Alexis hustled them into a waiting carriage. He mounted the carriage box with his friend Lieutenant Vasily Bibikov of the Guards and seized the reins. The faithful Shkurin perched himself at the back of the vehicle.

They set out at top speed, utilizing a roundabout route to escape the challenges of the Holsteiners posted at the main entrance of the Peterhof pavilion. As he urged on the horses, Orlov glanced over his shoulder from time to time, but there were no pursuers.

The two horses were soon driven to their limit, and one of the unfortunate animals flopped over into the dust of the road. The horse was propped up again, but Shkurin warned Orlov, "We can't keep up this pace!"

A cart pulled by two sturdy farmhorses pulled up. Orlov stopped the peasant and demanded his horses, leaving Catherine's exhausted but still intact thoroughbreds in exchange, plus a few gold coins. The flabbergasted rustic watched as the carriage bearing the fine ladies and gentlemen, now drawn by his own horses, vanished into the distance.

As they neared the capital, a city drozhky approached. In it was young Michel, Catherine's French hairdresser, on his way to Peterhof for his morning's work. The coiffeur squeezed his way into the carriage and prepared the future Catherine II's hair en route.

Within sight of the gates of St. Petersburg, they were greeted by the welcome sight of Gregory Orlov and his friend Prince Baryatinsky. The two men, mounted, were escorting a capacious carriage that would be more suitable for Catherine's triumphal entry into the city.

The change from one vehicle to the other was effected swiftly. Gregory, after fondly embracing his mistress, galloped with Baryatinsky to the nearby Izmailovsky Guards barracks to alert the men of Catherine's arrival.

Soon Catherine heard the blare of trumpets summoning the soldiers. It was seven o'clock on a sunny morning when the Izmailovsky gates were flung open for her carriage. She was greeted by Gregory Orlov on his horse, surrounded by officers and soldiers shouting enthusiastically.

Their Commander, Cyril Razumovsky, approached Catherine on foot. Bending one knee, he reverently kissed her hand. By his side the regimental priest raised a cross to signal the troops' oath of allegiance to their new sovereign.

Loudly, resoundingly, the Count read the manifesto, on which the ink was hardly dry. The officers and soldiers cheered "our Little Mother, Empress Catherine the Second," then lined up to kiss the cross and swear fidelity.

Catherine stood beaming amidst her jubilant warriors. A few days later she was to describe the scene in a letter to Poniatowski: "Each one of these officers and soldiers was sincerely convinced that he, precisely he, had made me Empress."

Some of the officers, particularly the younger ones, touched the hem of her mantle as if it were a sacred relic.

Her next stop was at the Semyonovsky Guards barracks. Now the procession was headed by the regimental priest of the Izmailovsky Guards, Alexis, who held his cross triumphantly above him, glittering in the sun. At the barracks, the officers and men, who had been told of the events, stood at the gates and greeted her with joyous protestations of fealty. Many of them had found the time to ransack the storehouses and to locate their beloved uniforms of Peter the Great's pattern. They had thrown aside the detested Prussian-style coats and breeches forced on them by Peter III and were now comfortable and merry, dressed as the Great Emperor, the founder of the elite units, would have wished them to be.

But then came a more difficult and uncertain task—Catherine's visit to the Preobrazhensky Guards barracks. Although two of the Orlovs were serving as officers in this regiment and numerous other adherents of Catherine's were in the rank and file, the Preobrazhensky unit was under careful observation by her husband's men, for it was here that her Captain Passek had been arrested and the plot nearly ruined.

Catherine's entourage at once sensed a certain hesitancy at the moment of their arrival. While some of the Preobrazhensky officers greeted her warmly, others stood apart as if undecided. Gregory Orlov started to address the skeptics, exhorting them to follow the example of the two other regiments, but Captain Simon Vorontsov and Major Fyodor Voyeikov leaped to the Emperor's defense.

The day was saved for Catherine by Major Prince Alexander Menshikov, immensely popular in the regiment. In his booming voice, drowning out the general clamor, he called out: "Men of the Preobrazhensky! Long live our Little Mother, Empress Catherine! She will lead us to new victories over our foes! Hurrah!" This brief and stirring call to arms, delivered to the soldiers with such conviction, carried the day for the rebels. Shouting their support, the rank and file and the handful of indecisive officers rushed to join their mates from the Izmailovsky and Semyonovsky regiments.

In vain did Vorontsov and Voyeikov try to rally them for the Emperor. Seeing that the cause was lost, both dejectedly broke their swords over their knees as Alexis Orlov's soldiers surrounded them and placed them under arrest.

და

And now, Catherine, in her splendid open carriage, was proceeding along the Nevsky Prospect—the heart of St. Petersburg. Noisy and enthusiastic crowds lined the route as she and her enormously swollen entourage made its way to the Kazansky Cathedral. Her three Guards regiments surrounded her, marching to sounds of drums, cymbals, and hurrahs.

Archbishop Dimitry met her at the cathedral, together with all of the Church functionaries who could be gathered at short notice. The Archbishop was ecstatic; Catherine had triumphed over the sinister Lutheran heretic, the Antichrist who was threatening the holy Russian Orthodox Church.

Solemnly, close to tears, he addressed Catherine as the sole sovereign and rightful autocrat of all the Russias and blessed her and her newly won throne on behalf of the Church for all times to come. Churchbells struck up from everywhere, and amid their bronze-and-copper din and the cries of the ever-increasing crowd, the Empress was escorted by Dimitry and the Bishops back to her carriage, which now took her to the Winter Palace. There, the Senate and Synod swore allegiance.

Nikita Panin led little Paul, the Heir Apparent, to Catherine, while outside, the immense crowd demanded her presence, her words. She took the boy to a balcony and lifted him high, showing her son to the populace, which now seemed to even exceed its previous jubilation.

Carriages rushed to the palace from all over the capital. Officeholders, aristocrats of categories high and low, rich merchants and not so rich ones, some foreign diplomats—all were eager to pay their respects to the new sovereign, to assure her of their admiration and loyalty which, of course, they said they had felt for her for many years.

And that day, June 28, 1762, thanks to the speed with which her co-conspirators had acted, copies of the manifesto were pasted on the walls of public buildings and private houses throughout St. Petersburg. Those in the crowd who were literate read this text aloud while the rest listened avidly.

Not once was the deposed Peter of Holstein mentioned as Catherine's husband. Instead she referred to him as a transgressor guilty of crimes, not only against the Russian empire and the Orthodox Church, but also against her, Catherine, whom he, "according to the admission of those who were commissioned to do this," had resolved to execute, as he had also planned to kill their son Paul "whom Peter, on his ascension to the throne, had refused to recognize as his own." The manifesto concluded with these words: "For all these reasons, and with God's aid and the sincere will clearly expressed by our faithful subjects, We have taken the decision to ascend the throne of Russia alone, as the absolute sovereign to whom our true subjects gave Us their solemn oath."

The coup was brought off smoothly and successfully, but now there were loose ends to tie up.

Word was brought to Catherine that some soldiers had gone berserk and were hunting down people they didn't like with cries of "Cut all the foreigners' throats!"

Non-Russians trembled in their homes. The palace of Prince George of Holstein was looted, and his servants, after being badly manhandled, were locked in the cellar.

The Empress immediately ordered army and police patrols

to put down the disorders, and the assignment was carried out with speed and efficiency.

All exits from the city were blocked: no one was to leave. Catherine meant to prevent anyone from reaching Oranienbaum and Peter with the news. She would first consolidate her power, then inform him of the *fait accompli* and deal with him, his mistress, and his Holsteiners.

Peter, as ever absorbed in his preparations against Denmark, had heard nothing of the momentous events, and apparently intended to settle accounts with his wife the next day, during the festivities. Rather than arresting or poisoning Catherine there and then, as rumors had it, he may have planned to incarcerate her in the Schluesselburg before going on campaign. History offers no evidence as to what means he hoped to use for her perdition.

We do know that on that historic Friday, June 28, he impulsively decided not to wait for the next day, but to pay Catherine a surprise visit. Having dined well at Oranienbaum, with ample amounts of choice French wines, he took his mistress and other favorites on a ride to Peterhof.

In the first of this string of open carriages, ornamented with the emblems of his Imperial crown and coat of arms, the Emperor relaxed in company with his Elizabeth and the seventy-nine-year-old Field Marshal Minikh, recently recalled from Siberian exile and now Peter's chief counselor. Behind them, Biron, Lestocq, and both sons of the late Osterman; Chancellor Vorontsov and Field Marshal Trubetskoy with their aides-de-camp; and still farther back, young and merry ladies of the court, Elizabeth's attendants, escorted by handsome Holstein officers, all happily chatting and laughing. Some of these doubtless were licking their chops over the insults their master would heap upon Catherine that beautiful June evening.

The royal procession halted not at the main Peterhof palace entrance but at the pavilion on the adjacent hill, to which Peter knew Catherine had moved when ordered by him to quit St. Petersburg. He now expected her and her retinue to rush down the staircase to greet him. But no one came out. In a rage, Peter ran through the rooms, calling, "Catherine! Catherine!"

For a moment he thought that, trying to regain his favor or at least placate him, she was playing hide and seek, in the kittenish manner of the early years of their engagement and marriage.

He was disabused of this hopeful notion when his aides reported back from their searches of all the buildings and the park that they couldn't find any of her servants either. At last the officer in charge of the Peterhof Guards appeared. Pale with fright, he informed the Emperor: "Her Majesty left early this morning with her attendants . . . for where, I don't know."

Pushing the officer aside, Peter frantically continued to search the pavilion, calling, "Catherine, Catherine!"

He heard footsteps coming along a corridor, as though responding to his summons. But it was his Chancellor, looking for Peter. Vorontsov, flushed and excited, told his master that a functionary from his office had managed to escape from the capital, going first to Oranienbaum, then to Peterhof in a peasant's cart. He brought the terrible news of the coup d'état.

Peter was crushed—what he had feared all his life had come to pass. In his agony he flung himself on the Chancellor, embracing him and imploring him to go to St. Petersburg, there to plead with Catherine on his behalf; to beseech her to compromise, to share power with him. Tears streamed down his face as he listened to the Chancellor's refusal.

Both Vorontsov and Trubetskoy countered that Peter himself must proceed to the capital without delay: "Your Majesty will speak to the Guards, to the officers, who must still be loyal to you, and appeal to them to resist the rebels. The prestige of the lawful sovereign is so high in Russia that at your very appearance they will fall to their knees, the rebels will repent, and once more they will obey your legitimate authority."

But Peter hardly listened as he sat down heavily in the dining room. His mistress brought him several bottles of red wine, and now he downed one tall glass after another, in a stupor of defeat.

At long last he roused himself sufficiently to start dictating to the Chancellor a countermanifesto. Putting this aside, he began to compile a list of Catherine's adherents to be arrested at once.

Suddenly the thought occurred to Peter that he still had his Holstein units with him. He sent for the officers, who would lead these troops against Catherine's Guardsmen. But when they arrived, he only looked at them and with a tired gesture dismissed them. He dreaded the possibility of a battle, of bloodshed. Once again he begged Vorontsov and Trubetskoy to intercede with Catherine.

At this point Field Marshal Minikh took over. In Peter the old soldier saw a fellow German expiring in the quagmire of Russian politics. He would rescue the Emperor. Taking his hand, he guided Peter into a study. Here they were alone—

"Your Majesty, there is only one certain way for you to save yourself and preserve your power. You must immediately proceed to Kronstadt, where you now have your entire navy ready for action against Denmark. Those seamen are disciplined. There are quite a few Germans among them. They will never be untrue to you. Instead of Denmark, your destination is St. Petersburg. Bring your navy through the Gulf of Finland into the Neva delta. The rebels will not be able to defend the capital from an attack by sea and will be compelled to throw themselves upon your mercy. You will then, with no mercy whatever, make short shrift of them and will reoccupy the Russian throne for good."

Minikh added that the court, and particularly its women, must remain at Oranienbaum. Agreeing to everything, Peter made an exception for his mistress; she must come with him on this expedition.

Late that evening Peter and Minikh, with their officers, boarded a vessel from which the Imperial flag fluttered. Countess Elizabeth joined them. But she was not the only woman on board, having successfully insisted that several of her favorite ladies-in-waiting accompany her.

The ship set sail. But Catherine had anticipated just such a ploy. Earlier that day, at the Winter Palace, while receiving St. Petersburg's high military officials and accepting their oaths of allegiance, she happened to notice Admiral Ivan Talyzin, who she knew had always been partial to her, being a cousin of Bestuzhev-Ryumin's and a kinsman of Panin's. Talyzin happened to be in St. Petersburg on navy business at the time of the coup, and hastened to Catherine's side. She beckoned him over to her, was charming, and, promising future favors, ordered him to go to Kronstadt and hold its forts and ships for her. He set out immediately, and soon after his arrival induced the officers and the lower ranks to swear fealty to the new Empress.

Once again hopeful, Peter, his mistress, and officers were celebrating with food and drink as their vessel approached the waters of Kronstadt. It was past midnight. An officer in charge of the guard at the port entrance* shouted a command to halt. Minikh called back in his voice of authority, "This is His Majesty, our sovereign Emperor Peter Fyodorovich." He pointed to the Imperial flag. "Report at once to me. I am Field Marshal Minikh—"

The officer interrupted rudely: "There is no Emperor anymore. There is only Her Imperial Majesty, our sovereign Empress Catherine Alekseyevna!" And added: "Now clear out of here!"

The Field Marshal attempted to remonstrate, but once more the officer cut him short: "The fleet and the garrison have sworn allegiance to Her Imperial Majesty. If your vessel doesn't turn back immediately, I'll order that you be fired on, and we'll dispatch you to the bottom of the sea—to the Tsar of the Deep!"

Peter, on deck next to Minikh, was drunk. The Field Marshal begged him to disregard the treasonous officer at the port entrance and order the ship's Captain to put in: "No one will dare fire on Your Majesty. The moment you come ashore, all those Russians will fall to their knees and repent. They will obey their lawful sovereign."

Peter's response was to burst into tears, to the accompani-

---

*According to one reliable historical source, the man was Admiral Talyzin himself.

ment of his mistress and her women, all in hysterics, all demanding that the ship reverse its course: "Don't listen to old Minikh! Don't risk your life and ours!"

The Field Marshal, with a gesture of disgust, ordered the Captain to return to safety, and the pathetic company sailed into the bay at Oranienbaum just before dawn, Saturday, June 29.

But Minikh would not give up: "There"—he pointed while Peter blinked dully—"a man-o'-war rides at anchor, ready for departure for Reval. Board it, Your Majesty, sail for Reval, take command of the Russian army there. Lead the army to St. Petersburg!"

Peter seemed to be reviving. The old warrior pressed on: "Listen to me. I wager my head you will win. In just six weeks St. Petersburg and all of Russia will be groveling at your feet."

No, Peter was too tired and not yet entirely sober. He sent everyone away, and, without undressing, flopped into his bed. He was beyond advice good or bad: he had caved in.

Saturday evening, Peter's nemesis called a council of war at the Winter Palace. Present were the Orlovs, Cyril Razumovsky, a number of Guards officers who had helped carry the day, and other high-ranking allies. It was time to make plans for further action.

Catherine ordered that an officer's uniform of the Preobrazhensky Guards be brought to her, and Gregory Orlov fetched it—the grateful contribution of a lithe young officer. The uniform was cut in the style of Peter the Great. Catherine changed into the coat and breeches, then sat down and wrote a memorandum to the Senate: "Honored Senators: I am leaving the city at the head of my army to vouchsafe the stability and peace of my throne. With complete confidence I entrust the Senate with my supreme authority, with the fatherland, with the people, and with my son."

As she descended the principal staircase of the palace, the Guards regiments awaited her, in parade formation, in the vast square. A skilled horsewoman since her childhood, Catherine gracefully mounted a spirited white steed and rode in review of her elite soldiers, who promptly greeted her with thunderous hurrahs as their new Commander-in-Chief. Here was a woman, a victor—who was already a legend among them. Oak leaves were pinned gaily to her hat, and her hair was loose and flowing.

Suddenly Catherine noticed that her saber was dangling, unsupported by the necessary sword-knot. A young noncommissioned officer, a giant of a fellow, took off his own sword-knot, and, springing forward, presented it to the Empress. The quick-witted soldier was Gregory Potemkin, then twenty-three, destined years later to be Catherine's principal lover.

Now it was on to Peterhof and Oranienbaum. By her side rode Princess Vorontsova-Dashkova, also wearing a Guards uniform. The two exultant Catherines were thirty-three and eighteen respectively.

At three in the morning, well along the way, the column halted for a rest near a village on the fringe of some woods. Quarters were prepared for the Empress and her companion at a modest inn. There were no beds, so a cot with a straw-filled mattress was fetched for the Empress, and an officer's greatcoat served as a blanket. She lay down, but could not sleep.

Two emissaries from Peter arrived at five that morning: Vorontsov and Trubetskoy. Catherine had long detested both of them, the Chancellor for his incessant intrigues against her and the Field Marshal because he had at one time been Alexander Shuvalov's colleague in the secret police. Both were extremely poor choices as intermediaries.

On Peter's behalf they offered equal dominion over the empire. Catherine must have smiled inwardly at the stupidity of the suggestion. Dryly she told the pair to present Peter with her ultimatum: "He must abdicate."

Both messengers then realized, if they hadn't known it before, that the game was up, that Peter was finished. Both lowered themselves to their knees and swore allegiance to Catherine.

At six o'clock Admiral Talyzin appeared. In jubilation he told Her Majesty of her husband's fiasco at Kronstadt. Catherine knew how thorough her victory was: now she had to prevent Peter from escaping to the Baltic provinces and

Germany. This should not be difficult. It was clear to her that
Peter was a broken man, at her mercy.

Bugles sounded and the Guards regiments resumed their
march. In two more hours they were at Peterhof. As she had
expected, there was no resistance. The few sentries at the palace, in their Holstein uniforms, surrendered to the Guards
without a fight.

The Empress entered her apartment, which she had left
such a short time ago as a fugitive. Her bedroom was as she
had left it, the bed unmade, the floor unswept. She called for
a secretary and sat down to dictate Peter's act of abdication:
"In the period of my absolute reign over the Russian empire I
came to understand how insufficient was my strength to carry
this intolerable burden. . . . Therefore, after my decision, arrived at following considerable reflection, I solemnly declare
to all of Russia and all the world, being under no compulsion
whatsoever, that I abdicate for all times any dominion over
this empire."

The secretary read the text aloud as Catherine listened. It
was handed to Gregory Orlov. In company with General
Mikhail Izmailov, Commander-in-Chief of the Guards regiments, Gregory galloped to Oranienbaum.

In the meantime the Holsteiners guarding Oranienbaum
had already surrendered. Peter met his wife's lover mutely.
On his personal stationery, ornamented with the Imperial
crown, he painstakingly copied the text dictated by his wife.
Later, on learning of all this, Frederick commented, "He
obeyed like a child being sent off to bed."

A closed carriage was brought to the door for the former
Emperor, his mistress, and General Gudovich. Under the supervision of Gregory Orlov and Izmailov, surrounded by a
strong Guards escort, the trio was taken to Peterhof.

Catherine was at Peterhof again! Upon hearing this, Peter
regained hope. He would plead with her, soften her heart toward him. He would remind his wife—for she was, after all,
just that—of what he now imagined to be their early good
years together, united in opposition to their harsh aunt, Elizabeth. Peter even fancied he was capable of talking Catherine

into proclaiming herself merely the regent, while Crown
Prince Paul became Emperor.

But these fond dreams vanished when the short, dusty road
from Oranienbaum ended at Peterhof. Catherine refused to
see him. Peter wrote to her, imploring her to reconsider this
cruel rebuff, to receive him, to allow him to explain, but Catherine would not relent, possibly fearing that a face-to-face
meeting with her husband might melt her resolve. She refused
even to write.

Instead, a group of officers, led by Alexis Orlov, burst into
the room where Peter was confined. They tore the ribbon and
star of the Order of St. Andrew from his chest, relieved him
of his gold, diamond-studded Imperial sword, and ordered
him to exchange his uniform for a civilian suit they found in
his wardrobe.

An hour later, Peter had another unwelcome visit, this time
from Panin, who announced Catherine's will: "From now on
you are to be considered a state prisoner. You will be under
arrest at Ropsha until your permanent residence is
determined."

Ropsha was a modest estate with a small mansion, presented
to Peter by the Empress Elizabeth. He had hardly visited the
place. And then? He pictured a cell in the dreadful
Schluesselburg, where he had interviewed that other pathetic
prisoner of the state, Ivan VI. He recalled the minuscule window under the dank, cobwebbed ceiling; the dingy, thin mattress; the bad food; the rude jailers; the absence of air,
sunshine, wine . . .

Bursting into tears, Peter fell to his knees before Panin, embracing his visitor's legs, kissing his hands: "Do not at least
part me from my Elizabeth!"

Sternly Panin replied, "Your request is denied. She will be
sent away to Moscow."

Peter's mistress, who was present, joined her lover in imploring Catherine's emissary not to separate them. Panin
stood immovable, implacable. It was, after all, not up to him,
but to Catherine. And the Empress had spoken.

In his memoirs, Panin wrote that he had never been so disgusted as by this spectacle of a royal prisoner on his knees, in tears.

≈

At eight o'clock in the evening of June 29, 1762, in a closed carriage with its shades tightly drawn, the deposed Emperor was delivered to the house at Ropsha. In what used to be Empress Elizabeth's bedroom, a huge, canopied bed was set aside for him. Two sentries stood grimly outside the door. Peter would be confined to that room and not even allowed a walk on the terrace.

From this comfortable prison, all night long Peter could hear the voices of sentinels stationed in the park. He slept poorly. In the morning he asked that his own bed be brought from Oranienbaum. It arrived the same day.

Heartened, he requested the company of his personal physician, his favorite Negro servant, his best German valet, and one of his little dogs. He also wanted the solace of his violin. Advised of these five wishes, Catherine was magnanimous. She wrote to General Vasily Suvorov, whom she had appointed the new Commandant of Oranienbaum, "Among the prisoners at Oranienbaum you are to find Liders, the physician; also Narcissus, the Negro; also Timler, the *Oberkammerdiener;* and order them to take along [to Ropsha] the former sovereign's fiddle as well as his Mops, the little dog."

In her memoirs one distant day she would write, "He had everything he wished except liberty."

Soon enough he would lose his life.

≈

On Saturday afternoon, June 29, at Peterhof, while Catherine was resting prior to her return to St. Petersburg, the indefatigable Vorontsova-Dashkova bustled about the palace, seeing to a multitude of things.

She was on her way to visit the Empress in her bedchamber when in one of the intervening rooms she caught sight of Gregory Orlov, sprawled on a sofa in a comfortable pose.

When he saw the Princess he did not rise but asked her in-
dulgence: "I injured my knee in all these disturbances."

He continued to open a large envelope. She glanced at the
seal and recognized it: with its double-headed eagle and the
Imperial crown, it was one of the most important of the state
seals. She had seen it in her uncle's study when he was readying papers for the sovereign's eyes only. By Gregory's side
were more such packets.

"What are you doing?" she cried out in amazement.

"The Empress told me to unseal these," Gregory replied
matter-of-factly.

"I doubt that!" the Princess exclaimed sharply. "These packets could very well have remained unopened for a few more
days till Her Majesty's appointment of proper persons to do
this. Neither you nor I are authorized for this."

She had not even by this time realized how close to the Empress this handsome Captain was, and would have continued
her ingenuous reproofs but was interrupted by someone rushing in to report that Catherine's soldiers, declaring themselves
thirsty, had burst into the cellar, broken open casks of choice
Hungarian wines, and were now drinking more than their fill
out of their *kivery*, the tall, round, and practical hats worn by
the Guards. The Princess flew down the stairs to stop them.

"Here's money." She dug into her purse. "When we return
to St. Petersburg all the taverns will be opened for you!"

Shouting with glee, the soldiers poured the wine onto the
cellar's earthen floor and left.

She remounted the steps to find that a table had been
pushed next to the divan on which Gregory was reposing and
that three dinner places were set. The Empress had joined
Orlov, and as the Princess reentered, her friend beckoned her
to her side.

As they dined, the trio conversed amiably. Suddenly Catherine said to the Princess, "Can you imagine—this Captain
wishes to retire from my service! Don't you think it would be
the height of ingratitude on my part if I were to permit him to
leave it?"

The Princess responded with stiff politeness, "Your Majesty

now has so many ways of rewarding anyone's services that in my opinion there is no need to thwart his intention."

The Princess saw through Gregory's coyness—he was not about to leave either his artillery post or, above all, his court position. As she dined with the pair, her suspicions grew. She began to see what by that time was known to practically everyone at court and in the barracks. The Princess was jealous—she would lose her friend to this handsome soldier.

When Catherine returned to St. Petersburg, at her request Vorontsova-Dashkova rode at her side. The Princess reveled in the cries of triumph with which the procession was greeted by the crowds that lined the way, and prided herself on her role in making all this happen. In her memoirs she writes, "And not a drop of blood was shed all those remarkable days."

At seven o'clock on that magic Saturday evening, the Guards regiments and several other units that had joined Catherine's cause began the march to the capital.

The Empress started out two hours later. For a while she exchanged her horse for an Imperial carriage, gilded and ornamented with crowns and double-headed eagles. Her escort was a detachment of Mounted Guards.

Halfway to St. Petersburg she decided to stop for the night at the villa of Prince Kurakin, a kinsman of Vorontsova-Dashkova's. Her excuse was that she had not eaten for many hours, but nonetheless she refused the proffered supper. The real reason for the halt was that Catherine did not want to enter the capital in the murky mist; she needed the brilliant sunlight to illuminate her triumph.

Begging the hosts' pardon, she retired to their magnificent bedchamber, where an enormous Versailles-style canopied bed, all in gold and velvet, was hurriedly made ready for her. Still wearing the Preobrazhensky Guards uniform she had donned two days prior, without undressing, the Empress sank among the fine-down pillows and was asleep at once.

In the morning her Maria came in quietly, bearing a silver tray filled enticingly with breakfast delicacies. The coffee was French; the pastries Viennese—Catherine's favorites. But there was no time. She waved the food away, swallowed a cup of coffee, splashed her face with cold spring water, and was on her way.

Early Sunday morning, June 30, the victorious Empress passed through the gates of St. Petersburg, riding her white stallion, the Imperial carriage following her. Princess Catherine rode at her side. The pair was preceded by a regiment of Hussars and other light cavalry. The procession was joined by the Mounted Guards Regiment that had helped in the coup d'état. On foot, behind the horsemen and the carriage, marched the three principal Guards regiments—the Preobrazhensky, the Izmailovsky, and the Semyonovsky, as well as the artillerymen, who proudly claimed Gregory Orlov as one of their own.

The city's streets and squares were jammed with crowds wildly cheering the new sovereign; windows, balconies, and rooftops were dense with citizens hailing Empress Catherine the Second. Choruses of hurrahs and the blare of the regimental bands mixed with the churchbells in a joyous cacophony. Clergy in gold and silver chasubles stood before every church on the route, ready to bless the passing soldiers and dignitaries and sprinkle them with holy water.

By noon the procession had reached the Summer Palace, where Panin, with little Paul, awaited Catherine, and the Senate, the Synod, and the court made their deep obeisances.

Patriotic fervor soon deteriorated into drunken tumult.

Gavriil Derzhavin, Catherine II's future poet laureate, in 1762 a youth of nineteen, thus describes it: "Sunday, holiday, triumph—the day was extremely beautiful, hot. The taverns, the winecellars, all were opened to the soldiers, and their drinking was at their maddest. In their infinite joy, the soldiers and their women carried off great tubs of wine, vodka, beer and mead, also champagne and other costly wines, indiscriminately pouring all these together into whatever small casks and other containers they happened to find."

The police were helpless and soon joined the revelers.

A disturbance broke out among the Izmailovsky soldiery, who were celebrating their part in the coup, boasting, "The Empress came to our barracks first!" Suddenly a drunken

Hussar galloped through their groups, shouting, "The Prussians have abducted our Little Mother, the Empress! Thirty thousand Prussians are on the way! To arms!"

The tipsy soldiers grabbed their muskets and formed a threatening mob. Gregory and Alexis Orlov, along with Count Razumovsky, rushed out to calm them, but to no avail.

That Sunday evening, Catherine had at last undressed and gone to bed when, at midnight, she was awakened by Captain Passek, who informed her of the Hussar's stupid prank and its consequences: "All our soldiers are drunk and marching here to the palace to make sure that you are not harmed. They say they haven't seen you in some three hours. They promise to go away once they make sure you are safe. They won't listen to their officers—not even to the Orlovs."

Catherine got up, dressed hurriedly, and climbed into an open carriage, taking two officers with her. Stopping near the disorderly rabble, she stood up in the carriage so as to be in everyone's view and declared in a ringing voice, "I am unharmed, as you can see. Give me some peace—I haven't slept for three nights and have just been aroused from my bed. Obey your officers, go to sleep."

Rough voices came from the mob: "The damned Prussians have upset us! We are ready to die for you!"

"Well, all right, thanks! But go to sleep!"

"Good night then! Be well!" And they staggered sheepishly away, some still looking back over their shoulder at her carriage for reassurance.

Catherine's first act on Monday morning was to order that the taverns be closed and that the police deal summarily with drunken revelers. The crowds dispersed and the capital soon returned to normal.

Three years later, Catherine's Senate was still gravely weighing complaints and the possibility of legal compensation for tavernkeepers and wine merchants "in the matter of the spiritous beverages carried off by the soldiery and other persons on the occasion of Her Majesty's ascension of the Imperial throne."

During that extraordinary June weekend of 1762, Catherine dealt swiftly and efficiently with the diplomatic community
in St. Petersburg.

On Friday, the day of the coup, not all of them hastened to
the palace to pay their respects to Russia's new autocrat; some
of the plenipotentiaries assumed postures of watchful waiting.
Credence was given to highly improbable rumors. Peter III
was reigning as before, but had decided to be crowned before
departing for the Danish campaign. The ceremony would take
place not in Moscow but in St. Petersburg; hence all the commotion. Another rumor said that Peter had ordered his wife
to be crowned while he was off at the wars.

To put a stop to this nonsense, Catherine notified the diplomats in no uncertain terms that "Her Imperial Majesty, having
this day ascended the throne in accord with the unanimous
wishes and urgent petitions of her loyal subjects and true sup-
porters of the empire, assures their excellencies, the foreign
envoys at her court, that Her Imperial Majesty intends to live
in harmony with their crowned sovereigns. The day on which
their excellencies are to come and congratulate Her Imperial
Majesty will be announced."

The day would be Tuesday, July 2. The envoys of Sweden
and Holland, having been favorites of Peter's, were depressed
and at a loss. For several days they tried to ignore the *fait
accompli*. Robert Keith, the British Ambassador, wrote stoically
to his superiors in London that, although England had lost an
ally, Catherine and her Russia were by no means enemies.

Maria Theresa's envoy, Count d'Argenteau, was ecstatic and
wrote Vienna that now "the best possible relations between
Russia and Austria will be restored." The French Ambassador
proclaimed his delight to all and sundry.

The Prussian Ambassador, von der Goltz, was disheartened.
His King, only yesterday Russia's leading ally, was now considered to be Catherine's most bitter enemy. The Ambassador
informed Frederick that a war was possible.

Von der Goltz was stranded in Oranienbaum. Catherine was
indulgent—she sent a special escort to bring him to St. Petersburg under her protection. Nonetheless, on July 2, he was
the only envoy to avoid the audience, using the lame excuse

that his new court uniform was not ready. In reality he was waiting for Frederick's instructions.

The Empress shrewdly ignored the slight and invited him again, this time to an informal card party with refreshments. The Prussian accepted, and found that he had been placed, not at the main card table with the Empress, but at the side, with officials of second-rate embassies. But at one point Catherine unexpectedly interrupted the game by coming over to von der Goltz's table to graciously bid him welcome and asked him to relay her best wishes to his King.

The envoys as well as the courtiers wondered who Catherine's new Chancellor was going to be.

Michael Vorontsov was under house arrest. It was known that Bestuzhev-Ryumin was being recalled from exile and that Catherine had made a point of sending Gregory Orlov to meet the old statesman at a post station many miles from the capital. She had bestowed on him estates and other rewards. Gregory brought him directly to her at the palace, both men still dusty from the journey.

She greeted him fondly, almost tearfully, for he had suffered at the hands of Empress Elizabeth because of her. Now she pinned on him the diamond star and the blue ribbon of the Order of St. Andrew, then sent him off to a mansion she had prepared for him, where the cuisine, wines, and carriages were from the Imperial pantries and stables.

But after an audience with Bestuzhev-Ryumin, she was appalled by how badly he was out of touch with the events and the political atmosphere of 1762, after four years of banishment, and yet how self-assured and insatiably ambitious he remained despite the fragility of his near-seventy years. He began by lecturing her: "The war against Prussia must be resumed." Mutely the Empress shook her head in compassionate disbelief. No, he was not fit to be her Chancellor. She would retain him as a revered elderly statesman to be occasionally consulted on matters of secondary importance.

The Sunday of the triumphant return from Peterhof, Vorontsova-Dashkova tore herself away from the festivities at the Summer Palace to make three visits.

She first called on her uncle, who was Chancellor no more—Michael Vorontsov. The home where the young girl had grown up so happily now resembled a prison. The Count greeted her with a weak smile and conversed with his victorious niece calmly, in a resigned tone, philosophizing on the mutability of human affairs.

From this place of sadness and defeat, the Princess, dressed in her Preobrazhensky uniform, then rode to the mansion of her father, Michael's brother, Count Roman Vorontsov. There, she was amazed to see armed soldiers—a hundred of them.

Count Roman was relieved to see his daughter, who had so suddenly risen to power. "They brought your sister Elizabeth here under arrest. But somehow, together with her, I am also a prisoner. Why? Only because I am her father? But I am your father, too. Like you, I have always hated Peter and his mistress—she who is unfortunately my daughter. I have not seen her in years. I have refused to see her ever since she first linked herself with Peter. Can you do something about my detention?"

Princess Catherine could, and did. She found the soldiers' commander, a certain Kakovinsky, and made a scene. Speaking in French, she castigated the officer: "You misunderstood the order of my dear friend, the Empress. Her Majesty sent you here with your soldiers not to keep my father as a prisoner, but only to safeguard him from drunken Guards privates. For this not one hundred, but ten or twelve sentinels would have been enough. Send back at least one-half of your unit to the palace! Right away!"

Her sister met Princess Catherine with streams of tears and loud lamentations over her misfortune. Restraining her contempt, the Princess tried to calm her, promising to ask the Empress for leniency.

The third visit was to her own home and family. Her husband, Prince Dashkov, was with his troops, but she hugged and kissed her baby Anastasia, and, still not changing from her dirty, sweat-soaked uniform into proper clothes, she hurried back to the Summer Palace to rejoin her beloved Empress. As she entered, she saw Kakovinsky, in company with Gregory Orlov, leave Catherine's rooms.

A shock awaited her. The Empress greeted her coolly. With a frown she reprimanded the Princess: "At your father's house you shouldn't have spoken to that officer in French in front of his soldiers."

By this she meant that because of the overheated nationalistic mood, all those close to her should take care to speak Russian—no foreign languages.

"Nor should you have ordered him to send any of his soldiers away. This was a violation of military discipline on your part."

The Princess flared up: "Only a short while has passed since Your Majesty's ascension to the throne. In this brief time our soldiers have shown me such trust that they could not truly feel offended by me, no matter what language I used in their presence."

She reached into her pocket, drew out the ribbon of the Order of St. Catherine, and handed it to the Empress, who, however, at once countered: "Easy, easy! Don't get so hot about it, my friend! In any case you have to agree that you had no business sending his sentries away from their posts."

"True. But how could I permit Kakovinsky to do whatever he pleased while leaving Your Majesty's palace defenseless?"

"All right, all right," the Empress said placatingly. "My remarks were only about your impulsiveness. Here—for your services." And she placed the ribbon across the Princess' shoulder.

But the other Catherine would still not be so easily pacified: "Forgive me, Your Majesty, but it seems to me that the time has come for the truth to take leave of this palace. Allow me to beg you to accept my return to you of this ribbon, this reward. As a decoration it is of no great value in my eyes, and as a reward it is not for persons who consider their services to be above sale."

The Empress still refused to be provoked. She stepped forward and tenderly embraced her friend, protesting her love. The Princess' haughtiness melted; fighting back her tears, she kissed the hand of the woman she adulated and would gladly have died for.

The Empress pondered hard but not long over a successor to Michael Vorontsov. It was clear that Bestuzhev-Ryumin would never do. Panin? No, she could use him to far better advantage close to her side.

Catherine made the extremely bold decision to restore Count Michael to his post as Chancellor. He was crafty and not entirely to be trusted, but his gratitude would ensure his pliability and submissiveness.

She ordered the guard to be removed from his house, and invited him to sup with her. He understood right away and inwardly rejoiced: he was being called to the service of this devilishly clever and masterful woman. Although Catherine said nothing about her plans for him, she did remark off-handedly, "I will not punish your niece Elizabeth. She will be sent to a place near Moscow, to live there quietly under necessary surveillance till I find a fitting husband for her."

A few days later, the court and the foreign diplomatic world were astonished to learn that Empress Catherine II had reappointed her former enemy Count Michael Vorontsov as Chancellor of the Russian empire.

The Empress then married off his niece Elizabeth to Alexander Poliansky, an obscure nobleman whom Her Majesty thoughtfully elevated in rank and provided with a generous income. Elizabeth, who was only twenty-three and who had recently stood a fair chance of mounting the throne at the side of her eccentric lover, was spared the anticipated horrors of public execution or a lifetime of harsh seclusion in a nunnery. But she was nonetheless condemned to live out her monotonous days as the wife of a titled nonentity whom she didn't meet until the day of her forced marriage. She thanked God for her good fortune.

From among the prisoners at Oranienbaum the Empress summoned Field Marshal Minikh to her throne: "Field Marshal, you intended to raise arms against me."

Slyly Minikh replied, "Could I have done otherwise or less for the sovereign to whom I was indebted for my release from exile? But from this moment on my duty is to fight for Your Majesty, and you will find in me the very same loyalty."

Wisely, the Empress resolved not to be vindictive in this case either. She pardoned Minikh and welcomed him to her court. She would use Minikh—and with him Bestuzhev-Ryumin— primarily as ornaments. They were superannuated but could come in handy and might even be capable of providing sound advice on occasion.

Minikh in particular proved to be valuable. As Vorontsova-Dashkova noted, the Field Marshal's *politesse* set him off from the brash new courtiers—the Orlovs and other officers who had risen to power because of the coup; *arrivistes* without education or even decent manners. Catherine grew fond of the old soldier she had saved from disgrace or worse, and loved to listen to his tales of bygone days at court or on the battlefield.

The new Empress soon showered honors and gifts on those who had had the foresight to back her. Panin was made a count and awarded a lifetime pension of 5,000 rubles yearly, and Cyril Razumovsky received a similar pension. Talyzin was decorated with the Order of St. Andrew and given 2,000 rubles.

The most sumptuous rewards were of course reserved for the Orlov brothers, all of whom were made counts. Logically, Gregory and Alexis were especially favored: both were promoted to generals of the Imperial armed forces, and Her Majesty personally affixed the exalted Order of Alexander Nevsky to Gregory's manly chest.

Additional distribution of the spoils would be made in a few months, at Catherine's coronation in Moscow.

But an unwelcome ghost from the past appeared in the midst of Catherine's triumphs—that of her former lover, Stanislas Poniatowski.

Both before and after the death of Elizabeth, and during Peter's short and disastrous reign, the headstrong young Pole had continued to write *billets-doux* to his idol. He longed to be at her side, to share her destiny, whatever it might be. It is likely that he knew about Gregory, but he confidently hoped that once Catherine beheld him, his charm would do the rest.

In any case, he had to be stopped, particularly at this stage of
the game. On July 1, dating her letter in the Western manner,
eleven days ahead of the Russian calendar, she wrote:

> This 12th day of July 1762
> I firmly request that you delay your return here, for your
> presence under the current circumstances would be dan-
> gerous for you and would harm me considerably. The
> Revolution, which has just ended in my favor, is a verita-
> ble miracle: it is difficult to believe that it all happened
> with such unanimity. I am so overburdened with work
> that I cannot describe all this in detail. For the rest of my
> life I shall strive to respect you and be of use to you and
> your family, but the mood here is a critical one and every
> step is of vital importance. I have not slept the three last
> nights, and I took food only twice in the last four days.
> God be with you. Keep well.
>                                                        CATHERINE

In short, foreigners were not welcome in Russia that summer of 1762, especially ones who might remind the court and
the nation of old affairs and entanglements. Besides, Catherine had that splendid male, Gregory Orlov, for her bed.

Even if the handsome Gregory didn't worry him, Stanislas
was aware of the insults and dangers that would be his lot
once the sneering gossipmongers and schemers of the St. Petersburg palaces and chancelleries heard of his presence in
that city. He could easily imagine the calamities he might
bring on himself and Catherine at the hands of her enemies,
now lying low but eager for any excuse to rise and devour her.
So for a time, Poniatowski stopped writing about his possible
return, even though he nurtured the dim hope that someday
he would hold his longed-for royal mistress in his arms once
again.

# Two Murders: Peter III and Ivan VI

The deposed Emperor Peter III was murdered on Saturday, July 6, 1762, exactly one week after his overthrow.

He died at Ropsha, near the capital, in the small mansion surrounded by a lovely park of fruit trees, lindens, oaks, and birches. From the moment of his arrival, he was not even allowed a breath of fresh air on the terrace, much less a walk under the trees.

In the week left to him, Peter wrote three letters to Catherine in his faulty French.

I beg Your Majesty to trust me, to remove the sentries from the room adjacent to mine, so that I could use it, as my bedroom is too small and I have difficulty moving around in it. As is known to Your Majesty, I always pace back and forth; my legs swell if I do not do this. I also petition Your Majesty to order the removal of the officers from my room. They are with me all the time, never leaving, and yet I have needs which I cannot discharge in their presence. I ask Your Majesty not to treat me like a criminal, since I have never offended Your Majesty. I rest my hope in Your Majesty's magnanimity and beseech you to deport me to Germany as soon as possible, with a certain person, and God will reward Your Majesty.

He signed, "Your most obedient servant, Peter," and added a postscriptum: "I assure Your Majesty that I will not undertake anything whatever either against you personally or against your reign."

That "certain person" was of course his Elizabeth. But Catherine had other intentions. On the day of her triumph she dispatched General Savin to the Schluesselburg to remove the broken and pitiful Ivan VI to another safe place and prepare Ivan's old cell in the fortress for Peter.

The men watching Peter at Ropsha took their orders from Alexis Orlov. While his officers and soldiers were contemptuous and rude to their prisoner, Alexis pretended to be a gentle exception, and feigned compassion. On Monday, July 1, as the captive and some of the officers sat down for a card game, Peter said timidly, "But I have no money."

"Here"—Alexis offered him a few gold coins—"any sum that you want will be given to you."

In the writings of Andrew Schumacher, Secretary of the Danish embassy in St. Petersburg, who personally knew both Peter and Catherine, we find this scene, apparently jotted down from the words of an eyewitness: "Alexis Orlov, who had just finished telling the former Emperor that any wish of his would be granted, agreed to a requested stroll in the park, but, while opening the doors, motioned to the sentries who, crossing their rifles, barred the prisoner from leaving the room."

Alexis allowed Peter to write a second letter to Catherine:

Your Majesty, if you do not want to kill this man, already unfortunate enough, do have pity on me and give me my only solace—my Elizabeth. This would be an act of your reign's greatest benevolence. . . . If only Your Majesty would be good enough to allow me to see you for one little minute, this would prove to be my highest happiness.

Your most obedient servant, PETER

Receiving no answer, the next day the heartsick prisoner wrote his last letter:

Your Majesty, once more I implore you, since I have submitted to you in everything and have obeyed your will, do let me leave for Germany with those persons about whom I have already petitioned you that they may accompany me. I hope that your magnanimity will not allow my request to be in vain.

Your most obedient servant, PETER

Catherine still refused to respond.

Peter was growing increasingly ill and weak. His stomach was upset and he suffered from headaches. He feared for his life—with good reason.

In St. Petersburg, a number of influential courtiers were openly complaining about Gregory Orlov's boasting and swaggering arrogance. Alexis knew this, and may have planned to arrange Catherine's marriage to Gregory in order to quash the discontent. Unfortunately Catherine already had a husband, one who could not be disposed of by a divorce decree from the Holy Synod or by Her Majesty's ukase. Only as a widow could Catherine be legally wedded to Count Gregory Orlov.

Alexis dropped his benevolent pose and along with the other jailers began to mistreat Peter. Peter's health and spirits deteriorated. Hearing of this from Alexis, the Empress sent over Dr. Paulsen, her personal physician. He arrived at Ropsha on Wednesday the third. Three days later the former Emperor was no more.

&

That Saturday morning, after a sleepless night, Peter was napping when his valet, who had also not slept because of his master's indisposition, stepped out for a breath of air. The officer in charge of the sentries ordered: "Seize him!"

The valet was pushed into a waiting vehicle and removed from Ropsha and his master—an ominous prelude to the events that followed.

No one knows whether the guards and their captive were dining or gambling. But there was a quarrel, then a fistfight, and somehow the fragile and sickly Peter was strangled.

The murderer was Prince Fyodor Baryatinsky, a close friend of the Orlovs and one of the hard-core plotters in the coup d'état. Alexis was present and saw the fight, perhaps even participated in it.

Alexis scribbled a hasty note to Catherine and then carried the news to St. Petersburg himself. Those who saw him on that mission describe him as being "in torn clothes, covered with dust and sweat, his hair in disarray, his face expressing extreme excitement, unrest and horror." One could read in his distorted features "the feeling of guilt tormenting him, the realization of his sordid, inhuman deed."

Historians surmise that his note bears signs that it was written while he was drunk, so confused is its content, so garbled the handwriting. Scribbled for Catherine's eyes only, it nevertheless has become the property of historians.

Little Mother, benevolent sovereign! How can I explain and describe what happened: you will not believe your faithful slave, but as before God I will tell you the truth. Little Mother! I am ready to go to my death, but I myself do not know how this misfortune happened. We are lost if you do not pardon us. But no one had any thought of this beforehand, how we could raise our hand against the sire. But O Sovereign, the misfortune occurred. At the table he got into an argument with Prince Fyodor; we had no time to pull them apart and he was no more. We ourselves do not remember what we did; but all of us bar none are guilty and deserve execution. Do spare me, if

only for my brother's sake. Here I have stated my responsibility, and there is naught to investigate further. Forgive, or order my early end. The world is no longer sweet
to me: we have angered you and we have destroyed our
souls forever.

In November 1796, upon Catherine's death and her son
Paul's ascension to the throne, the new Emperor instructed his
son Alexander (Napoleon's future conqueror) and a courtier
to go through the papers of the late Empress. It was then that
Alexis Orlov's letter was found in a small box.

Paul read it and ordered it destroyed immediately. It was
thrown into the flames of the nearest fireplace, but not before
Count Fyodor Rostopchin, who had the note in his hands for
some fifteen minutes, copied it. Rostopchin commented, "I
recognized Count Orlov's handwriting. The paper was gray
and not clean; the style showed the state of this criminal's soul
and clearly demonstrates that the murderers feared the anger
of the Empress."

On Sunday morning, July 7, the people of the capital
crowded in front of the walls on which copies of Catherine's
latest ukase were pasted. As in her prior edicts, she referred to
Peter not as her husband but only as Russia's former ruler,
and announced his death as God's will and the result of one
more seizure of "hemorrhoidal colics," from which the unfortunate man had suffered for many years. She expressed her
"greatest sorrow" over Peter's death and added that during his
final illness she had "in carrying out her Christian duty"
provided the patient with "all the necessary medical services."
And she sadly asked her subjects to pray for Peter's soul "with
no bitter memories."

On the night of July 7 or the morning of July 8, the body
was transported from Ropsha to the monastery of Alexander
Nevsky in St. Petersburg. It was laid out in the very same
rooms where in 1746 Catherine, then the Crown Princess, attended mass for Princess Anna Leopoldovna of Braunschweig, Ivan VI's prisoner-mother, and where in 1759
Catherine bade farewell to one more Anna, her baby daughter
by Poniatowski.

We have an account of the last honors rendered to Peter III:

> The walls of the two rooms are covered with black woolen cloth. The first room is empty. Sentries stand at its doors. Two steps lead to a raised platform on which the coffin rests. Red velvet and lace are affixed to the sides of the coffin, and it is draped with brocade which descends to the floor. There are no medals or other marks of distinction to be seen. Mourners pass from the first room into the second in a long, unbroken stream. The officers standing guard instruct them to make their obeisance and then move on. The former Emperor's body is dressed in the light-azure uniform of the Holstein dragoons. His hands are crossed, and in large gauntlets. The draft blowing in through the open doors stirs his thin hair ever so slightly. His face is black, even blacker than that of an apoplectic's. A wide scarf is wound around his neck, but the guards do not allow anyone to linger for a close examination.

It is said that when Alexis Orlov's befuddled letter was handed to Catherine and she had read it, she fainted. A lady-in-waiting who was present wrote in her memoirs that the Empress, upon regaining consciousness, exclaimed in tears, "My glory has vanished forever! Posterity will never forgive me this crime, of which I am innocent."

To Vorontsova-Dashkova she said, "I simply cannot express my horror at this death. It is a devastating blow to me."

Nonetheless, that evening, at a court reception, the widow smiled calmly and was attentive and charming to all.

The court, then the nation, and soon enough Europe, refused to believe the story of the colics. Rumors abounded, replete with details concerning the roles of Alexis Orlov and Baryatinsky in the death. In Russia, and even more so in the West, Catherine was widely held to be the brains behind the demise of her husband.

On July 12, the French chargé d'affaires, Béranger, who was known for his partiality toward Catherine, wrote to de

Choiseul in Paris, "Considered objectively, how does Russia appear? On the one hand, Peter the Great's grandson dragged from the throne and murdered. On the other, Tsar Ivan's grandson in chains. Meanwhile this nobody of a Princess of Anhalt usurps the crown of their ancestors, ascending the throne by regicide."

Nonetheless he added, "I do not believe that the soul of the Empress is so criminal that she could have taken part in the Tsar's death. But the terrible suspicion remains."

De Choiseul sent these policy guidelines to the French embassy: "We are aware of the hostility of the Russian court toward France. The King so thoroughly despises the Empress of Russia . . . that we do not wish to take a single step that would change her attitude. The King believes that Catherine II's enmity honors France far more than her friendship."

Catherine's alleged guilt has become a historical cliché. One encyclopedia of things Russian, published recently in the United States, categorically claims that Peter "was assassinated with Catherine's consent." Other scholars exonerate her of any conscious complicity. But the evidence weighs heavily on Alexis. Was it just carelessness that permitted a drunken quarrel among soldiers to result in murder? Possible, but not likely.

Catherine never punished Alexis or any of his companions, but to her life's end she carefully preserved that boozy, contrite letter, perhaps as tangible proof of her innocence—or perhaps as a device to keep Alexis in line.

Peter was interred by the side of Princess Anna of Braunschweig, the mother of Ivan VI. The Senate was unanimous in counseling Catherine to avoid the funeral, and she sagely followed their advice.

A month later she wrote, "I must proceed in a forthright manner—no suspicion shall fall upon me." But of course it did, deservedly or not, and Catherine II has gone into history texts and folklore as the murderer of her husband, Peter III.

ॐ

One of the men who could pose a threat to Catherine and her throne was safely in his grave, but there were others.

Sergei Saltykov, her first lover, was busy with his diplomatic duties in Germany, but Stanislas was becoming a definite nuisance.

Again he wrote to her in his insistent jealousy, demanding readmittance to Russia and to her favors. His news was bad. He had been so overwrought that he fell ill with a grave nervous disorder and sought health away from Warsaw, at Pulawi, the country estate of Prince Czartoryski, one of his uncles.

After two weeks, he returned to Warsaw. En route he met a courier who was bringing him a letter from his friend Count Mercy d'Argenteau, the Austrian Ambassador to St. Petersburg. To his joy the packet also contained a long letter from Catherine.

In it she told of the events of late June—the coup d'état and her role in it, and of Peter's captivity and death. But she omitted the important detail of Alexis Orlov's involvement in the murder.

Catherine reiterated her pledge to do everything in her power to aid Stanislas and his family, but requested him to stop writing: "I have no time to reply to love letters."

She went on to say that any regular correspondence between them would be dangerous, since Russians hated all foreigners, and that she could be subjected to extreme unpleasantness. Catherine finally informed him of the stunning diplomatic *démarche* she had in mind: "I am sending Kaisering, my Ambassador, to Warsaw. He will make you King of Poland."

The letter concluded, "God be with you! Strange things happen in this world.—Catherine."

It took some two years for her audacious scheme in Poland to bear fruit; meanwhile she was occupied with other urgent state matters.

Catherine vowed not to repeat her late husband's error: she would be crowned forthwith. Four days after the coup, she decreed her coronation in Moscow for Sunday, the twenty-second of September. She would depart for Moscow weeks ahead of the scheduled day—late in August.

Preparations were to be begun at once.

\* \* \*

Catherine planned every detail meticulously; no expense would be spared. Gregory was put in charge and Prince Nikita Trubetskoy was second-in-command. The state treasury was ordered to issue them the sum of 50,000 rubles to get things under way. From the Imperial storerooms one pound of gold and twenty pounds of silver were turned over to the court jewelers for the crown. Ermine skins were purchased for the coronation robe. Six hundred thousand rubles' worth of specially minted silver coins would be tossed to the crowds that would flock to the Kremlin or would be distributed to convicts, beggars, and exiles throughout the empire.

Catherine decreed that of the twenty-five senators, twenty were to attend the coronation; the rest would remain in the capital. The Holy Synod was summoned to Moscow, as were the high officials of the ministries. By the end of August, the dignitaries had arrived, including Panin, who brought Crown Prince Paul. Mourning his father, hating his mother, the eight-year-old Heir Apparent was morose but tried to hide it.

Card games and balls were prohibited: the participants had to be pure in spirit for the event. However, Catherine gave dinners, suppers, and receptions for her courtiers, and she held conferences in the midst of the hubbub so that the affairs of the empire would not be neglected.

She attended the endless masses that were the glory of Moscow, whose churches were said to be "forty times forty." From the day of her conversion to the Russian Orthodox Church, Catherine had demonstrated her piety at every possible occasion. Now, at her coronation in the ancient capital, she outdid herself in observing the rituals and the long, exhausting vigils.

If her late aunt had followed long nights of debauchery with equally protracted mornings of prayer, it was out of her sincere and naive belief in the tenets of the Church. Catherine's orthodoxy was different: coolly calculating, it was acquired out of political necessity. For this friend of Voltaire's and other Enlightenment thinkers had chosen to be the absolute ruler of an immense, half-barbarous, half-Eastern nation, for whom freethinkers were agents of the devil. She was no reformer and certainly not an apostate. She would be to her subjects what they demanded she be: the devoted daughter of their beloved Church.

As scheduled, the coronation took place in the Kremlin on Sunday, the twenty-second of September, 1762. From early morning on, the narrow streets and great squares, the rooftops, windows, and ramparts were dense with unwashed and enthusiastic humanity. By eight o'clock, Guards regiments and other crack units were drawn up in ordered ranks in strategic places. At ten, drums and trumpets announced the beginning of the royal procession.

The Empress appeared at the Kremlin and at that moment churchbells sounded and batteries of cannon added to the tumult.

The high representatives of the Church met Catherine at the entrance of the Uspensky Cathedral, together with the Holy Synod, twenty bishops, thirty-five archimandrites, and a swarm of lesser clergy. They broke into a psalm. The sacred delegation was headed by the Metropolitan of Moscow and the Archbishop of Novgorod. While the Metropolitan shook holy water over the delegation, Archbishop Dimitry carried the coronation cross to the Empress.

Yet Catherine permitted no clergyman, no matter how distinguished, to have the supreme honor of investing her with the gorgeous trappings of power. She herself donned the Imperial mantle of purple. Two of her ladies-in-waiting adjusted it and then pinned the ribbon of the Order of St. Andrew to her bosom. The faithful Count Razumovsky, assisted by a high-ranking member of the armed forces, brought the crown to her on a golden cushion. Catherine lifted the crown, and with her own hands placed it on her head. Only in the traditional application of myrrh to a patch of her skin, done in the cathedral by Archbishop Dimitry, was a cleric permitted to touch her person.

The Empress now approached a throne in the cathedral. She held the scepter in her right hand, while in the left glittered the golden globe surmounted by a cross—the *derzhava,*

Russia's ancient symbol of its sovereign's might. Handing these sacred objects to her courtiers, Catherine walked to the altar to perform a rite that dated to Byzantine times.

Afterward, again with the scepter and globe, she led the procession from the Uspensky Cathedral to the Arkhangelsky and the Blagoveshchensky cathedrals for lesser rites.

Catherine finally returned to her apartments in the main Kremlin palace. In the principal chamber of the Granovity Hall, from her canopied throne, Catherine now paid off her debts to the forty brave comrades who had stood by her during the stormy days of June. The gifts included diamond-studded swords, St. Andrew's ribbons, promotions and titles, and serfs and land. For the last two, purses of money were offered as a substitute if so desired.

Four categories were established.

In the first, three men were granted life pensions of 5,000 rubles per year. These were the two Counts, Cyril Razumovsky and Nikita Panin, and Prince M. N. Volkonsky, a senator and lieutenant colonel in the Mounted Guards. His precise role in the coup is unknown. Count Cyril smiled ever so slightly: the pension, measured against his fabulous wealth, was a pittance. Nonetheless he appreciated it as a token of Her Majesty's gracious esteem.

In the second category, the five Orlov brothers, now counts, were given 800 serfs apiece and the villages and lands that went with them. Twelve other officers and courtiers received the same or chose the money in lieu of the serfs—24,000 rubles, which amounted to thirty rubles per serf. Catherine Vorontsova-Dashkova found her name in this category. She proceeded to add up her debts, which came to about 24,000 rubles, and instructed her creditors to send their bills to Her Majesty's personal treasurer.

Eleven persons were in the third category, which meant each received 600 serfs or 18,000 rubles.

Those in the last category received 300 to 500 serfs or thirty rubles per "soul."

At three o'clock the Empress dined by herself, still on the throne. Colonels carried the dishes to her, and a high digni-

tary placed them before her with a bow. Generals and courtiers stood close by until the Empress commanded them to go
to the tables prepared for them in other chambers. Music and
song accompanied the feast.

That evening, the Kremlin and all the cathedrals, churches,
and towers were illuminated. Crowds streamed into the center
of the city. At midnight Catherine came out to watch her people enjoying themselves. She was disguised, but was recognized and greeted with cheers—a good sign.

On Monday, September 23, there were receptions for the
high Church officials, the ladies-in-waiting, and the diplomats.
That evening, fountains on the Ivanovsky Square gushed
streams of white and red wine for three hours, and oxen, together with all sorts of game and poultry, were roasted. Bread
was distributed, and from the Kremlin windows, courtiers
threw silver—and occasionally gold—coins to the throngs of
city folk and peasants milling below.

During the days and evenings that followed, Catherine received members of the nobility, officers of the Guards and
other regiments, and delegations of wealthy merchants. There
were balls and dinners, and for the common people the
squares were filled with wooden tables groaning with meats,
bread, beer, and other plebeian fare. Fireworks on a nearby
meadow delighted members of every social class.

In the churches, there were practically nonstop services,
which the Empress attended whenever possible, and she also
made frequent pilgrimages to shrines and monasteries in and
around the city. It was spring of the next year before the triumphant Empress, her Guards regiments, and her court returned to St. Petersburg.

Catherine never really liked Moscow, so sprawling, exotic,
tradition-bound, and proud. But she knew that it was not only
an ancient and rigid custom for Russian sovereigns to be
crowned there, but it was politically expedient for her to
spend as much time in the "heart of Russia" as she could. So
Catherine turned her swift, slight, taut smile of benevolence
on her Muscovites.

One day in the summer of 1762, while still in St. Petersburg, the Empress was dining with a group of her most intimate courtiers. The conversation was about the June coup d'état.

Gregory Orlov, as was his habit, was boasting of his influence in the Guards regiments. Addressing himself to Catherine, he said, "Should I want to, I could easily depose you in a month's time."

All were speechless. The Empress immediately made it clear that this amazing act of impudence did not sit well with her. Razumovsky turned to Gregory and said, making sure his tone was simultaneously jesting and serious, "Perhaps. But, my friend, not waiting for a month to elapse, we would have hanged you first."

Arrogant and vainglorious, the Orlovs, and especially Gregory and Alexis, were making numerous enemies at court and even among their fellow Guards. Officers were heard to mutter that the Orlovs were no longer the simple and approachable comrades-in-arms they used to be, and were now living high off the hog while their mates still ate plain fare and drilled in the muddy fields.

Vorontsova-Dashkova made no secret of her dislike of the Orlovs and their gross behavior at court. She once remarked that she could force herself to tolerate Gregory, but not Alexis. At the coronation she felt slighted when she was placed in a lesser position of honor in Catherine's entourage.

It is not surprising that the Princess ascribed her loss of prestige to the Orlovs' intrigues. However, it was the Empress herself who had begun to resent the credit which the Princess publicly claimed for her part in the conspiracy and the triumph. In time, Catherine II made the cooling of her favor obvious.

Catherine was also beginning to be suspicious of the Orlovs and their lust for power. Some of her courtiers were hopefully observing the ever-so-slight erosion of her enchantment with Gregory. On October 9, 1762, in his dispatch to Paris, Louis-Auguste de Breteuil wrote about Gregory, "Monsieur Orlov is a very handsome man. He has been in love with the Tsarina for many years. I remember that she once referred to him as being ridiculous. He is said to be a fool. However, since he speaks only Russian, it is difficult for me to judge."

Catherine shrewdly recognized the extent of the anti-Orlov sentiment, as did foreign diplomats at court. On May 23, 1763, Lord John Buckingham, England's new Ambassador, informed London: "People of all ranks are displeased with the great favors shown to the Orloff family, and express their dissatisfaction much more freely than has been usual in this country." Three months later, on August 22, he added: "Count Orloff is considered so much an upstart in this country, where there is little else, that all, but his own family, are his enemies."

Catherine was beginning to have doubts about her lover, that magnificently virile young stallion whom she had raised to such heights. In her memoirs, in retrospect, she idealized Gregory when she defined what she believed constituted a true Russian male: "Never had the universe created a manlier, steadier, more sincere man, a more humane, noble, devoted individual than the Scythian. No man could equal him in the regularity of his features, the handsomeness of his face, the gloss of his skin, or the proportions and grandeur of his body, with its strong, well-formed, and muscular members."

But in 1763 and 1764, Catherine was becoming more and more disturbed by the indiscreet behavior of her rough diamond. A French diplomat reported to Paris that her lover treated her, in public, in a manner that was cruder than any streetwalker in France would tolerate from her *maquereau.*

She still loved Gregory, but in her conversations with envoys as well as with her courtiers, she now and then revealed her misgivings about him. The Orlovs in consequence began to worry that their hold over her might be slipping. Alexis revived his plan to marry Catherine to Gregory, and Gregory agreed.

The two brothers approached Bestuzhev-Ryumin, who, although bereft of his former voice in Imperial politics, had been restored by Catherine to membership in the Council of State.

The sly old statesman fell in with the scheme, believing that his support would please not only the puissant brothers but Catherine herself, who at that time was keeping her cards facedown on the table. Bestuzhev-Ryumin could only guess what his sovereign's designs were, and he wasn't as clever as he was before his banishment.

A session of the Council of State was called. Those present listened to Bestuzhev-Ryumin in silence, staring at the table in front of them, eyes lowered in embarrassment.

Count Panin stood up. First looking at Catherine's portrait hanging over the throne, then at Bestuzhev-Ryumin, he said, "Our sovereign is free to act as she sees fit, but Madame Orlova will never be the Empress of Russia!"

No more had to be said. The session ended and the dignitaries filed out.

But the Orlovs and their spokesman refused to concede defeat. Bestuzhev-Ryumin requested an audience with Catherine in order to report to her on the meeting. He told her, "There is a precedent [for the marriage], Your Majesty. You could take advantage of that historic event—the secret marriage of the late Empress and Count Alexis Razumovsky. No doubt he has preserved the document certifying the marriage."

Catherine thought deeply. "All right," she said. "I will consider the matter. It is important to have that document if it exists."

That evening she conferred with Michael Vorontsov. In the end she instructed him to call on the aged Night Emperor. It is likely that she had seen Razumovsky ahead of Vorontsov, possibly to rehearse the suspiciously theatrical scene that ensued—a performance that Vorontsov records in his memoirs.

The Night Emperor was seated in his armchair by the fire, reading his Bible. He stood up slowly as Vorontsov was ushered in.

"I have come to you at Her Majesty's request," the Chancellor told him. "Can you give her the certificate of your secret marriage to Empress Elizabeth Petrovna? If you can, Her Majesty will officially recognize you as Prince Consort, widower of the late Empress, and I can assure you that on this basis you will be granted the title of Imperial Highness and the Grand Ducal pension that goes with it."

Razumovsky unhurriedly closed his Bible and walked across the room to a cupboard opposite the fireplace. He opened the door of the cupboard and took from the shelf a small black casket encrusted with silver and mother-of-pearl. He opened it and extracted a roll of parchment tied with a narrow, rose-colored silk ribbon, brought the roll to his lips with reverence, then tossed it into the flames. As the parchment burned, he turned to the Chancellor and said quietly, "Please tell Her Majesty that no such certificate exists."

Rumors of the matchmaking project had in the meantime led to a sinister conspiracy—a cabal of Guards officers would prevent the marriage by assassinating Gregory Orlov. However, the group was too small to be effective.

The plot was discovered, the participants arrested, and minutes of the interrogation of two of the ringleaders have survived.

The plotters were Captains in the Izmailovsky Guards, Fyodor Khitrovo and Michael Lasunsky. Their initial conversation was echoed in the interrogation:

*Khitrovo:* Have you heard about the marriage?

*Lasunsky:* What marriage?

*Khitrovo:* Surely you must have heard. Let's not talk politics, but it seems our Empress will marry Orlov.

*Lasunsky:* Yes, I have heard the rumor, but whether it's true or a sheer fable, I don't know.

*Khitrovo:* What do you think of it?

*Lasunsky:* What is there to think? Nothing can be done, we must submit to her will. No way to fight it.

*Khitrovo:* No—if this is about to happen, we must find the means to stop them. The rumor is being purposely spread in the city to see whether there would be any opposition.

*Lasunsky:* No opposition would come from the people or from anyone else.

The Captains and some other officers were charged with the assassination plot. By Catherine's decree, no mention of the conspiracy was made public, nor were any of the persons involved seriously punished. A few officers were banished to their estates, and the affair was discreetly swept under the royal carpets.

Still, that persistent voice from the past, Stanislas

Poniatowski, continued to haunt Catherine. Again and again he wrote imploring and affectionate letters to her. All through the winter of 1763–1764, he begged her permission to return to Russia.

"Oh, Sophie, Sophie"—he reverted to her earliest name as he had often done when they were lovers—"I don't want the crown of Poland. I dream of one thing only—to be with you. I cannot live without you. Do let me come back to Russia—and to you!"

The Empress turned a deaf ear to these words of entreaty and love, and continued to prepare her former lover's path to the throne of Poland. She had a good-sized army set to march on that turbulent land, as well as the backing of the King of Prussia, for the predatory, expansion-minded Frederick had agreed to lend his aid in return for new conquests.

The Polish nobility, corrupt and quarrelsome, were at one another's throats, seeing advancement in the offing. The Czartoryskis, who were Stanislas' relatives, were opposed by the equally influential Branickis and Radziwills. But the Czartoryskis had the advantage of Catherine's favor. They planned to depose Augustus III, King of Poland and Elector of Saxony. They wanted the crown of Poland—only that and none of Saxony—for their candidate, Prince Adam Czartoryski.

The dénouement was bloodless. In October 1763, Augustus III died of natural causes, leaving the throne in Warsaw conveniently vacant. Catherine dispatched a strong Russian army under Prince Nicholas Repnin and proposed to Frederick that Count Stanislas, not Prince Adam, be imposed on the Poles as their King. Frederick was quick to assent.

And so, in April 1764, under the watchful eye and the ready sword of Prince Repnin, the Polish nobles "elected" as their King Catherine's former paramour, the suave, elegant, but heartbroken Stanislas Poniatowski.

He was crowned on September 7, 1764 (by the Western calendar). Quickly accustoming himself to the pomp and perquisites of his new role, Poniatowski, now Stanislas II Augustus, sent forth diplomatic missions to his fellow sovereigns announcing his ascension to the throne. His mission to the Sultan of Turkey included his singular aide-de-camp

Charles Lee, later to be prominent in the War of Independence as second-in-command to George Washington—while secretly on London's payroll.

That year also witnessed the murder of the Ivan VI, the only legitimate sovereign during the coups of 1741 and 1762. As great-grandson of Ivan V, the feebleminded half-brother of Peter the Great, he was the only male descendant of the elder of the two brothers who reigned in the Muscovy of the late seventeenth century, and so, by Russia's ancient laws of succession, he and only he was entitled to the Imperial throne.

In early 1756 an escaped convict named Ivan Zubarev was, upon his recapture, delivered to Alexander Shuvalov's secret police. At his interrogation the convict had much of interest to tell. In his years of freedom he had wandered to Western Europe, where he had tried to offer his services to foreign governments—unsuccessfully until he reached Berlin and came to Frederick's attention.

The King received Zubarev, listened to him, and decided to use him. Provided with money, the adventurer was sent back to Russia to organize an uprising of Old Believers, religious dissenters, against Elizabeth. Their goal was to free Ivan, then an adolescent, and recapture the usurped Romanov throne in his name.

This was at least Zubarev's story as Shuvalov's henchmen questioned him under torture. Results of his deposition were at once brought to Elizabeth, who was greatly upset. What disturbed her most was the realization that Frederick, through Zubarev or other sources, knew that Ivan was alive and a prisoner at Kholmogory, near Arkhangelsk, in the frigid White Sea region. Shuvalov cunningly played on her fears.

Measures were to be taken at once—the boy prisoner was to be transferred to a more secure prison. General Savin of the Guards was in all haste dispatched to Kholmogory. In March 1756, in the early hours of the morning when everyone was fast asleep, the fifteen-year-old prisoner was awakened and swiftly prepared for a long journey. He was driven westward in a carriage whose windows were tightly shut and shades carefully drawn, a sack over his groggy head, with two slits in the rough canvas for his eyes.

A tighter guard was thrown around the rest of the family at Kholmogory. An elaborate fiction was to be maintained: reports on Ivan, now called Gregory, were to be sent to Shuvalov as if the boy were still in Kholmogory, not in his new and last place of confinement in the Schluesselburg.

On March 20, 1756, Shuvalov instructed Major Ivan Berednikov, the recently appointed Commandant of the fortress, that when the ice cleared and a boat could freely reach the fortress, the Kholmogory prisoner was to be delivered there. "The soldiers bringing him are not to be let into the fortress but sent back." The instructions came into Berednikov's hands on the afternoon of March 31. Ivan was most likely given into his custody that night.

Berednikov had a number of officers and soldiers under him, and, of these, several were appointed to be in direct charge of the celebrated captive. Of Ivan's guards, two— Danila Vlasyev and Luka Chekin—were with him from 1756 to the very end of July in 1764. Eighteen months after Ivan's arrival at the fortress, Captain Ovtsyn of the Preobrazhensky Guards was placed over both Vlasyev and Chekin, but Ovtsyn seemed to have served at the fortress only until early 1762.

The cell's only window, near the ceiling, was narrow and covered with white paint; no sunlight could struggle through it. The furniture was sparse. In this near-cubicle the two guards, Vlasyev and Chekin, had to keep an eye on the youth day and night.

As at Kholmogory, so now at Schluesselburg, neither guards nor anyone else who came near the prisoner could reveal to their family or friends outside what the nature of their service was. Their correspondence was read by Shuvalov himself, who struck out anything suspicious. The same went for incoming mail.

Ovtsyn wrote to Shuvalov regularly and in detail. On May 29, 1759, he reported that "the prisoner is in good health but has lost his mind. . . . Some ten times each hour he repeats that he is being bewitched by guards' whispering at him, by their blowing at him of air, fire, smoke, and the like. He gets angry if he hears a sentry outside his door cough or just blow his nose. I don't know what to do with him. Every hour is a worry."

The Captain's sad tale continued.

On June 10 Ivan had an angry fit because Ovtsyn would not let him have a pair of scissors. Grabbing the Captain by his sleeve, he shouted, "When I tell you I am bewitched, you are to look at me with respect! Don't you speak rudely to me!"

At another guard, a sublieutenant, he yelled, "Swine, how dare you talk to me!"

On the fourteenth he again complained to Ovtsyn of being "malevolently magicked." Ovtsyn told him, "Stop it—I don't want to hear any more of this nonsense!"

Whereupon, in his rage, Ivan grabbed the Captain's arm, tearing his coat. Later Ovtsyn reported to Shuvalov that he feared he would be murdered by the prisoner: "In my fright I yelled at him, 'Are you trying to kill me?' If I hadn't left the barracks just then, he might have killed me."

This was of course unlikely, since Ovtsyn himself wrote to Shuvalov that Ivan, then not quite twenty, was "delicate and pale." Still, Ovtsyn insisted in his reports that the prisoner's behavior intimidated his captors. Ivan stared into the eyes of each guard, puckered his mouth to blow air and snort at them. At dinner he grimaced at them, shaking his head, swinging his spoon, and waving his arms at them, thus "frightening the entire table."

Yet, quite early in his litany, Ovtsyn admitted, "To tell the truth, I can't understand whether he is really insane or only pretends to be."

If at Kholmogory the prisoner had still been sane his sufferings at Schluesselburg could have unhinged him. And yet, there is the possibility that Ivan pretended to be insane, perhaps hoping that as a deranged man he would not be feared as a pretender to the throne; that they wouldn't harm a poor idiot.

Sane or not, he constantly voiced his contempt for his persecutors.

Bored more than frightened, they teased him, and he reacted with curses and by throwing things at them. During such disturbances Ovtsyn would be called to calm Ivan. As the Captain entered the cell, the prisoner would try to tell him that he was a prince and an emperor, but Ovtsyn would not listen and would walk out.

In his report to Shuvalov for June 1759, the Captain wrote that he was beginning to worry about his own sanity.

Shuvalov then instructed Ovtsyn to question the prisoner point-blank: "Who are you?" On July 11 there was this answer: "I asked the prisoner, 'Who are you?' He replied at first that he was a man of high station, then said he was a prince. I ordered him to cease this nonsense and lying. He, greatly angered, rushed at me, shouting twice that he was a prince."

His face darkening, Ivan jumped around his tiny cell in such outrage that from then on Ovtsyn would not enter it alone.

Shuvalov, uneasy, finally sent a court physician to attend to Ivan. This was probably the only time a medical man saw the prisoner in all the long years of his captivity. Ivan met the doctor calmly, but soon became violent and yelled obscenities at his guards, particularly Ovtsyn, to whose orders to stop he responded at the top of his voice, "How dare you shout at me? I am a prince of the empire, I am your sovereign!"

He proclaimed himself not only a great man and a prince but also a disembodied spirit. Yes, he had a body, he said, but it was not his. The spirit of Saint Gregory had occupied it.

At times, more matter-of-factly, Ivan declared that he wished to become a monk. His guards, unknown to him, had specific instructions on this score. They nodded to him, agreeing: "You will be named Father Gervasy."

"Oh no. I will be Father Theodosy."

Refusing to bow before anyone, he announced that on taking Holy Orders he would be made Metropolitan: "I will then ask God's permission to bow before icons and perhaps even before some people. But without this, short of becoming a metropolitan, I will not bow to anyone."

Thus, with increasing violence, it went on for years, well into 1761.

Once he threw a cup of boiling water at a sublieutenant who

luckily jumped aside just in time. Out of the firewood brought in for the little stove, he saved a log to attack his guards with. Benches, chairs, and other objects sometimes served the same purpose.

The guards retaliated with threats to take his clothes away as punishment or to deprive him of tea or food. Shuvalov instructed Ovtsyn to remove from the cell loose bricks or anything else that could serve Ivan as weapons to injure himself or others; to prohibit forks, knives, and other utensils; and to feed him "by the guards' hands only," like a child. In case of a raging fit he was to be tied up.

These and similar instructions were faithfully carried out. Even his glass cup was replaced by a wooden one. He would break bits of plaster off the walls and try to hide them. The guards thought he planned to use them as writing instruments (although they didn't know whether he could write or read), and took these away, too.

One day Ivan succeeded in beating Ovtsyn with his fists on the head and the chest. The Captain's men dashed in to the rescue. Seizing Ivan, they bound him and held him on the floor, tied up, for two hours, while he cried, "I am God! Fetch the Supreme Judge to me!"

When he was in a peaceful mood, and muttering to himself, it was, in Ovtsyn's words, "rare that even a word could be understood, perhaps just one word a week was comprehensible, but hardly of any importance."

On one occasion, closely observing the youth, Ovtsyn decided, and so reported to Shuvalov, that the prisoner was physically ill, "with hernia, like myself."

When Peter III ascended to the throne, he had Shuvalov issue stern instructions to Prince Ivan Churmanteyev, the newly appointed Captain in charge of the captive in the fortress, that Ivan was not to be given up alive into anyone's hands trying to free him. Extraordinary strictness was to be maintained: "Should the prisoner create disturbances or resist you, or utter anything indecent, you are to chain him until he quiets down. But if even this proves to no avail, then you are to beat him with a cane and a whip."

Ivan's erratic behavior and chaotic mutterings must have convinced Peter that he had nothing to fear from this wretch. If an emergency should arise, Peter would—as he assured Frederick in his messages to Berlin—simply order Ivan's head to be chopped off.

But while alive and innocuous, Ivan should by all rights be given a better lot; his quarters and treatment should be improved. So Peter told his courtiers soon after his visit to that grim cell that he would have a special, comfortable room built for Ivan, befitting his noble origins. This plan was vague and ended abruptly when Peter was overthrown.

Now Catherine II had inherited Ivan.

Almost from the beginning of her reign, for the solution of delicate questions she turned not so much to her lover, Gregory Orlov, as to the sage Nikita Panin, who, still officially Crown Prince Paul's mentor and tutor, had become Catherine's most trusted statesman.

Count Nikita suggested to Catherine that Peter be put into Ivan's cell—after Ivan's transfer from Schluesselburg to the minor and obscure fortress of Kexholm, on a far-off shore of Lake Ladoga, close to Finland.

Catherine agreed. On July 3, with a sack over his head, Ivan was being escorted by General Silin to his new destination. However, bad weather struck while the vehicle was en route, and the journey was interrupted short of Kexholm. By the time the weather cleared, word reached Silin that Peter was dead and that Ivan was to be returned to Schluesselburg.

This was done, and now Ivan found a pleasant surprise: his old cell was freshly plastered and whitewashed, the floor was clean, and though the window near the ceiling was covered with paint as before, there were no cobwebs over it. A new oaken table and a massive chair graced his cubicle, and a new shelf was in a corner. A shiny metal washbasin, a good pitcher, and a fine toilet pot were other welcome changes.

Yet he was still treated brutally, and was the butt of his guards' hatred, badgering, and blows, for the cell had been renovated for Peter III, not Ivan VI.

And then, in the second month of her reign, Catherine came secretly to Schluesselburg to see Ivan.

She must have remembered that in her late aunt's time rumors had circulated that Elizabeth someday would free and marry Ivan, despite the differences in their ages, thus would she once and for all legitimize her reign. (In that century, as in previous ones, dynastic factors often prevailed over age gaps.) But in Elizabeth's case there was a far more serious hindrance: the Orthodox Church would have stood firm against any such marriage of two fairly close blood relations. Catherine was now, even more than before, playing her cards cautiously. She would not marry Gregory, that was clear. Whom then, if anyone? Folk rumors linking Elizabeth and Ivan may have come to her mind. Perhaps her own union with Ivan, while firmly legitimizing her hold on the throne, would not be opposed by the Church, for there were no blood ties between them.

The morning before her arrival, the prisoner saw an armchair upholstered in velvet brought into his cell. For the first time in all his captive life he was most respectfully served a cup of coffee with milk and given tasty buns to eat, with jam and butter. Then a handsome lady appeared, sat at the table, and invited him to sit at its other end. The guards stood ramrod-straight by the walls and the door. General Silin took his obedient station behind the lady's armchair.

Catherine tried to talk to Ivan, and was shocked. He spoke indistinctly, as if tongue-tied. He slobbered. With one hand he constantly supported his jaw. Then he began to grimace. Dismayed, she soon left. In time she would write that Ivan was a physical and mental invalid, a retarded human being; she would clearly hint that there could be no future reign for him.

Nonetheless, as did Peter during his short reign, she knew that at the courts of Europe the thought of Ivan was very much present, and she probably knew of Frederick's warnings to Peter regarding Ivan. Now, recently crowned, Catherine was aware that Louis XV had hopes for the boy.

Indeed, Louis wrote to de Breteuil, his envoy to St. Petersburg, the man who had so badly miscalculated in refusing the money Catherine needed for her coup, "The fate of Prince Ivan should enter into your calculations. The very fact that he is still alive is significant. Attempt, but of course with the utmost discretion, to establish contact with him. It is said that he has followers. Try, without arousing suspicions, to get to the bottom of this matter."

Conspiracies and rumors of conspiracies were gathering about Catherine. In October 1762, Nikita Panin reported to her that a clique of more than seventy Guards officers intended to overthrow her and enthrone Ivan. Four of the ringleaders were seized and questioned: a certain Peter Khrushchev and three Guryev brothers. They confessed. Panin proposed that these four scoundrels and their cohorts be tortured and court-martialed, but Catherine wisely pardoned them all, thus winning the admiration of some of her enemies and even a few new allies.

She recalled with pity her visit with Ivan—that delicate face, so aristocratic in spite of the dreadful rictus, so un-Russian, so Western, with its tragic gray eyes. She had wanted to reach out and pat his red hair. Nonetheless she reaffirmed her late husband's order of January 1, 1762, not to allow Ivan alive into anyone's hands. On her instructions Panin wrote to Prince Ivan Churmanteyev, "Should, contrary to our expectations, anyone come with an order signed by me, or by the Commandant of the fortress, or by any other officer, and demand to take the prisoner away, you are not to surrender to him, but to consider all to be a forgery or the hand of the enemy. And should that hand be so strong that there is no other solution, the prisoner is to be killed. But he is not to be turned over to anyone."

As in Elizabeth's time, so now during Catherine's reign, the search went on to find and destroy state papers, coins, and medals bearing Ivan VI's name as Emperor. Manifestoes, oaths of fealty, passports, and other documents bearing his Imperial title, liturgical books mentioning him as Emperor— all were to be burned. Coins and medals struck in his name were diligently sought, confiscated, and melted down.

Increasingly, Catherine was considering having Ivan ordained as a monk, for he would then forever cease to be a candidate for the throne. "My orders are that he is to remain in perpetual captivity and thus prevented from causing any sort of mischief. He is to become a monk and exchange his present residence for a monastery located neither too near nor too far; one to which there are no pilgrimages. There he is to be kept under surveillance of his present guard."

In accordance with these plans, Panin directed Captain Vlasyev and Lieutenant Chekin to "use your conversations with the prisoner to inspire him to seek the destiny of a monk. As a monk, he would be called not Gregory but Gervasy. Convince him that this path is predestined by God."

They were to exhort him daily, together or separately, until he gave in. One or the other was to sleep in the same cell with him so they could work on him during every waking moment. Both men performed this politico-religious duty day and night. They soon begged Panin to give them other assignments after all these long years as Ivan's keepers, for they too had become prisoners. There was never any leave for them, and they could see no one on the outside. They were cut off from their families, with whom they could correspond only through the St. Petersburg authorities, without telling them precisely where they were or what their service was.

But their petitions were refused. On August 3, 1762, they were promised early relief. This did not come. On November 29, 1763, both petitioned again. On December 28 Panin responded: Her Majesty rewarded them with one thousand rubles each and asked them to be patient, at least "until the early summer months."

The curtain rang down, suddenly and dramatically, and relief came on the night of July 4–5, 1764.

The man responsible for the death of Ivan VI was a young lieutenant, Vasily Mirovich, ambitious but ill-starred, precisely the same age as Ivan.

At times in history it appears that the sins of the grandfathers, as well as the fathers, are handed down to their descendants. Mirovich's troubles began before his birth, in 1709, when, on the Ukrainian steppes, Cossacks rose against Elizabeth's father, Peter the Great. Under the leadership of Ivan Mazepa, their Hetman, they joined the invading Swedish army of Charles XII, with whose aid they hoped to split the Ukraine from the Russia they hated so.

But on June 27, 1709, in the battle of Poltava in the Ukraine, the Swedes and their Cossack allies were defeated by Peter's forces. Charles, wounded, fled to Turkey, and with him Mazepa, who died later that year.

Among their adherents, Colonel Fyodor Mirovich fled across the border, settling in Poland, leaving behind his wife and two small sons in the Ukrainian town of Pereyaslavl. His estates in the Smolensk province were confiscated.

The boys, Yakov and Peter, were taken by an uncle, first to his home in Chernigov in the Ukraine, but soon, in his search for better fortune, to St. Petersburg. However, the uncle was thrown into a dungeon on charges of treason. The boys were now homeless, living in the streets. Learning of their plight, Catherine I ordered them sent to school, but by the time they were in their teens, Yakov and Peter decided to shift for themselves, complaining that no money was given them to live on while studying.

Fortune smiled briefly in 1728 when Princess Elizabeth, then nineteen, heeded Peter's plea and took him on as a secretary. In 1729 he was with her in her Moscow residence when his brother Yakov joined the staff of Count Potocki, the Polish-Saxon representative in St. Petersburg.

Trouble came once more. The runaway Colonel Mirovich was still alive in Poland, and Yakov secretly visited him. By 1732 the secret was out, and Yakov was arrested by the Imperial Russian authorities, grilled, and exiled to Siberia along with his wife and a few other members of the family.

In Siberia, in 1740, Vasily was born. The boy grew up with the stigma of his clan as traitors, and he and his three sisters shared the bitter poverty of all the Miroviches. Upon reaching military age, he was permitted to become a sublieutenant in the provincial Smolensky Regiment. If it hadn't been for his grandfather's treason of 1709, Vasily would have now been a Guards officer, with a handsome income from the Smolensk estates. But it was all gone.

In 1763, he petitioned Catherine for the return of at least some of his grandfather's property, pleading that he and his three sisters would be satisfied with "whatever of those estates and lands the magnanimity of Her Imperial Majesty would allot" to them. Catherine refused. So generous with gifts to the nobles who had recently helped her to the throne, she scribbled on Vasily's request, "On the basis of what is written here, the petitioners have no claim whatever, and therefore the Senate is to refuse this."

Vasily then tried, through the Senate and other channels, to obtain a pension for his impoverished sisters. Again he was rebuffed.

But he refused to give up. In 1763, he somehow succeeded in obtaining the position of aide on the staff of Peter Panin, brother of the all-powerful Count Nikita Panin. A general and senator, Peter Panin was in charge of administering Courland, a province which he and his office controlled by proxy, preferring to remain in St. Petersburg, with its social whirl.

Mirovich enjoyed the good life in the capital with a sort of morose desperation, brooding on the injustice done him and wasting his time drinking, gambling, and dueling.

He was mired in debt, and once even went to the extreme of writing his mother for a paltry forty rubles. On the back of her letter of refusal he wrote remorsefully, "May Saint Nicholas hear my vow that from the year 1763 to my death I will not smoke, take snuff, or play cards."

And on another fragment of paper he swore that, come his twenty-fifth birthday, he would reduce his drinking to "a very little brandy."

And still he gambled, caroused, and avoided work. Peter Panin was a tolerant man, and tried to give some fatherly advice. Mirovich was grateful. Shortly before mounting the scaffold he wrote, "His Excellency in the goodness of his heart repeatedly lectured me on the need for restraint. He was generous in his favors and ceaselessly urged me to mend my ways, but when these exhortations failed to halt my escapades, I was let to go from my job and made an officer in a field regiment."

His position with Peter Panin had lasted only three months.

Mirovich also tried to solicit the acquaintance and assistance of Princess Vorontsova-Dashkova, but with no success. She even refused to meet him. There is evidence that he once caught the attention of her husband, Prince Michael Dashkov, but this was no help to him either.

Cyril Razumovsky, a fellow Ukrainian, listened to Mirovich's story about his grandfather and how the late Colonel had ruined Vasily, and advised him to forget his ancient grievances: "The dead do not return from the grave. Carve out your own career, young man. Seize fortune by the forelock as others have done."

Sound enough advice, but given to the wrong man. Mirovich was deeply impressed by these words and resolved to act accordingly.

He was aware of how the surreptitious loyalty of certain officers to Elizabeth and Catherine had burst forth to raise these women to the throne. He hated the memory of Peter the Great and his daughter Elizabeth, and detested the *parvenue* Empress Catherine, while calculating that her power was still shaky.

This dark, muscular, intense young man had the drive in him, and his aim was at last clear. What means would he use to humble the might of Catherine II? Whom would his hobnailed soldier's boots escort up the marble steps to the throne? The answer was former Emperor Ivan VI.

≥∿

It was October 1763. Mirovich's Smolensky Regiment was ordered to winter quarters at the Schluesselburg. The soldiers were on foot, and behind them Mirovich and a fellow lieutenant rode in a *kibitka,* a covered cart. Near St. Petersburg, having passed through the village of Rybachye, Mirovich decided to take a walk, ahead of the soldiers.

Leaving the slowly lumbering cart and his dozing companion in it, Mirovich wandered along a riverbank and met a man approaching from the opposite direction, a musket on each shoulder. Mirovich stopped him: "Who are you?"

"I am a former soldier, sir, a drummer in retirement," the man replied respectfully. "I am walking to Petersburg because some scoundrel has stolen my boat. I had it tied near the Nevsky Monastery and left for a minute to sell my catch of fish, but look here, sir, they stole my boat! So vile are folk these days. But then, sir, you won't find justice now anywhere in the world!"

"How so?"

"Well, what justice can there be when our lawful sovereign has been kept a prisoner some seven years now in the very fortress where you, sir, are taking your regiment?"

"Do they let anyone into the fortress freely?"

"Just you officers and your soldiers. And now and then a general who has the need to be there on the state's business. But no one else is permitted, except perhaps those who wish to pray in the fortress church, but this only on a pass each time from the Commandant no less."

"What sovereign is it, and what do they call him?"

"'Tis Tsar Ioann Antonovich whom they keep captive in the stone chamber down below, sir."

This was perhaps the first time Vasily Mirovich heard that Ivan was still alive. Later he would testify that for a while this information made no particular impression upon him, but that gradually he came back to it again and again, until one day—April 1, 1764—he realized that here at long last was his golden opportunity. He would free Ivan from the dungeon, proclaim him Emperor, and do away with Catherine.

Yet, early on, Mirovich felt that he could not do it alone. He needed help.

He would approach his fellow officer and best friend in the regiment, Lieutenant Appolon Ushakov, like himself an aristocrat from a poverty-stricken family, with some minor connections at the Imperial court, who, however, had not so far proved useful for his advancement.

One day Mirovich asked Ushakov, with a seeming casualness, "Would you join me in an enterprise like that of the Orlov brothers'?"

At first his friend was taken aback, but quickly recovered his composure. "Something like what the Orlovs did! And with what aim?"

Calmly Mirovich declared, "To free our sovereign Ioann Antonovich, who is imprisoned right where we are, in the Schluesselburg."

"Yes," mused Ushakov. "I too once heard from an engineer officer that Ioann Antonovich is being held here."

The two talked further. For a time Ushakov would not believe that Mirovich was in earnest. But in time he became convinced of the seriousness of his friend's intentions and agreed to join him.

One day they went to the fortress church, and, making sure there were no witnesses, placed their hands on the Holy Gospel and exchanged oaths to carry out their awesome project in God's name to restore justice.

They then composed a manifesto in which Catherine was denounced as a usurper and a whore and which proclaimed Ivan as lawful Emperor of all the Russias. Mirovich was responsible for most of the wording.

Mirovich was about to set the date for his coup d'état when fate intervened. On May 23, Ushakov was detailed by his superiors to transport 15,000 rubles in silver coins to Smolensk in order to pay military expenditures in that region. With him, as his orderly and coachman, went a soldier named Novichkov.

Lieutenant Ushakov fell ill at a village rest stop. He instructed his orderly to proceed westward with the money and stayed behind to recuperate. Novichkov completed the mission alone, delivered the trunk containing the money, and returned to the village for his commander.

But the villagers informed him that Lieutenant Ushakov, feeling better, had decided to return to St. Petersburg. Novichkov hastened after him, but en route some peasants told him excitedly that on June 6 a tilt cart lined with coarse matting had been found half submerged in the nearby Shelona River. In it were a cushion, an officer's hat, a sword with a gilded handle-knot, a shirt, and eight rubles.

Soon after the discovery of the cart, a corpse had floated to the surface. The unthinking peasants buried it without Church rites and only then notified the authorities. In the presence of Novichkov, the authorities dug up the body. Novichkov affirmed that he recognized both the body and the objects found in the cart. The dead man was his commander, Lieutenant Appolon Ushakov.

There was a small wound on the left temple. Ushakov was reburied without further investigation, and the cause of his death remained a mystery. Perhaps it was just another case of highway robbery and murder; perhaps there was foul play involved on the behalf of some mysterious upper level of the Imperial bureaucracy; perhaps the officer committed suicide because of guilt over the plot into which his comrade had drawn him.

❧

Vasily Mirovich was again alone, but he persisted in his attempts to enlist aid. He had to hurry. Catherine was visiting her Baltic provinces that early July 1764, and Mirovich felt he had to act while she was away from her capital, her center of power.

On July 3 it was Mirovich's turn to share a week's watch at the main gate of the Schluesselburg. In the words of a subsequent report by Colonel Ivan Berednikov, Commandant of the fortress, while on the watch "Vasily, son of Yakov, Mirovich, a sublieutenant of the Smolensky Infantry Regiment, by his own request replaced another officer."

On the fourth, at five o'clock in the afternoon, Mirovich caught sight of Captain Danila Vlasyev, chief of a special unit posted at the little terrace which, Mirovich knew, led to the barracks in whose dungeon Ivan was incarcerated.

The two officers saluted, then strolled along a gallery near the terrace, chatting about nothing in particular.

Mirovich suddenly took the plunge: "Would you betray me before hearing my plan?"

Vlasyev displayed no curiosity regarding this cryptic question, but would not allow Mirovich to continue, cutting him short by saying evenly, "If the undertaking would mean your ruin, I don't want to hear about it."

The two men silently descended from the gallery to a nearby pier, sat looking at the water for a while, and returned to the fortress. At the main gate, Mirovich invited Vlasyev to come to the guardroom, but the Captain refused: "We are forbidden to visit anyone."

At that point Mirovich decided he would have only his own soldiers to count on.

He summoned Yakov Pisklov, his orderly, to his tiny office in the guardroom, greeted him pleasantly, then burst out:

"Our Tsar, Ioann Antonovich, is imprisoned here. We are going to liberate him. Join me and talk the rest of the men into it!"

The orderly gave his consent at once: "If my comrades agree, so do I!"

Mirovich then sent for a private named Basov, and in the same blunt manner recruited him into the conspiracy. He dispatched Pisklov to bring him the three corporals of his guard unit, one by one. With astonishing speed and ease he induced these men to join him.

Mirovich postponed setting the machinery in motion that he hoped would carry him to power and wealth: he would take his time in choosing the most advantageous time for the deed.

He had, however, reckoned without Captain Vlasyev. The Captain had been taken aback by his fellow officer's rash confidence, for the two hardly knew each other, and his mistrust and suspicions were growing.

That evening he told his friend Lieutenant Luka Chekin about the enigmatic Mirovich and about his own misgivings. The two decided to act without further delay.

Per their instructions in such situations, they bypassed Commandant Berednikov and wrote directly to Panin: Berednikov had to send the report on to the Count without knowing its contents.

That night Mirovich remained awake. At half past one, Sergeant Lebedev, in charge of the watch, came to him: "The Commandant just ordered me to let some boats go in and out of the fortress and not to tell you about it."

Much later that night the noncom returned, this time to inform Mirovich that a military scribe was accompanying the boats in their shuttle.

The Lieutenant's heart skipped a beat. Vlasyev must have reported him! Any more delays would be fatal.

He made his decision. Without stopping to dress, he picked up his uniform, sword, and hat, then bounded down the stairs into the barracks in which his men were sleeping. From the doorway he called, "To arms!"

Some of his soldiers were billeted elsewhere. Quickly sending messengers to rouse them, feverishly donning his uniform, Mirovich was finally ready to review and lead his rudely awakened infantrymen as they stood before him outside the barracks, half dazed, trying to straighten out their lines.

"Load your muskets!" he commanded.

He then detailed a corporal and two privates to guard the main gate: "No one leaves!"

At the head of his troops, he rushed to the Commandant's quarters and hammered on the door with all his might. The Colonel had only a short time before been talking with Vlasyev and was not yet asleep, although he was dressed for bed. He threw his officer's greatcoat over his nightshirt and opened the door. Astonished by the sight of Mirovich and his soldiers, he shouted, "Lieutenant! What on earth are you doing? Why, without my orders, have you gathered these soldiers with their weapons?"

Mirovich's response was a blow on the head with his musket, "cracking my skull," as the Colonel ruefully reported to Panin.

"Why are you holding our innocent sovereign?" Mirovich yelled at the reeling Colonel.

Stunned and covered with blood, Berednikov nonetheless had the strength to reply, "There is no sovereign here. I am holding a convict given into my keeping."

Mirovich turned to his men: "This scoundrel is keeping our sovereign Ioann Antonovich under guard in this fortress! Take him away—our duty is to die for our Emperor!"

The soldiers echoed: "Our duty is to die!"

Prodding Berednikov with their bayonets, they led him away. "And thus did I remain, the rebel soldiers holding me prisoner until the fifth hour of the morning," the Colonel later wrote.

Mirovich led the main body of insurrectionists at a run to the central area of the fortress. As they neared the entrance to the dungeon, a sentry called out, "Who goes there?"

To which the rebel leader replied, "I am on my way to the sovereign!"

At that point shooting began.

Vlasyev later reported to Panin that he and Chekin had heard the call to arms. After the initial attack on the barracks, Vlasyev ordered the attackers to cease and desist: "Seeing that the enemy nonetheless continued their onslaught, I commanded my men to fire on them. I stole along the upper rampart as best as possible, then descended to where my soldiers were making their stand under Lieutenant Chekin. He and I strengthened our unit, and from our protected position we drove off the enemy."

Mirovich ordered his troops to hold their fire because, as he testified after his arrest, he was afraid the Emperor might be hurt. Falling back, he shouted at his enemy, "Stop shooting! Surrender or I'll bring out a cannon!"

Vlasyev and Chekin were preparing to order their soldiers to loose another volley when a cannon, small but sufficiently lethal, was dragged from a nearby bastion, pointed at the defenders, and made ready. "Seeing the enemy's superiority," Vlasyev wrote, "and the impossibility of further resistance, we were forced to yield."

Mirovich sent a messenger to them with the further warning: "Hold your fire. We are ready to use the cannon."

Vlasyev capitulated, the defenders laid their muskets at their feet, and victory appeared to be within the grasp of the rebels.

The soldiers seized Vlasyev and Chekin and wanted to bayonet them, but Mirovich restrained them. Instead, he grabbed Chekin by the wrist and demanded at the top of his voice, "Where is our sovereign—the Emperor?"

Struggling to free himself, Chekin retorted, "There is no Emperor. There is only our sovereign, Empress Catherine Alexseyevna!"

Mirovich's response to this audacious taunt was to hit his captive on the back of the neck: "Go! Point out the Emperor! Unlock the door!" The victorious soldiers shoved Chekin roughly to the door and forced him to unlock it.

Catherine's investigators later wrote that a total of 124 shots were fired that night by both sides, but no one was hit. The reasons were poor visibility owing to fog, the fact that neither side had a clear line of fire, and because "the soldiers were sleepy."

The wretched twenty-four-year-old captive on whose behalf

Mirovich had conspired and fought was the only casualty of this farce.

He was butchered by Vlasyev and Chekin during a break in the fighting. Ivan, wakened by the shouting and gunfire outside, was out of his bed when the two officers loyal to the Empress rushed into his cell with their swords drawn and proceeded to hack him to pieces. Ivan, almost naked, tried to resist, but was soon bleeding from numerous wounds. One of the officers gave him the coup de grâce by running his sword through his body.

When Lieutenant Chekin unlocked the door, Mirovich and his men beheld, in the light of a lantern swung by one of the soldiers, Ivan's body lying in a pool of blood on the stone floor.

Out of the young man's lacerated throat sounded the death rattle. Then all was still.

Glaring with hatred at the two assassins—his captives—Mirovich shrieked, "Pitiless men! Do you not fear God? Why did you shed this innocent blood? How did you dare to slay this great man? I will order my men to bayonet you!"

Then he changed his tune: "Now I am done for! But you are more fortunate than I. No, I will not kill you."

One of the officers told him defiantly, "We did this by Imperial order." And demanded: "Who sent you?"

Mirovich drew himself up proudly: "I did it on my own."

"We have done our duty—here is the order," was the reply.

They showed him the decree, which they always carried with them. It might have been Peter III's order of January 1, 1762: "Should anyone, against our expectations, try to take the prisoner away from you, you are to resist to your utmost and never to surrender the prisoner alive." Or it might have been Panin's later confirmation of the same order, done on Catherine's instructions. But Mirovich would not read it, even touch it.

The game was lost. Mirovich knelt before the body. Weeping hysterically, he kissed Ivan's arms and legs. His tears were for himself as well.

He directed his soldiers to place the corpse on the bed. Later, aided by his followers, he carried it onto the parade grounds of the fortress. He sent for the military chaplain, who performed a brief funeral service. Everyone present, on their knees, chanted the Orthodox "Eternal Memory."

Officers and common soldiers flocked to the ceremony from the various barracks, wanting to know, "What happened? Who is he?"

So thoroughly had Ivan's captivity been kept secret even in the fortress that many were learning of his presence for the first time, and were amazed.

Rising from his knees, Mirovich, through his tears, addressed the singular gathering: "Brothers! This was our sovereign, Emperor Ivan Antonovich! Great misfortunes will now descend upon us. But you are innocent, for you did not know my intentions, and I will take upon myself all the guilt and all the punishment. I alone will suffer!"

Mirovich kissed his rebel soldiers on the mouth and the cheeks. Later that day Vlasyev reported to Count Panin: "He then pronounced his own arrest and we were freed from detention."

The Count responded with orders to arrest Mirovich and his cohorts, a total of thirty-nine men. They meekly laid down their arms and bowed their heads to fate.

Panin ordered that Ivan be buried immediately, within the fortress, and with a minimum of ceremony. A simple stone cross was to be placed over the grave, with no inscription.

By a singular oversight, the gate nearest the fatal dungeon was for many years afterward called the Ioannovsky Gate, and only much later renamed the Trinity Gate. But the date 1741, the year when Ioann's pathetic star shone for a brief moment prior to its extinction, remained chiseled on the gate.

Catherine had been on her Baltic junket since late June, and was enjoying her triumphant progress when a courier from St. Petersburg, covered with dust, was shown into her presence at the ducal palace in Riga. The first urgent message from Alexis Orlov was handed to her during a game of cards. After reading about the events of July 5 at Schluesselburg, she was at first speechless and her pretty hands trembled. As more couriers arrived, from Orlov and Panin, she regained her composure and was able to write to the latter, "Wondrous and mysterious is the Lord's plan. Clearly Providence protects me, having freed me from this burden."

The threatening ghost from the past that dwelt in the Schluesselburg dungeon had been laid to rest.

Now it remained to get to the bottom of the plot. The Empress sent urgent notes to the highest functionaries in the capital, particularly to Panin, demanding further details and issuing near-frantic instructions.

So fragmentary and contradictory were the initial reports pouring into Riga that for a while she thought that Lieutenant Ushakov was alive and under arrest with Mirovich. She ordered Panin to "make sure that Mirovich and Ushakov do not commit suicide. . . . I'm told that Ushakov has quite a few connections with various minor members of my court."

But as certain papers were uncovered at Mirovich's lodgings in the Schluesselburg, and depositions by the rebel soldiers and other participants were taken, they were sent to Catherine, now on her way back to the capital.

The Empress was outraged to learn that on the fateful night, before leading his cohorts into action, Mirovich had found time to address their sleepy ranks with this fiery and treasonous appeal: "In God's name stand up for our lawful sovereign, free him from his vile captivity, and elevate him to the throne usurped by the foreign woman Catherine!" He had followed this perfidious act by reading from the manifesto, in which she, Catherine II, was called a whore, among other things.

When she was given the actual text of the manifesto, Catherine was even further offended to read that "having stolen the throne, she had her own husband poisoned and is now in her weakness living with an ordinary officer named Gregory Orlov, notorious for his vices, and is even preparing to marry him."

She wanted all available information on Vasily Mirovich, and her secret police were quick to forward the Lieutenant's life story to her. His dubious character was amply depicted: a gambler deep in debt, quarrelsome at the card table and elsewhere, a heavy drinker, a schemer with high ambitions but limited intelligence.

Panin, who had observed Mirovich the closest and the longest, described his former employee as "a man with no education whatever, arrogant in his ignorance, and lacking even the capacity to weigh the consequences of his undertaking."

Having learned of this appraisal by Count Peter, his kinswoman Princess Vorontsova-Dashkova maliciously entered in her memoirs that the Empress "in this horrible portrait . . . must have recognized an astonishing resemblance to Gregory Orlov."

The Orlovs kept well informed about the affair, for they intended to use the godsent gift of the Schluesselburg fiasco as the means to settle accounts with some of their enemies. First among them would be the acid-tongued Vorontsova-Dashkova. In his initial message to the Empress at Riga, Alexis Orlov announced that earlier in the summer Mirovich had several times been observed entering a dacha belonging to the Princess, each time early in the morning, and that the Princess should be considered as suspect in the attempted coup.

The summer of 1764, Princess Catherine was ill, as was her little daughter Anastasia, so she took herself, her child, and her son Paul to the estate of one of her numerous kinsmen, Prince Kurakin, at Gatchina, near the capital. She remembered this magnificent villa well, and fondly; two summers before, on Saturday evening, June 29, 1762, the newly triumphant Empress, having deposed Peter III, had rested there with her retinue, and after a relaxing night at the Kurakins' had proceeded to be acclaimed in the capital.

Things were different this summer, two years later. The Kurakins let her have this large and comfortable villa as practically her own, but the Princess lived here in self-imposed solitude, receiving but few visitors and leaving the house rarely, for occasional rides in the lovely countryside on her docile horse. Excitement came only on the days when couriers brought her periodic letters from her husband, Prince Michael Dashkov, who was at the vanguard of the Russian troops entering Poland to seat Stanislas Poniatowski on the throne at Warsaw. The Prince wrote of the fevers from which he was suffering intermittently, but begged his wife not to worry. He was, however, soon to die of them.

So life at Gatchina was tranquil. However, things were happening literally next door, for the Princess had judged the dwelling too large for her needs and placed the larger part of it at the disposal of Panin, whom she called Uncle Peter, since they were related. That summer, petitioners came to his door in a steady stream, and among them was Panin's former aide, Lieutenant Mirovich. Until the very last he was imploring his erstwhile patron to intercede for him and his sisters at the Senate about the estates confiscated from his rebellious grandfather half a century previously. But the Princess never knew him, had never, as she later indignantly protested, "laid my eyes on him."

When he heard about the unjust accusation, Panin hastened to assure both the investigators and the uneasy Catherine that Mirovich had, on his leaves from Schluesselburg, come to see him, Panin, not the Princess.

However, it took some time for the clouds to dispel and for the ruffled Princess to forget the insults to her. The historian Ilovaisky puts it as follows:

> The Princess was no longer harassed, but the very possibility of being under suspicion placed her in an extremely unpleasant situation and caused her increasing alienation from the Empress. And the mistrust of the Empress is not at all surprising. Catherine knew that the Princess was a woman of restless and enterprising character who by the age of nineteen had achieved fame as a skilled conspirator. She could imagine without difficulty that such a woman, considering herself slighted, might seize the first chance to repay her ungrateful friend, thus once again gaining the attention of all Europe.

Foreign writers of the era were fond of linking the name of this dynamic and intelligent young woman with every intrigue that marked the early years of Catherine's reign, basing their suppositions on rumors that at the same time could have had a semblance of truth to them. Again and again the Princess, outraged, denied the accusations. In Ilovaisky's words, "She doubtlessly gave much freedom to her tongue, but in the absence of any clear proof, history has no right to ascribe to her any revolutionary activities, for she understood too well the difference between Peter III and Catherine II."

In her memoirs Princess Catherine writes, "It was sad and pitiable to see the false influence that fogged Catherine's brain to the point where she was ready to suspect genuine patriots and her most loyal friends. When Mirovich was executed, I, not having any reasons to mourn his fate, blessed my own destiny for not having ever seen him. Else his head, in my memory the very first one to fall under the ax in Russia, would have plagued my imagination."

In the early and middle 1760s anonymous anti-Catherine propaganda letters were being surreptitiously left about in the streets and buildings of St. Petersburg and Moscow. Called *podmetnye pis'ma*—secretly dropped or anonymous letters— they were addressed to anyone who would or should be interested. Some of them of course found their way into the hands of the government.

In June 1764, on the day of Catherine's departure for her Baltic provinces, an anonymous and particularly venomous example was found in front of the house of one Antonov, a copying clerk with the Senate. It was delivered to the authorities and eventually to Count Nikita Panin.

Its contents, after the events of July 5, made the Count reflect that there might be a connection between this crude, blustering manifesto and the bungled plot against Catherine. Panin forwarded it to the investigators. It read:

O what is nowadays being done to the people of Russia by this foreign Tsarist rule! They intend to destroy our Russian nation and hurl it into perdition. But no matter how terrible our sufferings, they cannot destroy Russia. They will only lead themselves into the abyss, for the time of our rising is near. We will first of all take Count Zakhar Chernyshev into the torture chamber and will whip him with knouts mercilessly, then quarter him and have his head chopped off. Secondly, the same for Alexis Razumovsky. Thirdly, the same for Gregory Orlov, so that afterward no one will dare violate the rights and laws laid down by our previous Tsars. The Tsarina herself should be sent back to her country. And we must consecrate on the Tsarist throne the pure and innocent Ioann Antonovich, to whom all Russia longs to swear an oath of loyalty with the utmost zeal and faith. All these beasts must be done away with, for they have ruined many men of the military and other classes, who curse and denounce them. And then the salvation of the Russian armed forces will result.

No punctuation graced this clumsy diatribe, but the handwriting appeared to be that of some professional scribe in government service. On the back, in another hand, a laconic comment was scribbled—a brief, humorous folk ditty, followed by the words "'Tis truth itself that is written on this paper."

En route to Panin's office, the document had gone through several readings by citizens who had picked it up, perused it, and dropped it, to be retrieved by others. The author was not discovered despite all the efforts of the authorities.

Mirovich was taken from his cell, shown the treasonous handbill, and asked, "Was it you who ordered the writing and distribution of this?"

Mirovich, confused, denied all knowledge of it. The interrogators urged him to be frank, to confess: "Whose hand is it in? To whom did you delegate its copying and dissemination?"

"I neither wrote the text nor instructed anyone else to write it or distribute it."

The prisoner was cooler, more at ease, when Panin personally questioned him about the Ivan VI conspiracy: "Why did you undertake such as villainous scheme?"

"To be what you have become," Mirovich told him cynically.

Meanwhile the Empress felt compelled to explain to Russia and to Europe the regrettable matter of the murdered Ivan. In her ukase of August 17, 1764, she wrote:

When by the unanimous desire of our loyal people God deigned that We ascend the throne of all the Russias, and We, seeing still alive Prince Ioann, born of Prince Anton Braunschweig-Wolfenbuettel and Princess Anna of Mecklenburg, who for a certain time, as the whole world knows, was in his infancy unlawfully made Emperor of all the Russias, and while still an infant by God's counsel dethroned forever, and the lawful scepter received by the daughter of Peter the Great, our most beloved aunt, the late deceased Empress Elizabeth Petrovna, the very first thing occurring to Us, after rendering praise to God Almighty, was the wish and the thought in Our natural humanity to see to it that this human being, dethroned by God's design, have his lot lightened in his life so circumscribed since infancy. We resolved personally to see this Prince, so as, on ascertaining his spiritual qualities, to assure him of a calm life in accordance with his natural essence and the upbringing as given him by that time. We perceived in him, besides his tongue-tied state so difficult for him to bear and for others to understand, his lack of human mind and sense. All those who were with Us on that visit saw how Our heart ached with Our humane pity. Finally all saw that nothing was left for Us to do for this ill-born and yet more unluckily grown man but to leave him in the same abode in which we had found him under arrest, and to give him all possible humane satisfaction. And this We ordered to be done immediately, though in his state there could be little improvement, for he knew neither people nor any sense, could not differentiate between good and evil, nor could he spend his life in bookreading, for his only pleasure was in his own senseless thoughts. Yet, so that no one for his own ill plans would disturb him or cause a rebellion in society by whatever enterprise, We ordered reliable guard to be maintained, appointed such faithful and honest noblemen-officers as Captain Vlasyev and Lieutenant Chekin . . . to take care of him.

She ordered Nikita Panin to press on with the investigation.

To the original two score of rebels several more soldiers were soon added. The Empress wanted the trial of Mirovich and his men to be held as soon and as publicly as possible. An Assembly of judges was selected from heads of the Collegia, and the Synod members. Not only chiefs but deputy chiefs of the government departments and even generals were to participate. Catherine proclaimed on the subject of Lieutenant Vasily Mirovich that "this malefactor intended to pull me down from the throne of Russia. For that offense against my person I magnanimously forgive him. But insofar as the integrity of the state, and the general welfare and tranquillity are concerned, I am obligated, on the basis of his crime, to hand him over to my loyal Assembly."

She obviously intended to make a Roman holiday of the trial.

A preliminary, lengthier draft of this decree shows how deeply wounded Catherine was by the tone of the attack on her contained in the scurrilous manifesto. In the early draft she wrote that Mirovich had insulted not her, but "the One who by His Godly designs raised me to the throne." Catherine spoke of the difficulty of being the supreme ruler, of tasks accomplished "at what price to me, each and every justice-loving citizen knows." Sadly she reminded her loyal subjects that the plot, had it succeeded, would have brought "calamitous disturbances to our Empire and ill fortune to many of its citizens."

The trial of Mirovich and the soldiers whom he drew into his scheme began on August 23, and a Supreme Council appointed by the Empress for this purpose proclaimed the Assembly's verdict on September 9. Mirovich was to have his head chopped off; his followers were to suffer a variety of savage punishments.

On September 10 the Council decreed: "The scaffold, with its pertinent accessories, shall be erected by the police, who shall be reimbursed by the state treasury. The military unit to attend the execution, as required by the head of the police, shall be detailed by the War Department, while the executioners and their tools shall be provided by the Province of St.

Petersburg. The official proclamation of the crimes to be punished shall be the responsibility of the police."

A huge crowd came to enjoy the execution at the Obzhorny Marketplace in St. Petersburg on September 15, 1764—so many that one of the wooden bridges leading to the market collapsed.

Vasily Mirovich mounted the scaffold calmly and knelt, bowing his head matter-of-factly. The ax fell. A roar, then a sigh rose from the crowd as the executioner, according to custom, raised the severed head to the mob, swinging it a little.

In the evening the scaffold, together with the head and the rest of the corpse, was burned, and the ashes were fired from a cannon.

That same September day, in the same marketplace, six of the Lieutenant's principal co-conspirators ran the gauntlet between two rows of approximately one thousand soldiers wielding cudgels. There were three corporals and three privates. Yakov Piskov, the first infantryman to join the plot, endured the ordeal twelve times; the other five suffered ten times.

One source relates that all of the victims died on the spot, but others say that some survived to pass their lives at hard labor.

But there were other malefactors to be dealt with—forty-one privates who had the poor judgment to follow Mirovich. These unfortunates ran the gauntlet not in the capital but on the Schluesselburg parade grounds. Those who lived went to Siberia to serve in the penal brigade of three newly formed infantry regiments.

For years it was assumed that none of the conspirators survived the terrible punishment, but some documents published in 1966 indicate the contrary.

Catherine generously rewarded those who stood by her. Vlasyev and Chekin were given several hundred thousand rubles each and immediate honorable retirement at full salary. They were enjoined, however, to live discreetly, away from the world, and not to discuss the affair.

For months afterward, all Europe buzzed with the rumor

that Catherine herself had masterminded the conspiracy that ended in Ivan's assassination, that she had bribed Mirovich to stage this ugly farce and then sacrificed him.

Both in Russia and abroad it was widely believed that Mirovich mounted the scaffold so cooly because he was certain that Catherine would follow Elizabeth's practice of arranging mock executions only, of commuting death sentences at the last moment to mutilation and Siberia. In the fact that Catherine decreed the ax to fall, many saw proof that she was guilty, that she had been the Lieutenant's co-conspirator and wished to silence him forever.

In his memorandum of July 20, 1764, to his King, the French chargé d'affaires Béranger wrote, "The suspicion is that the Empress conceived and organized this murder. . . . What a woman this Empress Catherine! And what a theater is Russia. . . ." Jean le Rond d'Alembert commented ironically, "It is most unpleasant when one must get rid of so many people and then write that we are very sorry about it but that it is not our fault."

Some diplomats in St. Petersburg informed their governments that Mirovich had sympathizers among the populace. Count von Sacken, the Saxon-Polish envoy, while relaying to Dresden the news of the August 17 ukase, added that many of the common people prayed for the soul of Mirovich and were bold enough to have priests hold services for him openly, in the squares.

From Paris, Madame Geoffrin wrote to the Empress that she should not have promulgated the ukase, which only added oil to the fire. Like Geoffrin, Voltaire was convinced of Catherine's innocence of Ivan's murder. He blamed her enemies: "This entire Ivan matter was so horribly stupid that one can swear it was carried out by fanatics."

But as time passed, the two crimes were increasingly laid at Catherine's doorstep. In 1770, in her account of her travels in Western Europe, Vorontsova-Dashkova wrote that she was "often compelled to talk of this . . . and defend the Empress from this double slander." On each occasion she voiced her angry amazement that the notables of Europe could believe such absurdities.

# Epilogue

Catherine the Great died at the age of sixty-seven, on November 10, 1796. During her last weeks she had sores on her legs, but the rumor that she died of syphilis was never reliably confirmed. Whether or not she was afflicted with a venereal disease, the cause of death was a stroke.

As for her first three lovers:

Her last encounter with Sergei Saltykov was in the spring of 1755, when Elizabeth sent him as her representative to Hamburg.

He reached that city in early July, dawdling en route, enjoying the hospitality of friends. Among other stopping-off places was Zerbst, where he delivered a letter to Princess Johanna Elizabeth from Catherine wherein she commended him to her mother as one of her closest and most devoted friends. The mother extended a warm welcome to him.

Then, for several years, while he was at his Hamburg post, Johanna Elizabeth used Saltykov to correspond with Catherine

regarding conspiracies against Elizabeth. It was by way of Saltykov that Johanna Elizabeth also kept in contact with Bestuzhev-Ryumin. When, in February 1758, the Chancellor was
arrested and exiled, Saltykov feared that his part in the
Zerbst-Berlin-St. Petersburg connection would be uncovered
by Elizabeth's intelligence officers and that he would be recalled home and punished. He was in a panic upon learning
of Bestuzhev-Ryumin's plight and Catherine's interrogation
and close escape from her aunt's wrath. He sighed in relief
when the storm spared her and completely passed him.

After the coup d'état of 1762, the new Empress remembered her first lover, at least in his Hamburg role, gratefully.
A mere three weeks following her seizure of the throne, in a
ukase of July 22, she appointed him Ambassador to Louis XV,
instructing the Senate to issue the sum of 10,000 rubles for his
moving expenses to Paris.

Saltykov could hardly wait to savor the delights of that
splendid post in the French capital, and both Paris and St.
Petersburg soon heard about his extravagances. Already in
early 1763, the French envoy in Russia reported to Louis that
rumors abounded at Catherine's court about Saltykov's impending dismissal. Doubtless there were enough envious courtiers hovering near her throne who looked forward to his
disgrace.

By then Louis had received numerous complaints about
Saltykov's mounting debts. The French government duly relayed these claims to St. Petersburg.

The Empress acted. In August 1763 she ordered Saltykov's
transfer from Paris: he was to be her representative at Regensburg, the permanent seat of the Diet of the Holy Roman
Empire, where he would replace her envoy, Ivan Simolin, who
was posted to Dresden.

But the French authorities would not permit Saltykov to
leave Paris until he paid up. A long and involved correspondence ensued. Saltykov remained in France one more year
while things were straightened out. At last, drawing on her
personal funds, the Empress sent her debauched former lover
enough money to quiet his creditors and to rescue the splendid Order of St. Catherine, which was languishing in the

pawnshop—the ultimate mark of his decline in the world. On April 4, Saltykov wrote his sovereign an abject letter of thanks.

Then it was revealed that he did not redeem the Order; it was still at the *mont-de-piété*. The money had gone for other purposes, probably for whores, for by then Saltykov's formerly clean features had sagged, and he had difficulty obtaining mistresses gratis. The distressed Catherine sent a note by way of Nikita Panin, in which Saltykov was castigated for his lapse into vice and commanded to redeem the Order without further delay—the state treasury would foot the bill.

When the French authorities were finally willing to allow their now unwelcome Russian guest to leave the country, a new difficulty arose. For some reason Simolin could not go to Dresden; thus Saltykov was not to replace him at Regensburg. In late April 1764, Nikita Panin suggested to the Empress that Simolin remain at Regensburg and Saltykov be sent to Dresden.

Catherine replied, "Has he not by now performed enough of his pranks? Still, if you are willing to vouch for him, send him to Dresden. But he will always be a fifth wheel on the carriage."

Thus ended the saga of Sergei Saltykov. There is no further mention of him in the Imperial archives or elsewhere. We do not know when he returned to Russia, or if he ever returned. There is no record of where or when he died.

The trail of Catherine's second lover is much easier to follow.

Stanislas II Augustus Poniatowski, the last King of Poland, although not elevated to the throne by his own virtues or efforts, did not consider his lofty position as a gift from his former mistress. As Stanislas II, he tried hard to mend the fortunes of Poland and Lithuania. A Lithuanian historian, Constantine Jurgela, generally hostile toward him, concedes that Stanislas was "a well-educated man of gracious manners, intent on improving the situation of the two nations." But the tide of history opposed him: after 1767 Catherine's envoys, particularly Prince Nicholas Repnin, openly and almost contemptuously dominated him. "King Stanislas lacked courage,

energy, and firmness," Jurgela writes. "He submitted to Repnin's will."

And in a few years, Catherine launched her plan to carve
up Poland between herself, Frederick of Prussia, and Maria
Theresa of Austria.

It required a quarter century and three brutal partitions—
1772, 1793, and 1795—and Poland was no more. Poniatowski
ruled as Stanislas II Augustus till the final curtain fell and he
was almost lynched by his outraged subjects.

Frederick, gloating over his first share of the spoils, sent
Catherine his profuse thanks: "God said, let there be light,
and there was light. You speak, and the world is silent before
you."

In 1772, as she signed the first treaty of partition so inge-
niously drawn up by Frederick, Maria Theresa shed tears: "I
sign because so many great and wise men want me to. But a
long time after my death, the world will witness the results of
an act that has gone against all precedent of what is accepted
as sacred and just."

On hearing of her tears, the King of Prussia commented
cynically, "She is always weeping, but always annexing!"

When d'Alembert, by then the French envoy in Berlin,
minced no words in stigmatizing the partition as a violation of
international law and morality, Frederick laughed: "Empress
Catherine and I are a duo of criminals; but, I wonder, how
did the Empress-Queen [Maria Theresa], so full of devotion,
arrange it with her confessor?"

Prior to Catherine's death in 1796 and Stanislas' demise two
years later, this couple who had once lived for each other met
only once. This was on the occasion of Catherine's celebrated
journey of 1787 down the Dnieper to inspect the southern territories wrested from the Turkish yoke. This voyage was im-
mortalized in the history books because of the so-called
Potemkin villages, merely façades, which lined the route, and
the peasants, coached to appear happy, who were transported
down the great stream ahead of the Empress' festive barges.
All this theater was supposed to demonstrate to Her Majesty
and her entourage the successful colonization of the area.
Later researches tended to dispel the theory of fraud by Pot-

emkin as a malicious invention of one of Catherine's guests who hated him.

In any case, the triumphant warrior and statesman, Catherine's favorite lover, stood by her side. Rumor had it that they were secretly married. By her decree he was now Prince Potemkin-Tavrichesky; that is, of the Taurida, as this vast region of the southern Ukraine and the Crimea was then called. She had recently bestowed on him this honorific title in recognition of the military and diplomatic skill that had driven the armies of the Sultan from southern Russia.

Also hovering near Catherine's majestic presence was her latest Adonis, Alexander Mamonov, twenty, present thanks to Potemkin's complaisance. Among the crowned heads that graced that splendid boating party were Emperor Joseph II of Austria, son of the late Maria Theresa, and King Stanislas II Augustus.

In 1787, Catherine was fifty-eight and Stanislas fifty-five. As he looked at her, he beheld not his youthful, demure Sophie of those long-ago white nights of St. Petersburg, but a stout, matronly-looking, regal woman of the world, a dowager whom the ever sharp-tongued Frederick had wittily characterized as a veteran of sin and crime.

Stanislas yearned for the least sign that something remained of their love, but Catherine was pleasantly aloof, receiving the Pole graciously, then dismissing him promptly and categorically.

Soon after the boat trip, Catherine advised Stanislas, through her ambassadors, to marry.

Over the years there had been no lack of willing beauties at his court in Warsaw, and women of titles—Polish, French, Russian, and Austrian—competed for the privilege of climbing into his bed. One of them, his cousin, Princess Elizabeth Czartoryska-Lubomirska, wrote to him that she had been in love with him ever since his boyhood: "You were extremely handsome. . . . I just cannot find words for the feeling I had when I saw you passing. . . ."

The woman he finally did marry, Elizabeth Grabowska, seventeen years his junior, was born into a modest Polish family named Szydlowski. Married to Lieutenant General Jan Grabowski, she was a stunning blonde with pure white skin who immediately aroused His Majesty's passion. When informed of the King's desire, General Jan expressed his humble assent to share his wife with his sovereign.

She bore the King two sons: Michael, born in 1773, and Stanislas, born in 1780. Both were given the name of Grabowski, not Poniatowski, and both made solid careers in the Imperial Russian military and diplomatic services.

The General died in 1784, and within a few years Stanislas married Elizabeth in a church ceremony. The wedding took place in the royal chapel late at night, privately, with the Primate of Poland (Michael, brother of the King) and Elizabeth's brother as the only two witnesses. She was never crowned, and the marriage remained morganatic.

R. Nisbet Bain, a British historian of Polish-French origin, writes of Elizabeth Grabowska, "She was the only sweetheart of Stanislas who was sincerely attached to him. She asked nothing from him either for herself or her friends. She never intrigued or plotted against him. She shared with him both his good and ill fortune and was always ready with salutary and disinterested advice. . . . After his marriage with Grabowska the King led a much more regular life, renounced *les autres petites* and gave himself almost entirely to affairs of state."

Among those earlier "other little ones" Bain named one Elizabeth Rozhanska, a Princess Sapieha, and an actress known as Todi. The actress had "enchanted him with her beautiful voice," and their "usual rendezvous was the studio of the artist Bacciarelli where a great court-lady, Pani Malczewska, used to go through her celebrated 'mythological poses *au naturel.*'"

Of the several Frenchwomen who at one time or another traveled to Poland in pursuit of the King, a certain Marquise de Lulli was the most successful charmer. As Bain writes: "At the age of eighteen she accompanied her aunt to Warsaw and soon acquired such an absolute dominion over the King that she interfered in affairs of state and became a source of emolument and promotion to which many had recourse. She lived in the Krakow suburb, and her equipages and her diamonds were the admiration of the Polish capital. Every penny of the millions, which she banked securely abroad, came out of the King's pocket."

The wily Marquise managed to cling to her influence even after the King's marriage to Grabowska, and well into his sixties. She visited him for a month, from early July to early August of 1795, after Catherine had deposed him and consigned him to a palace in Lithuania.

After the first partition, many Polish officers and soldiers migrated to other countries. Some served in the French forces, others sailed across the ocean to fight for American independence. Kasimir Pulaski organized a cavalry unit under George Washington's command in 1778 and was mortally wounded in an attack on Savannah the next year. The even more famous Thaddeus Kosciusko fought valiantly in the same cause and survived to return to Poland for the last attempt to save his fatherland from the predators that were destroying it.

The *Prince Radziwill,* a schooner owned by Felix Miklaszewicz, was among those raiding British shipping under the letters of marque and reprisal issued by the Continental Congress. Count Michael Grabowski, the youthful son of King Stanislas and Elizabeth Grabowska, joined the 6,000 French regulars who under Count Jean-Baptiste de Rochambeau landed at Newport, Rhode Island, in 1780 to aid Americans, and fought with Washington against the British on the Hudson in 1781.

Fearing the loss of his throne and his country, Stanislas vainly tried to enlist the aid of France, then of England, against Russia and her partners in crime.

Time was running out. Among other mishaps was his choice of an English-language secretary. This was a young American, Lewis Littlepage, for a time known as a protégé of John Hay's. In the 1780s Stanislas, still King, was already an exile in his Lithuanian palace at Grodno (Gardinas). Littlepage, arriving at Grodno in 1784, quickly made what his enemies called "a career in greed."

After winning the King's trust, he was sent on secret missions to Western Europe. In Paris in 1788 Thomas Jefferson frowned upon his countryman's high living and low morals. Littlepage sold his King's favors for cash, which he pocketed. Behind the scenes he was a Russian agent, also for a price. After the King's death, the American adventurer filed a claim against the estate, which was paid in full by the Russian government. He returned to Virginia and died two years later.

During the sad days of exile at Grodno, Stanislas' morganatic wife, Elizabeth, was a ray of sunshine. A French observer, De Poulet, entered in his memoirs that she "played the foremost role . . . everyone respected her; not Poles alone but also Russians preferred her to the King's sisters and nieces." Prince Repnin, officially Catherine's envoy but in reality there to act as the power behind the throne, called on her frequently, as did Russia's Princess Volkonskaya and Countess Panina.

There were numerous uprisings of Polish patriots against their King, whom they considered to be the tool of the Russians, and under this popular pressure Stanislas at long last halfheartedly sided with the rebels. In 1791 he attempted a constitutional reform. In 1794, when Kosciusko led the last uprising against Russia and Prussia, Stanislas threw in his lot with the insurgents. The revolt was crushed and Catherine forced him to abdicate.

Shorn of the last vestiges of power or prestige, he had to remain at Grodno one more year, until Catherine's death. Her son and successor, Paul I, brought him to St. Petersburg, where, in 1798, Stanislas Poniatowski passed away in luxury.

There is reason to believe that Catherine remained the only woman he ever truly loved, from 1755, when they met, to practically the end of the century, when both died, two years apart.

Gregory Orlov remained with Catherine the longest.

Increasingly, it was an ambivalent relationship, particularly toward the end of his life. Malicious tongues at her court and in Western Europe whispered that the Empress, although requiring his services in bed, on occasion also felt the urge to rid herself of his crude person, and even went so far as to occasionally ensure that he was exposed to mortal dangers.

An outstanding instance of this occurred during the late

summer of 1771, when she sent her lover to Moscow to deal with the black plague which had broken out there.

Thousands were dying in Moscow's homes and on the streets, and the survivors were running short of coffins and priests. The dead were tossed into pits, then covered with lime, without proper funeral ceremonies. Friends and loved ones often refused to surrender corpses to burial details unless a mass were said.

Churches were packed with worshipers demanding that priests lead them in public prayer to the Almighty for the cessation of the plague. Mobs collected in the marketplaces to kneel before the icons and stormed monasteries and clergymen's homes in futile entreaties to arrange masses and other services—all this despite orders from authorities to disperse, since the crowds only spread the infection.

The Metropolitan Augustin himself rode to one of the Moscow squares to plead with the hysterical rabble to go home. Enraged, they rushed at the old man, tore off his robes, mauled him, knocked him to the ground, and killed him.

It was at that point that the Empress announced she was dispatching Gregory Orlov to Moscow with orders to calm the populace and see to it that the plague abated.

The court was astonished: Catherine was sending her lover to a certain and inglorious death. Foreign envoys reported to their capitals that Orlov's career—his life, in fact—was finished, and this on Catherine's instructions. It was clear to them that she wanted him out of her life permanently, for in the past she had prohibited him, in spite of his requests, from taking part in dangerous military expeditions. She had wanted him by her side, safe and robust.

Gregory Orlov left for Moscow on October 2, 1771. He returned late in January, exhausted and thin but very much alive, and covered with glory as the man who had personally conquered the Black Death. During those terrible 105 days, with his accustomed vigor, Orlov had led soldiers and police against the howling, half-maddened mobs, scattering them with brutal efficiency. He had rallied the available doctors and made sure there was enough lime for burials, and sufficient medicines. He had visited hospitals and private houses to supervise the removal and burial of the dead, and the burning of their clothing.

Catherine erected triumphal arches to greet his arrival in the capital and praised his extraordinary behavior. She ordered the Imperial mint to strike a gold medal in his honor, inscribed with the words "To the Savior of Moscow." But she showed no emotion toward him.

That winter, sharp-eyed courtiers noticed that Gregory did not appear at her side as frequently as in the past, and that on many nights her bedroom door remained closed to him. The Savior of Moscow could not help but realize that by degrees Catherine was cooling toward him.

For a long time she would not admit this. Occasionally, with a hint of sadness, Catherine would remark to a confidante that Gregory was tiring of her, but the fact was that she was also tiring of him. After twelve years both needed a change. Orlov was now in his late thirties, and her eye began to linger on the younger Guardsmen who graced her court.

In the spring of 1772, she conceived another mission for him. Her war against the Ottoman Empire had been successful, and the Sultan seemed to be ready for terms. The site for the conference was Fokshany, a small Moldavian town that once belonged to the Turks and is now part of Rumania. She named Gregory as her chief negotiator and assigned him high-ranking aides.

Soon Catherine was to write to a woman friend that her "angels of peace" were already at Fokshany, facing "those ugly Turks and their beards," and that surely her Count Gregory Orlov "must really look like an angel compared to those louts." She praised Orlov as being "without exaggeration the handsomest man of his time. His person eclipses everyone around him. He is such a remarkable person, this Ambassador; Nature has been so extraordinarily liberal with him from the point of view of face, mind, heart, and soul!"

She had kind words for his staff, too: they were "brilliant and select." Yet it was in that retinue that Nikita Panin, possibly at her suggestion, had planted his agents, who dutifully reported Orlov's appalling blunders at Fokshany.

Historians have speculated that Orlov's gaucheness and general ineptitude at the peace conference needlessly prolonged the war for two years. He seldom addressed the representatives of the Ottoman Empire in anything but a shout. He outdid them in ostentation, arriving at Fokshany in a gold-trimmed carriage, accompanied by secretaries, aides-de-camp, pages, and servants. He wore Catherine's latest gift: a magnificent court uniform embroidered in real gold. Its buttons were blue diamonds of the first water. He would barely shake the hands extended to him by the dignified Turkish delegates, and behaved as though he were not only the head of the Russian diplomatic team but of Russia itself. His speeches were long-winded and pompous.

High-ranking Russians, especially Field Marshal Peter Rumyantsev, who had defeated the Turks, could not get a word in edgewise. Orlov rudely interrupted him and even on one occasion threatened to hang him "on the nearest aspen tree" if he dared argue with him.

Orlov repeatedly cut short bargaining sessions, preferring to stage glittering receptions and luxurious banquets, claiming that these displays would do more to impress the recalcitrant Turks than tedious negotiations. But the Turks did not react as predicted; instead they rejected every Russian proposal and tried to bypass Orlov, addressing themselves to Rumyantsev.

When Panin learned of all this through his informers and special couriers, he wrote to Orlov that the Empress wished him to let up a bit. In vain. Orlov refused even to read the instructions from his sovereign.

Panin's agents were careful to inform their employer about the orgies that Orlov took part in between bargaining sessions, for Catherine's lover had discovered that in nearby Yassy there were beautiful Moldavian maidens and choice local wines available. To make access to these joys more easy, he transferred the headquarters of his delegation to that town.

Then, Orlov suddenly announced that the negotiations were terminated, and without a word to either Catherine or Panin, packed up and left for St. Petersburg.

He had a good reason for this precipitous step: from his

spies at court he had just learned that Catherine had taken a new lover—the twenty-eight-year-old Alexander Vasilchikov.

Orlov was denied permission to enter the capital. By Catherine's orders he was stopped on the outskirts on the pretext that a quarantine was required since he had come from a disease-ridden province of the Ottoman Empire. Orlov was to remain at the outlying Gatchina palace until further notice.

He was in a jealous rage but had no choice but to obey. Catherine was even more furious, for on the day her lover departed for the botched peace conference, she was given indisputable proof of his gross infidelity. Orlov had, she was informed, enjoyed the favors of a young and beautiful lady-in-waiting, Nelidova. Furthermore, Nelidova was one of her favorites; a close confidante.

Catherine was to write in her memoirs that it was then she decided she "could no longer trust him, a thought that hurt me cruelly and forced me, out of desperation, to take a step which I deplore to this day more than I can say."

Thus began her liaison with Vasilchikov, fifteen years her junior. Again according to her memoirs, Catherine, now forty-three, did not enjoy herself to the extent that his vigorous performance should have warranted: "His caresses provoked nothing in me but tears, and I believe that not since my birth have I cried as much as I did during those eighteen months. At first I thought I would grow accustomed to the situation, but it became worse and worse."

Clearly she missed her Gregory. Yet she would be implacable. She made an effort to feign satisfaction with her new protégé. Moving the young man into her palace, into what used to be Orlov's apartment next to her rooms, she named Vasilchikov her "Aide-de-Camp-in-Chief" (which by then was the well-known euphemism for her bed partner if the affair was of any duration), showered him with lavish gifts, foremost among them a purse of 100,000 rubles, and pinned the most distinguished medals of the empire on his chest.

She wrote Vasilchikov flaming letters of love, but her paramour sensed her pain and aloofness. He also resented her moody possessiveness and later complained to a foreign diplomat that "I was treated as though I were a kept woman." He felt trapped: "I was not allowed to receive any guests nor to absent myself to go any place."

In her mélange of affection and hatred toward her dismissed lover, Catherine began to be afraid of him. She had the locks in the Winter Palace changed, increased the sentinels at every door, and surrounded herself with additional guards. She told her confidantes, "You don't know him. He is capable of killing me."

Gregory Orlov, in his fury and outraged pride, would undoubtedly have murdered the man who replaced him, but it was much more romantic for Catherine to imagine that she and Crown Prince Paul—not her new bedmate—would be the objects of Orlov's thirst for vengeance.

Catherine summoned the courage to send Nikita Panin to Orlov, demanding the immediate return of her gift dating back to their early, happy days: a medallion bearing her portrait, its frame studded with diamonds, which he always proudly wore on his chest in token of their liaison. Vehemently Orlov refused to surrender it. Panin offered a compromise: "Return just the portrait. You may keep the frame with its diamonds."

"No, a thousand times no!"

To Sabatier de Cabre, a French diplomat, the disgraced soldier and courtier mused sadly, "I can live in a simple tavern with no regrets for my former grandeur, but I am pained to see the Empress lower herself to this man, with the ensuing gossip about it all over Europe."

Gradually calm replaced outrage, and he began to solace himself with any and all sorts of women, some brought to him from the streets.

Another French diplomat reported, "Nature created Gregory Orlov a Russian peasant, and this he will remain until the end of his days. . . . He spends from dawn to dusk with his female admirers who live in the palace. He does not leave his rooms, but takes his meals there. The tableware is filthy, the meals are atrocious, but this Prince considers his life to be something splendid. . . . Stupidities amuse him; both his soul and his appetites are satisfied. As he feeds, so does he love, and he is as happy with some Kalmuck or Finnish woman as with a court beauty. In short he is a boor."

Now Catherine stripped him of all the honors she had heaped upon him as well as of his military and political responsibilities. As compensation she gave him a lifetime pension of 150,000 gold rubles per year, an outright gift of 100,000 rubles, and the right to select any estates he wished to make a total of 10,000 serfs. He was accorded the right to inhabit any palace in the empire except in the capital. But, relenting even in this matter, Catherine allotted him the Marble Palace, then under construction in the capital, with all its furniture and furnishings. For the time being, however, he had to leave Russia. For how long, she did not say.

He promised to go. At Christmastime in 1772 she primly received him to bid him a formal bon voyage. He left in January 1773, but went no further than Reval, on Russia's Baltic shores, and in March returned to St. Petersburg.

The Empress received him again, benevolently but coldly. On May 21 she restored all his former ranks and posts and presented him, out of her personal collections, with a superb set of Sèvres porcelain for which she had paid 250,000 gold rubles. But never again would she admit him to her bed.

In appreciation of her magnanimity, and in memory of their love, on the occasion of Catherine's saint's day, November 24, 1773, Gregory presented her with the fabled diamond then known as the Nadir Shah Stone. Two hundred carats after its initial cutting and polishing, it was azure-blue and of unprecedented beauty and sparkle.

The gem was discovered in India's famed Golconda fields, in Andra Pradesh, in the early seventeenth century. During the course of that century, a Mogul ruler ordered it to be recut, which reduced its size somewhat but increased its brilliance. In 1737 Persia's Nadir Shah, upon capturing Delhi, appropriated its riches, the great diamond not the least of them.

The stone was then stolen by a daring thief. Implanted into his leg, it was carried for thousands of miles across India, Persia, the Caucasian mountains and the Russian steppes, and thus brought to St. Petersburg. An Armenian merchant showed the diamond to Orlov, who promptly paid 460,000 gold rubles for it.

Delighted with the gift, the Empress had it mounted at the tip of her golden scepter, in close proximity to the double-headed Imperial eagle of black enamel, to remind posterity that in 1762 a Guards Captain and his brothers had elevated her to the throne of all the Russias. Today in the Soviet state treasury in Moscow, it is known to the world as the Orlov Diamond.

By 1774, Alexander Vasilchikov, proving to be merely a short-term lover, was slowly but irrevocably being edged out of Catherine's bed and life.

A far more gifted, though older, Guards officer replaced him. This was Gregory Potemkin, then thirty-five, known to Catherine since 1762 and his participation in the coup. For a while she and Potemkin played a transparent comedy of conducting their liaison behind Vasilchikov's back, but finally she wrote Gregory a note: "Tell Panin that he should send Vasilchikov away to take a cure somewhere. His presence upsets me a great deal, and at the same time he complains about pains in the chest. After his cure we will send him as ambassador somewhere where there is not much work to do. He is a nuisance and a bore."

Potemkin was to remain at Catherine's side, not only as a lover and possibly even a secret husband, wed in a church, but also as her trusted statesman, until his death in 1791.

Orlov left for Europe in early 1775, and for years was intermittently seen in Italy, Austria, England, and elsewhere. Still ambitious, he schemed from afar to ruin Potemkin. In 1780, he encountered Vorontsova-Dashkova and her son Paul in their foreign travels and annoyed her by insisting that the boy be returned to Russia at once. Paul would oust Potemkin, then become Her Majesty's latest and youngest Aide-de-Camp-in-Chief, meaning of course Catherine's lover. Indignantly the Princess turned her back on this suggestion and took Paul away.

In 1777, rather late in the season, there came into Gregory Orlov's life one final passion. At the age of forty-three he fell in love with his fifteen-year-old cousin, Catherine Zinovyeva, daughter of Nicholas Zinovyev, Senior Commandant of the city of St. Petersburg.

Fresh at court, only recently appointed a lady-in-waiting, this comely girl, like so many others, responded to Gregory's advances with enthusiasm. They became lovers and spoke of marriage. However, the Orthodox Church was strict about what they considered to be incest—no marriage between cousins. The Holy Synod declined Orlov's request.

But a country priest, tempted by a considerable sum, performed the ceremony. A storm was raised, not only by the Synod but by the Senate as well, until the Empress stepped in and told the Synod to ignore canonic law and approve the marriage. She added her special blessing by promoting the bride to a higher position at court and bestowing the coveted Order of St. Catherine upon her. Neither the Synod nor the Senate opposed her.

But Orlov's young wife soon fell ill with tuberculosis, and her doctors ordered her to go to Switzerland, where she died in 1782. Orlov's enemies whispered that he was to blame—his insatiable carnal demands had driven the poor woman to exhaustion, illness, and death.

His wife's death destroyed Orlov. He took to his bed, and deep depression soon turned into insanity.

It was rumored that the Empress visited him in his St. Petersburg palace during the last stages of his agony, sitting long hours by his bedside. If so, it is doubtful that he recognized her or anyone else.

In November 1782, Alexis Orlov and the other brothers transported the pitiful wreck to his palace in Moscow. There, on April 13, 1783, the Metropolitan Platon came to hear his last confession, which, however, proved impossible. The celebrated man of God administered the last rites a few minutes before Gregory's death. He was forty-nine years old.

Catherine's principal lovers total up to an even dozen. They are listed here with their birth and death dates, but it is impossible to determine with any degree of accuracy the periods during which they enjoyed her favors.

1. Sergei Vasilievich Saltykov, 1726–17—
2. Count Stanislas Augustus Poniatowski, 1732–1798.
3. Prince Gregory Gregorievich Orlov, 1734–1783.
4. Alexander Semyonovich Vasilchikov, 1744–1803.
5. Prince Gregory Alexandrovich Potemkin-Tavrichesky, 1739–1791.
6. Count Peter Vasilievich Zavadovsky, 1739–1812.
7. Semyon Gavrilovich Zorich, 1745–1799.
8. Ivan Nikolaievich Rimsky-Korsakov, 1754–1831.
9. Alexander Dmitrievich Lanskoy, 1758–1784.
10. Alexander Petrovich Yermolov, 1754–1834.
11. Count Alexander Matveievich Dmitriyev-Mamonov, 1758–1803.
12. Prince Platon Alexandrovich Zubov, 1767–1822.

The intensity of her attachment to these men varied greatly. The liaison with Potemkin was the most enduring, and possibly included morganatic marriage, for the couple recognized each other's talents and got on very well together. In addition to his services in the regal bed, Potemkin fought the Empress' battles, both on the military and the diplomatic fronts, and helped her to achieve her ambitions of expanding the Russian empire.

In realizing that his sexual appeal to Catherine was waning, and in finding handsome young replacements for her, Potemkin once again demonstrated his superior foresight and discretion. This remarkable couple enjoyed for years a warm relationship totally free from jealousy or interference. The Empress and her esteemed friend must have compared notes about their savory adventures and laughed heartily. Potemkin had many wondrous tales to tell, including the famous episode when he took to bed all five of his young nieces, the daughters of his younger sister Maria Engelhardt, one after the other and sometimes simultaneously, for the quintet was madly in love with their illustrious uncle.

Among the men whom Potemkin sent to her, Catherine favored one, Alexander Lanskoy, with a special tenderness. Lanskoy died at twenty-six, literally in her arms, and she wept deeply felt tears over him. Of his death in 1784 she wrote to

Baron Melchior von Grimm that it left her in a state of desperate prostration. And when in 1796 she herself was dying, she parted from her very last lover, the nineteen-year-old Prince Platon Zubov, with profound affection and regret. At sixty-seven she could easily have been his grandmother.

In her rich and tumultous bedroom career Catherine dismissed four—Vasilchikov, Zavadovsky, Zorich, and Yermolov—quite casually because their mediocrity bored her early on. Two lovers—Rimsky-Korsakov and Dmitriyev-Mamonov—were sent packing because, like Gregory Orlov, they were found to be sleeping with other women.

In addition to the twelve, there were numerous casual affairs, but these usually took place when Catherine was not involved with one of her preferred lovers or when she knew that she was being betrayed.

During her long rule, and for nearly two centuries afterward, scabrous stories circulated concerning Catherine's phenomenal erotic life, and her entire adult existence was depicted as being an uninterrupted lascivious epic. The few historians who have recognized her political abilities have halfheartedly tried to play down these tales.

There is no doubt that they were grossly exaggerated. For example, well into the twentieth century not a few aristocratic Russian clans had their proud family legends of a strapping young ancestor who was invited into Catherine's capacious bed. Had all these stories been authentic, there would not have been enough nights or idle afternoons during Catherine's reign to account for the number of offspring thus engendered.

On the other hand, though not as promiscuous as her aunt, Empress Elizabeth, there is no question that Catherine II was known to give free rein to her appetites. And some of the men who passed through her bedroom were indeed remarkable: John Paul Jones in his reminiscences boasts of sleeping with Catherine and even adds that both had syphilis at the time and helped each other with their attempts to cure it.

There is a colorful if somewhat less reliable tale that appears from time to time in historical documents, claiming that two of Catherine's confidantes were known discreetly at court as *les épreuveuses*—the testers. These were Anna Protasova, known as "the Queen of Golconda," and the chambermaid, Maria Perekusikhina. They were, according to gossip, assigned to test candidates for Catherine's bed, and their sovereign depended on their assessments of the candidate's skill and stamina. If the reports were favorable, the man was received in the royal bed.

Sympathetic biographers, in their attempts to justify Catherine's frequent need to change partners, have speculated that this was not so much owing to any innate promiscuousness as to her early disappointment with her inadequate husband, Peter. They maintain that this ugly experience marked her for life, causing her to seek not only a lover but a mate on whom she could depend while bearing the enormous responsibilities of administering and expanding an empire. During those innumerable nights she was seeking a husband, but found only male animals, primitive, uncultivated, and incapable of satisfying her spiritual, intellectual, or emotional needs. This was the intimate tragedy behind the façade of power.

The closest to an ideal man in Catherine's life was Poniatowski, then Potemkin. But the former was a Pole, a foreigner unacceptable to nationalistic Russia, and in time he turned out to be shallow. The latter was too much like her in his need for variety. The early experiences of Catherine and Potemkin spoiled them for monogamy.

That is, if Catherine the Great ever indeed prized monogamy.

The ghost of Peter III would not be stilled. In September 1773, while Catherine's best troops were off fighting the Turks, a daring Cossack of the Don, Yemelian Pugachev, declared himself to be her husband, Emperor Pyotr Fyodorovich Romanov.

The pretender said that eleven years previously he had escaped from the men who had tried to kill him. He now was at the head of fierce hordes of escaped serfs, Cossacks, Tatars, Bashkirs, and other malcontents sworn to punish the faithless German seated on the throne of Russia.

This imposter, an illiterate veteran of wars against Prussia, Turkey, and Poland, was as volatile and fearless as he was shrewd. He did not at all resemble the murdered Emperor, but this was no problem, for Pugachev promised liberty and loot to all who would follow him.

The Pugachev Rebellion began in the Urals and went on to capture one Imperial fortress after the other in the Volga steppes. Important cities such as Kazan, Penza, and Saratov soon fell.

Outnumbered loyal units that stood in his path surrendered or fled. Captured officers were executed, as were clergymen and members of the aristocracy. Entire families were hanged from the gates of their mansions, parents and children strung up in orderly rows according to age.

Foreigners or even Russians in Western dress were murdered. A German botanist was surprised while peacefully collecting specimens. He was promptly stripped and impaled.

In 1773 and 1774, the Russian earth seemed to shake. Some were convinced that Moscow was threatened and St. Petersburg would then fall. Catherine's reign seemed to be tottering.

But in 1774, the war with Turkey finally ended, and first-line troops were freed for action against the rebels. In a series of bloody engagements Pugachev's ragtag army was crushed. His own Cossacks, dispirited by the defeat, jumped him, tied him up, and delivered him to Catherine's generals. He was taken to Moscow in a cage, tortured, and, on January 10, 1775, executed.

All over the Eastern territories his panic-stricken followers were hunted down, knouted, and branded. Tongues, noses, and ears were hacked off, and the worst offenders were hanged on gallows erected on rafts, which were then sent floating down the Volga and other rivers as an object lesson for the cowering survivors.

About the same time, another claimant to the throne appeared—a young woman who recalled the epoch and the sins of Catherine's aunt. Calling herself Princess Elizabeth Tarakanova, she traveled from one European capital to the other, declaring herself to be the daughter of Empress Elizabeth by her Night Emperor, Alexis Razumovsky, and the only legitimate heir to the Romanov throne.

The year 1774 was the high point of Tarakanova's bid for power, for she apparently had won support in Poland and elsewhere in Western Europe. But the victorious end of Catherine's campaigns against the Turks on one front and Pugachev on another freed her to deal with her new enemy. In November of that year she instructed Alexis Orlov, then with the navy in the Mediterranean, to use his wiles to entrap the attractive young woman.

Alexis carried out his orders with consummate skill. He managed to meet the woman, turned on his considerable charm, told her he loved her. In Italy he enticed her onto a Russian man-o'-war, where a cleverly faked Orthodox marriage ceremony was performed. The ship then set sail for Russia along with the "bride."

From her dungeon in the Peter and Paul Fortress, the pretender wrote piteous letters to Catherine, begging in vain for mercy. She died on December 4, 1775, of consumption, not drowned in her cell by the rising Neva floodwaters as a popular legend and a celebrated Russian painting would have it. Her real origin and name remain a mystery to this day.

And there were Catherine's increasing problems with her son, Crown Prince Paul.

While Elizabeth lived and reigned, it was she, not his mother, who saw to Paul's upbringing, away from Catherine. For too long he was smothered by fond but ignorant and superstitious nurses. His early childhood was filled with frightening fables and ugly fairy tales; he became afraid of his own shadow.

When Elizabeth recalled Nikita Panin from his ambassadorial post in Sweden to take charge of Paul, the suave diplomat did his best to straighten the boy out, but the damage was already done. His dread of the world was exacerbated when his father, whom he worshiped, was deposed and assassinated. Paul was then nearly eight.

He first disliked, then positively hated, the powerful, devious woman who happened to be his mother, and deeply resented her lovers, particularly Gregory Orlov, whose role he understood from early on. In 1762 he knew that the Orlovs were behind his father's dethronement and death, and was equally certain that they had acted on his mother's instructions. In short, he regarded his mother as his father's murderess. This conviction remained with him until Catherine's death, when Alexis Orlov's frantic note was found in her papers, proving Catherine's innocence of the crime.

As he had adored his father before that fateful summer of 1762, so he continued to revere his memory forever afterward. The boy resembled Peter III in appearance and temperament. During his adolescence he seemed to his mother the very picture of Peter when she first met him upon her arrival in Russia. Paul even walked with the same nervous, half-bouncing gait, as though propelled by a pair of springs concealed in his spindly legs. He was devoted to playing at soldiers, and his outbursts of hysterical anger were similar to those of his father's.

It was as though Peter III had risen from the tomb.

During the last few years of her life, Catherine was alarmed by her son. By no means a liberal, the Crown Prince nonetheless favored certain changes, and submitted to his mother a memorandum in which she seemed to read evidence of his wish to undo much of her empire-building and to cast aspersions on or even nullify the achievements of Peter the Great.

Catherine increased the distance between herself and Paul, and turned her attention and affections toward his two young sons, Alexander and Constantine. She was in the process of drafting a ukase in which she would disallow Paul's claim to the throne in favor of Alexander when her stroke of November 1796 cut her short.

Thus did Paul become Emperor. He was forty-two, and full of a lifetime's pent-up hatred and energy.

He proceeded at once to punish all the surviving favorites of his late mother and to befriend those whom she had slighted or persecuted.

On December 4, a high official came to the sickbed of Princess Vorontsova-Dashkova in her Moscow mansion. In a low voice he announced, "You are to leave for one of your estates in the provinces, there to reflect on the events of 1762."

Young Platon Zubov, Catherine's last lover, was banished abroad for an indefinite term. Gregory Potemkin, dead since 1791, was disinterred from his splendid tomb at the St. Catherine Church in the Black Sea port of Kherson and his bones contemptuously scattered.

The most bizarre example of Paul's retribution was the glorification of his murdered father's skeleton. A few days after his mother's death, the new Emperor united Catherine II and Peter III. By Paul's instructions, his father's bones were lifted out of their tomb at the Alexander Nevsky Monastery, where they had rested for over three decades. The skeleton was then ceremoniously carried the length of the Nevsky Prospect to the Winter Palace and there placed by Catherine's body. A banner was hoisted above the two coffins: DIVIDED IN LIFE, JOINED IN DEATH.

The grandees and foreign diplomats at court were commanded by the new Emperor to pay homage to both his parents, now lying in state among the great columns of the palace.

He then ordered a double funeral. The bodies, in a slow, solemn cadence, were brought to the Cathedral of Saint Peter and Saint Paul.

The Emperor was imaginative and malicious in his revenge. By his decree, the aged, humbled, and fearful Alexis Orlov headed the macabre procession on that subzero day. In his arms was the old crown of Peter III, resting on a cushion. Two other men responsible for his father's undoing, Baryatinsky and Passek, were publicly humiliated by being forced to act as the pallbearers of their victim.

Emperor Paul I, head high, face stony, marched immediately behind the coffins, followed by his wife, Empress Maria, with the Grand Dukes and the highest court dignitaries.

No liberal, Paul nonetheless recalled a noted dissident from Siberia and released a prominent Freemason-writer from a Schluesselburg dungeon because they had suffered under

Catherine's decrees. He made a special visit to Kosciusko, living under guard at the Marble Palace, presented the courageous Pole with gifts, and allowed him to return to America. Other Polish captives of the late Empress were also liberated. Paul said to one of them, "You have suffered greatly; you have been mistreated for a long time. But under the preceding reign all honest men were persecuted, myself first of all."

One of Catherine's former lovers was not only spared but honored and pampered—Stanislas Poniatowski, whom Paul promptly invited back from his exile at Grodno to a pleasant existence at St. Petersburg. Paul did this for two reasons. First, because his mother had dealt harshly with the Pole, but also because, decades earlier, when Crown Prince Paul and his wife were touring Western Europe, King Stanislas II had given them a truly royal reception at the court of Warsaw. In his luxurious quarters in St. Petersburg, Catherine's second lover breathed his last in 1798, a contented man.

Paul detested everything Western that his mother had loved and fostered, and his wars against France and England were coupled with an adulation of Prussia that reflected the spirit of Peter III. Once again his soldiers were squeezed into tight uniforms, and harsh discipline and endless drilling were the order of the day. It was said that at one parade, incensed by what he considered laxness, he barked out: "To Siberia, march!" The regiment forthwith began to plod eastward, to be halted and recalled several days later, when Paul's anger had finally abated.

In 1800 the Emperor ordered a unit of Cossacks to cross the wastes of Asia and wrest India from the British. But the expeditionary force was given neither adequate provisions nor even usable maps. It was a mad undertaking dreamed up by a half-mad tyrant.

The Cossacks would most likely have perished miserably en route had not fortune intervened. On a March night in 1801, Emperor Paul was strangled behind a screen in his bedroom where vainly he had tried to hide. The assassins were a cabal of high courtiers who had, if not the aid, then the mute consent of his son, Crown Prince Alexander. When mounting the throne as Alexander I, he promptly signed a ukase recalling the Cossacks.

Unlike the embittered Paul, Alexander I and his successors, down to the 1917 Revolution, revered the memory of Catherine the Great, and, following in the footsteps of the Romanovs, Russian historians loyal to the monarchy insist that posterity also bend its collective knee before the memory of this extraordinary autocrat. She must never, they say, be referred to merely as Catherine II, but must be known as Catherine the Great. In their opinion Catherine was not sexually unbalanced, but was a woman who was given the almost unique opportunity to live out in reality the suppressed fantasies of many ordinary women. The difference was of course that she was in no way ordinary.

The historians who side with Catherine write that her efforts resulted in the creation of a vast empire, and that it was she, more than Peter the Great, who was responsible for this achievement. For this, an intellect capable of decisiveness and able to read the minds of those surrounding her as well as to judge events distant in time and space was needed. According to them, discussions of her sex life are superfluous.

Her defenders concede that she committed criminal acts, the most notorious being the partitions of Poland. But they point to her cultivation, linguistic ability, and knowledge of literature, philosophy, and even some science, and the balance tilts in her favor.

Prominent foreigners were frequently awed by Catherine. Voltaire, as a rule no friend of crowned heads, said of her, "Catherine surpasses all the other monarchs of Russia. . . . She changed the eighteenth century into a golden age."

Maurice Paléologue, a member of the Academie Française, was the last French Ambassador to live in Russia prior to the Revolution, and knew that country and its people well. He compared Catherine favorably with the most brilliant of French kings, Louis XIV:

Catherine, who was even bolder, lacked neither common

sense nor perspicacity, and that is why she was able to accomplish her huge task. By her internal policies she constructed the durable scaffolding that upheld the Tsarist regime for over a century. In her foreign policy she superbly carried on the projects initiated by Peter the Great. She dealt a death blow to the power of the Ottomans in Europe. She conquered the Crimea, the shores of the Black Sea, and two-thirds of Poland. Finally, she implanted in the Russian soul a splendid and enduring dream, one that recurs by fits and starts—the yearning for Constantinople. . . . In the course of modern history, there have been few such strong and original personalities. Few have been gifted with such energy, captivating charm, and luminous brilliancy as Catherine the Great.

There have been numerous dissenting voices, particularly among Western scholars. Professor Robert R. Palmer of Princeton University writes that Catherine's stature has been exaggerated, that in spite of her grandiloquent phrases in letters to Voltaire and others, she was no social reformer, and her much praised sublime literary style was little more than verbal dexterity, although many were impressed by it. This *soi-disant* liberal, remember, extended serfdom in her domains.

And not all Tsarist historians joined the chorus of praise for Catherine. The eminent Vasily Klyuchevsky was sharply critical, and Lev Tolstoy refers to her angrily as "that sinful, narrow, evil-hearted woman."

Even Catherine's admirers concede that her methods were out of the pages of Machiavelli—but one can easily ask what man or woman seated on a throne in the Europe of those days could survive without guile and treachery? Catherine was a harsh and adroit practitioner of absolutism, but that was *de rigueur,* with the possible exception of some English and Scandinavian rulers. Catherine tolerated, indeed encouraged serfdom, but what choice did she have, since the serf-owning aristocrats had raised her to the throne and were her mainstay there? Had she tried to undermine them, they would have made short shrift of her.

The world was, and remains today, more fascinated by

Catherine the Great's sex life than by her statecraft. But it is impossible to differentiate clearly between the two, for her sexual dynamism was an integral part of her political genius. So often geniuses are cursed with extraordinary sensuousness, which they usually try to keep hidden. The singularity of Catherine the Great was that she seldom, if ever, tried to conceal her carnality.

# Bibliography

*Primary Sources*

Catherine's memoirs were the chief primary source for this bibliography. They were written in French and published in Russia for the first time in 1907 by the Imperial Academy of Sciences, in the original, with a Russian translation. The editor was A. N. Pypin, a member of the Academy. The memoirs are complete except for a section in which she claims that her son, the future Paul I, was the issue not of her husband Peter, but of Saltykov. This deletion was ordered by Nicholas II when he authorized the publication.

*Sochineniya Imperatritsy Yekateriny Vtoroi* [The Works of Empress Catherine II], ed. by A. N. Pypin. St. Petersburg: Academy of Sciences, Vol. XII, 1907, *Avtobiograficheskiya zapiski* [Autobiographical Memoirs], in French and Russian.

Various editions of the memoirs have been published outside of Russia. Chronologically they are:

*Mémoires de l'impératrice Catherine II. écrits par elle-même, et pré-cedés d'une préface par Alexandre Herzen.* London: N. Trübner & cie, 1859. The second edition of this book, by the same publisher in the same year, has this addition to the title: . . . *augmentée de huit lettres de Pierre III.*

*Memoirs of the Empress Catherine II., Written by Herself, with a Preface by A. Herzen.* Translated from the French. London: Trübner & Co., 1859.

*Zapiski Yekateriny II, imperatritsy Rossii.* Translated from the French. Leipzig: E. L. Kasprowicz, 1876 (second edition).

*Errinerungen der kaiserin Katharina II. von ihr selbst geschrieben; nach Alexander Herzen ausgabe neu hrsg. von G. Kuntze. Mit mehreren portraits und einem Nachtrag aus den Errinerungen der Fuerstin Daschkoff.* Stuttgart: R. Lutz, 1908 (seventh edition).

*La jeunesse de la grande Catherine; souvenirs autobiographiques de l'impératrice, annotés d'après les documents d'archives et les Mém-oires. Illustrations documentaires.* Paris: L. Michaud, 1910.

*Memoirs of Catherine the Great.* Translated by Katherine Anthony. New York and London: Alfred A. Knopf, 1927.

*Mémoires de Catherine II, écrits par elle-même. Texte établi et prés-enté par Dominique Maroger. Introduction de Pierre Audiat.* Paris: Hachette, 1935.

*The Memoirs of Catherine the Great.* Edited by Dominique Maroger with an introduction by G. P. Gooch; translated from the French by Moura Budberg. London: H. Hamilton, 1955; New York: Macmillan, 1955, and Collier Books, 1961.

*The Memoirs of Catherine the Great. With the Preface to the First Edition (1859), by Alexander Herzen.* Translated, with foreword and epilogue, by Lowell Bair. New York: Bantam Books, 1957.

*Avtobiograficheskiya zapiski. Na osnovanii podlinnykh rukopisei i s ob'iasnitel'nymi primechaniyami A. N. Pypina* [Autobiographical Memoirs. Based on Authentic Manuscripts and with Explanatory Notes by A. N. Pypin]. As published in St. Petersburg by the Imperial Academy of Sciences in 1907 and reprinted in Cyrillic characters in Osnabrück, West Germany: Biblio Verlag, 1967.

LETTERS

Buckinghamshire, John, Earl. *The Despatches and Correspondence of John, Second Earl of Buckinghamshire, Ambassador to the Court of Catherine II, of Russia 1762-1765.* Edited by A. D. Collyer. London: Longmans, Green & Co. Volume I, 1900, for the period from September 1762 to the end of February 1763.

*Correspondance artistique [avec Grimm].* Edited by Louis Réau. *Archives de l'Art français.* Paris: Nouvelle période, 1932, vol. 17, pp. 1-206.

*Correspondance inédite du roi Stanislas-Auguste Poniatowski et de Madame Geoffrin (1764–1777), précédée d'une étude sur Stanislas-Auguste et Madame Geoffrin et accompagnée de nombreuses notes par M. Charles de Mouÿ, ouvrage orné d'un portrait a l'eau forte de deux fac-similes.* Paris: E. Plon et cie, 1875.

*Documents of Catherine the Great: The Correspondence with Voltaire and the Instruction of 1767; in the English text of 1768.* Edited by W. F. Reddaway. Cambridge, England: the University Press, 1931; and New York: Russell & Russell, 1971.

*Filosoficheskaya i politicheskaya perepiska imperatritsy Yekateriny II s g. Volterom. S 1763 po 1778 g. Perevod s frantsuzskago* [Philosophical and Political Correspondence of Empress Catherine II with M. Voltaire. From 1763 to 1778. Translated from the French]. St. Petersburg: Imperial Printery, 1802. A more complete edition is by the Senate Printery, also 1802. Translated by Mikhail Antonovsky.

Grimm, Friedrich Melchior, Freiherr von. *Lettres de Catherine II à Grimm.* (In French and Russian.) St. Petersburg: I. Grot, 1878.

Larivière, Charles de. *Cathérine la Grande d'après sa correspondance: Cathérine II et la Revolution française d'après de nouveaux documents; avec preface de A. Rambaud.* Paris: H. Le Soudier, 1895.

*Lettres d'amour de Catherine II à Potemkine.* Edited by Georges Oudard. Paris: Calmann-Lévy, 1934. Introduction and notes by Oudard.

*Lettres de Catherine II à Stanislas-Auguste Poniatowski, roi de Pologne (1762-1764).* Paris: n.p., 1914.

*Les lettres de Catherine II au prince de Ligne (1780-1796) publiées avec quelques notes par la princess Charles de Ligne.* Brussels and Paris: G. van Oest & cie, 1924.

*Lettres de Grimm à l'impératrice Catherine II, publiées sous les auspices de la Société impériale d'histoire russe, par Jacques Grot.* St. Petersburg: Imperial Academy of Sciences Printery, 1886.

*Lettres inédites du prince de Ligne à Catherine II. Revue Européenne,* Paris, August 1923, vol. I, pp. 1–8.

Ligne, Charles Joseph, Prince de. *Letters and Reflections of the Austrian Field-Marshal Prince de Ligne. Edited by the Baroness Staël-Holstein, Containing Anecdotes Hitherto Unpublished of Joseph II, Catherine II, Frederick the Great, Rousseau, Voltaire and Others* . . . Translated from the French by D. Boileau. Philadelphia: Bradford & Inskeep, 1809. Two volumes in one.

*Pis'ma i zapiski Imperitritsy Yekateriny Vtoroi k grafu Nikite Ivanovichu Paninu* [Letters and Notes of Empress Catherine II to Count Nikita Ivanovich Panin]. Moscow: University Printery, 1863.

*Pis'ma k datskoi koroleve Yuliane Marii* [Letters to Queen Juliane Maria of Denmark]. The original French is accompanied by a Russian translation and a summary in Danish. Copenhagen: I. Frimodt, 1914.

*Les plus belles lettres de Catherine II, présentées par Georges Oudard.* Paris: Calmann-Lévy, 1962.

Williams, Sir Charles Hanbury. *Correspondence of Catherine*

*the Great Whęn Grand-Duchess, with Sir Charles Hanbury-Williams,
and Letters from Count Poniatowski.* Edited and translated by the
Earl of Ilchester and Mrs. Langford-Brooke. London: T. Butterworth, Ltd., 1928.

MEMOIRS

Allonville, Armand François, Comte d'. *Mémoires secrets de
1770 à 1830.* Paris: Werdet, 1838-1845. Six volumes.

Choiseul Stainville, Etienne François, Duc de. *Mémoires de m.
le duc Choiseul . . . écrit par lui-même, et imprimés sous ses yeux,
dans son cabinet, à Chanteloup, en 1778 . . .* Chanteloup and
Paris: F. Buisson, 1790. Two volumes.

Dashkova, Catherine, Princess (née Countess Vorontsova).
*Memoirs of the Princess Daschkaw, Lady of Honour to Catherine II.
. . . Written by Herself; Comprising Letters of the Empress, and Other
Correspondence. Edited from the Originals, by Mrs. W. Bradford.*
London: H. Colburn, 1840. Two volumes.
A German version of these Memoirs appeared in 1857, a
second English edition in 1858, and a Russian translation was
issued by Alexander Herzen in 1859 as: *Zapiski kniagni Ye. R.
Dashkovoi pisannyia eyyu samoi. Perevod s Angliyakago yazyka*
[Memoirs . . . written by herself. Translation from the English
language]. London: Trübner & Co., 1859. The common sup-
position has been that both the German and Russian editions
were translations from the French, but Dr. Robert V. Allen of
the Library of Congress says, "As best I can tell, these were all
based on the 1840 English version." The 1859 French edition
is clearly indicated as a translation from the English, as
follows:
*Mémoires de la princesse Daschkoff, dame d'honneur de Catherine
II . . . écrits par elle-même, avec la correspondance de cette impératrice et d'autres lettres. Pub. sur le manuscript original par Mistress
W. Bradford. Tr. de l'anglais par M. Alfred Des Essarts.* Paris: A.
Franck, 1859. Four volumes in two.
Another Russian edition was issued by E. L. Kasparovich in
Leipzig in the late 1850s (exact date not known), possibly

based on the Herzen version: *Vospominaniya knyagini E. R. Dashkovoi* [Memoirs of Princess E. R. Dashkova]. It reached its third edition in 1876.

All the Dashkova memoirs appeared outside Russia as translations from the French, and in the case of the Paris edition of 1859 as a translation by Des Essarts from the English version of the French original. Dr. Allen of the Library of Congress suggests, "Since the Vorontsova-Dashkova memoirs were originally written in French, it is the text in the latter language that would be the guiding one. According to N. D. Chechulin's article on the Princess in the *Russky biographichesky slovar'*, it was not until the French manuscript was published in volume 21 of *Arkhiv kniazia M. L. Vorontsova* (Moscow, 1870-1895) that the original was made available."

The best and most complete version of the Vorontsova-Dashkova memoirs is *Zapiski . . .* , edited by N. D. Chachulin, St. Petersburg; published by A. S. Suvorin, 1907. The most recent French and English translations are:

Dachkov, Princesse Catherine. *Mémoires.* Paris: Mercure de France, 1966.

*The Memoirs of Princess Dashkov (1743-1810).* Translated and edited by Kyril Fitzlyon. London: J. Calder, 1958.

Esterhazy de Galantha, Valentin Ladislas, Comte. *Mémoires du Comte Valentin Esterhazy, avec une introduction et des notes, par Ernest Daudet.* Paris: Plon-Nourrit et cie, 1905.

Frederick II the Great, King of Prussia. *Mémoires de Frédéric II, roi de Prusse, écrits en français par lui-même; publiés conformément aux manuscrits originaux conservés du cabinet à Berlin, avec des notes et des tables par MM. E. Boutarie et E. Campardon.* Paris: H. Plon, 1866. Two volumes.

Golovine, Varvara N., Comtesse (née Golitzine). *Souvenirs.* Paris: Plon, 1910. Also in English: Memoirs of *Countess Golovine, a Lady at the Court of Catherine II.* Translated from the French by G. M. Fox-Davies. Edited by K. Waliszewski. London: D. Nutt, 1910.

Helbig, Georg Adolf Wilhelm, von. *Russiche Günstlinge.* Tübingen: J. G. Cotta, bookseller; the publisher is anonymous, 1809. Reprinted by J. Scheible in Stuttgart in 1883, with a portrait of Catherine II. This German diplomat is particularly revealing about Gregory Orlov and his brothers.

Khrapovitsky, Alexander. *Pamiatnyia zapiski A. V. Khrapovitskago, stats-sekretarya imperatritsy Yekateriny Vtoroi* [Aide-memoire and Diary of A. V. Khrapovitsky, Chief Secretary of Empress Catherine II]. Moscow: University Printery, 1862; reprinted in 1874.

Masson, Charles François Philibert. *Mémoires secrets sur la Russie, et particulièrement sur la fin du règne de Catherine II et le commencement de celui de Paul I. Formant un tableau de moeurs de St. Petersburg à la fin du XVIIIe siècle.* Paris: S. Pougens, an VIII (1800). Two volumes.
English translation: *Secret Memoirs of the Court of St. Petersburg, Particularly Towards the End of the Reign of Catherine II and the Commencement of That of Paul I, Serving as a Supplement to the Life of Catherine II. Translated from the French.* London: T. N. Longman and O. Rees, 1801–1802; Philadelphia: G. Barrie & Son, 1898; New York: Arno Press and the New York Times, 1970, in the series Russia Observed.

*Die Memoiren des letzten Königs von Polen Stanislaw August Poniatowski.* Introduction by A. V. Guttry, translation by I. von Powa. München: G. Muller, 192?

*Mémoires du duc de Choiseul, 1719-1785.* Paris: Plon-Nourrit et cie, 1904. Two volumes.

*Mémoires secrets et inédits de Stanislas Auguste comte Poniatowski, dernier roi de Pologne, relatifs à ses rapports intimes avec l'impératrice Catherine II et son avenement au trône. Journal privé du roi Stanislas Auguste pendant son voyage en Russie. . . . Suivi d'une relation de ses funérailles, depuis 12 février jusqu'au 8 mars 1798.* Leipzig: W. Gerhard, 1862.

Rulhière, Claude Carloman, de. *Histoire, ou Anecdotes sur la révolution de Russie; en l'annee 1762.* Paris: Desenne, an V (1797).

Sabatier de Cabres. *Catherine II, sa cour et la Russie en 1772.* Preface by Sergei Aleksandrovich Sobolevski. Berlin: A. Asher & Co., 1862.

Ségur, Philippe Paul, Comte de. *Histoire et mémoires.* Paris: Firmin Didot frères, 1873. Seven volumes.

Sherer, J. B. *Anecdotes intéressantes et secrètes sur la cour de Russie.* Paris, 1792.

## DOCUMENTS

*Archives of the Russian Empire.* Vol. I of the Imperial State Council during the reign of Catherine II, St. Petersburg, 1869. *Bumagi imperatritsy Yekateriny II, khranyashchiyasia v Gosudarstvennom arkhive Ministerstva inostrannykh del* [Papers of Empress Catherine II, Kept in the State Archive of the Ministry of Foreign Affairs]. St. Petersburg: Printery of the Imperial Academy of Sciences, 1871-1874. Three volumes (Vol. III edited by I. K. Grot).

*Prussian Archives.* In addition to the memoirs of Frederick the Great, see: *La cour de Russie il y a cent ans. Recueil de lettres et de dépêches.* Berlin, 1864.

Stasov, V[ladimir] V. *124 vystrela v Shlissel'burgskoi kreposti. Istoricheskoye issledovaniye* [124 Shots in the Schluesselburg Fortress—An Historical Quest]. Edited by Professor G. Novitsky. Moscow: illustrated Sunday supplement *Nedelya* [Week] to the daily *Izvestiya* [News], February-March 1966: numbers 10, 11, 13.
*124 vystrela* . . . represents the first publication of the secret Tsarist documents on the imprisonment and death of Ivan VI. These papers had long been known to exist, but the fact of

their existence was initially confirmed in print only in 1900. In excerpts from the memoirs of Baron (later Count) M. A. Korf, published in *Russkaya starina* [Russian Old Times], St. Petersburg, May 1900, volume 102, pp. 276–277, Korf told how in 1849, when appointed to head the Imperial Public Library, he visited Nicholas I at Tsarskoye Selo to thank him for the appointment. Korf related to the sovereign that he had seen in the Library "the authentic file regarding the confinement of the unfortunate Ioann Antonovich and his family at Kholmogory; the file where Empress Elizabeth Petrovna appears in an entirely different light than history depicts her. This apparently interested the sovereign, who was always greatly attracted to annals of all kinds, especially those having to do with his dynasty, and he at once instructed me to transfer the file, as not properly belonging in the Library, to the State Archive."

In general, Nicholas I wished such papers to be kept under lock and key. By his order of December 3, 1833, he forbade "anyone to unseal the Mirovich matter." The prohibition was relaxed after his death in 1855. Vladimir Stasov, an historian, gained access to the Ivan VI-Mirovich papers in the early 1860s. He researched and completed his study sometime before his death in 1906, but his manuscript was found in the archives by Soviet officials and scholars only in the mid-1960s. The above publication in *Nedelya* is a condensation of two chapters of his manuscript, but it abounds in the original reports by Ivan's wardens and the government's directives to the latter.

*State Archives of France.* Memoirs, reports of the French ambassadors, etc., in *Archives du Ministère des Affaires Etrangères. Correspondance politique de Russie.* Vols. LXVIII to CXXXIX.

*Secondary Sources: works on Catherine II and her times*
   Almedingen, Martha Edith, von. *Catherine, Empress of Russia.* New York: Dodd, Mead and Co., 1961. Reissued as *Catherine the Great.* London: Hutchinson, 1963.

   Anthony, Katharine Susan. *Catherine the Great.* Garden City,

N.Y.: Garden City Publishing Co., 1925; New York: Alfred A. Knopf, 1925.

Ausubel, Nathan. *Superman: the Life of Frederick the Great.* New York: Ives Washburn, 1931.

Bil'basov, Vasily A. *Istoriya Yekateriny Vtoroi.* St. Petersburg and Berlin, 1890-1896.
German versions of above:
*Geschichte Katharina II . . . übersetzt aus dem Russischen von M. Pezold.* Berlin: S. Cronbach, 1893. Two volumes.
*Katharina II. Kaiserin von Russland im Urtheile der Weltliteratur übersetzt aus dem Russischen mit einem Vorwort von T. Schiemann.* Berlin: J. Rade, 1897. Two volumes.

Bradford, Gamaliel. *Daughters of Eve.* Boston and New York: Houghton Mifflin Co., 1930; the New Home Library, 1930.

Brückner, Alexander. *Istoriya Yekateriny Vtoroi.* St. Petersburg: 1885. Three volumes.

Brusendorff, Ove, and Henningsen, Poul. *A History of Eroticism.* New York: Lyle Stuart, Inc., 1966. Originally published in Copenhagen. Thaning & Appels Forlag, 1961.

Bryanchaninov, N. V. *Catherine II, impératrice de Russie.* Paris: Payot, 1932.

Castéra, Jean Henri. *Vie de Catherine II, impératrice de Russie.* Paris: F. Buisson, an V (1797). Two volumes. Also by this author: *Histoire de Catherine II, impératrice de Russie.* Paris: Buisson, an VIII (1800).
———. *The Life of Catherine II, Empress of Russia.* A translation from the French, with additions by W. Tooke. London: T. N. Longman and O. Rees, 1799. Three volumes.
Another English edition: *History of Catherine II, Empress of Russia.* Translated from the French by Henry Hunter. London: J. Stockdale, 1800.

First American edition of the same: Philadelphia: William Fry, publisher; M. Maxwell, printer, 1802. Two volumes.

Coughlan, Robert. *Elizabeth and Catherine, Empresses of All the Russias.* New York: G. P. Putnam's Sons, 1974.

Cronin, Vincent. *Catherine, Empress of All the Russias.* New York: William Morrow and Co., 1978.

Firsov, N. N. *Pyotr III i Yekaterina II; pervyie gody yeya tsarstvovaniya, opyt kharakteristik* [Peter III and Catherine II; the First Years of Her Reign, an Experiment at Characterization]. Petrograd and Moscow: M. O. Wol'f Company, 1915.

George, Walter Lionel. *Historic Lovers.* London: Hutchinson & Co., Ltd., 1926.

Grey, Ian. *Catherine the Great, Autocrat and Empress of All Russia.* London: Hodder & Stoughten, 1961; Philadelphia: J. B. Lippincott Co., 1962.

Haslip, Joan. *Catherine the Great, a Biography.* New York: G. P. Putnam's Sons, 1977.

Hodgetts-Braylay, E. A. *The Life of Catherine the Great of Russia.* New York: Brentano's, 1914.

Hyde, Harford Montgomery. *The Empress Catherine and Princess Dashkov.* London: Chapman & Hall, Ltd., 1935.

Ilichester, Earl of, and Mrs. Langford-Brooke. *The Life of Sir Charles Hanbury-Williams, Poet, Wit and Diplomatist.* London: Thornton Butterworth Ltd., 1929.

Ilovaisky, D. I. "Yekateriny Romanovna Dashkova," in *Sochineniya* [Works]. Moscow: A. L. Vasilyev, 1884, pp. 223–443. Originally published in *Otechestvennyia Zapiski* [Native Notes], St. Petersburg, 1859, numbers 9–12.

Kauffret, P. E. *Catherine II et son règne.* Paris: n.p., 1860. Two volumes.

Kaus, Gina. *Catherine la Grande.* Paris: Grasset, 1934. In English: *Catherine, the Portrait of an Empress.* Translated from the German by June Head. New York: Literary Guild, 1935.

Klyuchevsky, V[asily] O. *Sochineniya. Kurs russkoi istorii* [A Course in Russian History]. Moscow: Publishing House of Social-Economic Literature, 1958. Volume IV treats Empresses Elizabeth and Catherine; also Emperor Peter III on pp. 338–347, and devotes pp. 348–355 to the overthrow and murder of Peter III. Volume V is devoted almost in its entirety to Catherine.

Kobeko, Dmitry. *Tsesarevich Pavel Petrovich (1754–1796). Istoricheskoye izsledovaniye* [Crown Prince Paul, Son of Peter (1754–1796). A Historical Study]. St. Petersburg: n.p., 1882.

Kochan, Miriam. *Life in Russia Under Catherine the Great.* London: B. T. Batsford, Ltd., and New York: G. P. Putnam's Sons, 1969 (European Life Series).

Lavater-Sloman, Mary. *Catherine II et son temps.* Paris: Payot, 1952.

Lorenz, Lincoln. *The Admiral and the Empress: John Paul Jones and Catherine the Great.* New York: Bookman Associates, 1954.

Madariaga, Isabel de. *Russia in the Age of Catherine the Great.* New Haven, Conn.: Yale University Press, 1981.

Murat, Marie de Rohan-Chabot, Princesse. *La vie amoureuse de la Grande Catherine de Russie.* Paris: Flammarion, 1927. In English: *The Private Life of Catherine the Great of Russia.* Translated by Garnett Saffery. New York and London: L. Carrier & Co., 1928.

Oldenbourg, Zoe. *Catherine de Russie.* Paris: Gallimard, 1966.

In English: *Catherine the Great*. London: Heinemann, 1965; and New York: Pantheon Books, 1965.

Olivier, Daria. *Catherine la Grande*. Paris: Librairie académique Perrin, 1965.

Palewski, J. P. "Stanislas-Auguste Poniatowski et Catherine II (1754-1798)." Paris: *Revue de France*, 1932, vol. 3, pp. 415–448 and 605–630.

Pingaud, Léonce. *Les Français en Russie et les Russes en France; l'ancien régime, l'émigration, les invasions*. Paris: Perrin & cie, 1886 and 1889.

Polovtsov, Alexandre A. *Les favoris de Catherine la Grande; préface de Maurice Paléologue*. Paris: Plon, 1939. In English: *The Favourites of Catherine the Great*. Foreward by Maurice Paléologue. London: Herbert Jenkins, Ltd., 1940.

Raeff, Marc, editor. *Catherine the Great: A Profile*. In the series World Profiles, Aïda DiPace Donald, general editor. New York: Hill and Wang, 1972.

———. "The Domestic Policies of Peter III and His Overthrow." *The American Historical Review*, June 1970, vol. LXXV, number 5, pp. 1289–1310.

Reboux, Paul. *La grande Catherine et ses petits amis*. Brussels: Les Editions de Chabassol, 1947.

Romanov, Alexander Mikhailovich, Grand Duke. *The Evil Empress: A Romance of the Court of Catherine the Great*. Philadelphia and London: J. B. Lippincott Co., 1934.

Schilder, N. *Histoire anecdotique de Paul I-er*. Paris: Calmann-Lévy, 1899.

Schloezer, Kurd von. *Friedrich der Grosse und Katharina die Zweite*. Berlin: W. Hertz, 1859.

Sergeant, Philip Walsingham. *The Courtships of Catherine the Great*. London: T. W. Laurie, 1925; and New York: Brentano's, 1925.

Shaw, Bernard. *The Great Catherine*. Drama. Prompt book, property of the New York Public Library. n.p.
———. "Great Catherine; A Thumbnail Sketch of Court Life in the Eighteenth Century." New York: *Everybody's Magazine*, 1915, vol. 32, pp. 193–212.

Sideau, F. G. *La cour de l'impératrice Catherine II: ses collaborateurs et son entourage. Cent quatre-vingt silhouettes*. Preface by Alexander Krougly. The text, including the title page, is in both Russian and French. St. Petersburg: n.p., 1899. Two volumes.

Taigny, Edmond. *Catherine II et la princesse Dashkoff*. Paris: Hachette, 1860. Reissued by Hachette in 1969 in an expanded version (from the original 40 pp. to 333 pp.).

Tourneux, Maurice. *Diderot et Catherine II*. Paris: Calmann-Lévy, 1899.

Troyat, Henri. *Catherine la Grande*. Paris: Flammarion, 1977. In English: *Catherine the Great*. Translated by Joan Pinkham. New York: E. P. Dutton, 1980.

Valloton, Henry. *Catherine II* (in French). Paris: A. Fayard, 1955.

Waliszewski, Kazimierz. *Autour d'un trône. Catherine II de Russie, ses collaborateurs, ses amis, ses favoris*. Paris: Plon-Nourrit et cie, 1894 (fourth edition); same publisher, 1913 (tenth edition).
———. *Le roman d'une impératrice, Catherine II de Russie*. Paris: Plon-Nourrit et cie, 1898 (seventh edition). In English: *The Romance of an Empress: Catherine II of Russia*. New York: D. Appleton, 1894.

Whishow, Frederic J. *At the Court of Catherine the Great.* New York: Frederick A. Stokes Co., 1899.
————. *An Empress in Love.* London: S. Paul & Co., 1910.

# Index